University
of Michigan
Business
School Management Series

INNOVATIVE SOLUTIONS TO THE PRESSING PROBLEMS OF BUSINESS

The mission of the University of Michigan Business School Management Series is to provide accessible, practical, and cutting-edge solutions to the most critical challenges facing business-people today. The UMBS Management Series provides concepts and tools for people who seek to make a significant difference in their organizations. Drawing on the research and experience of faculty at the University of Michigan Business School, the books are written to stretch thinking while providing practical, focused, and innovative solutions to the pressing problems of business.

Also available in the UMBS series:

Becoming a Better Value Creator, by Anjan V. Thakor

Achieving Success Through Social Capital, by Wayne Baker

Improving Customer Satisfaction, Loyalty, and Profit, by Michael D. Johnson and Anders Gustafsson

The Compensation Solution, by John E. Tropman

Strategic Interviewing, by Richaurd Camp, Mary Vielhaber, and Jack L. Simonetti

Creating the Multicultural Organization, by Taylor Cox

Getting Results, by Clinton O. Longenecker and Jack L. Simonetti

A Company of Leaders, by Gretchen M. Spreitzer and Robert E. Quinn

Managing the Unexpected, by Karl Weick and Kathleen Sutcliffe

Using the Law for Competitive Advantage, by George J. Siedel

Creativity at Work, by Jeff DeGraff and Katherine A. Lawrence

Making I/T Work, by Dennis G. Severance and Jacque Passino

Decision Management, by J. Frank Yates

A Manager's Guide to Employment Law, by Dana M. Muir

The Ethical Challenge, edited by Noel M. Tichy and Andrew R. McGill

Competing in a Service Economy, by Anders Gustafsson and Michael D. Johnson

Energize Your Workplace, by Jane E. Dutton

For additional information on any of these titles or future titles in the series, visit www.umbsbooks.com.

Executive Summary

N onfinancial executives often would rather leave finance to financial experts. Lacking a clear understanding of the financial aspects of strategic decisions, they tend to unquestioningly delegate the numbers aspects of decision making to their finance colleagues. But finance is too important and too integral to the general manager's responsibilities to be delegated without a clear idea of what is going on. As a general manager you do not need to know everything about finance that your financial experts know, but you do need a framework for evaluating financial analysis, making decisions based on it, and monitoring their implementation.

This book provides that framework. Through a series of case-based discussions, it will demystify the financial implications of the major types of strategic decisions for which you are typically responsible. The increased sophistication of financial markets gives your firm innovative options in raising and managing capital, in structuring deals, and in managing operating risks. This book will equip you to provide the necessary leadership to evaluate alternative strategies in this sophisticated market and make full use of your financial experts.

All decisions examined in the book are analyzed from the perspective of maximizing shareholder value. Chapter One elaborates on this concept and the role of finance in corporate strategy.

Chapters Two and Three tackle the basic resource allocation decisions that you are often expected to make. What are the value drivers of a project? How much will the capital cost and do the benefits derived offset this cost? If the project is likely to be a good investment, how much value will it create for shareholders? These are the basic questions that these foundational chapters will answer.

Chapter Four expands on the issue of capital structure. Its basic question is, in the course of financing new projects, what mix of debt and equity capital should the company choose in order to minimize cost of capital and thereby maximize firm value? Chapter Five explores the complementary question of payouts (dividends or share repurchases). For example, does it make sense to hoard as much cash as possible in order to reduce the need to borrow? What sort of payout policy is appropriate for your firm?

Mergers, acquisitions, and divestitures are important resource allocation decisions that change the scope of the firm. In Chapters Six and Seven you will learn how to judge whether such a sweeping move really is likely to serve the interests of your shareholders.

In the volatile product and financial markets that managers face today, it also important to understand how to manage a number of risks. How can specific risks be reduced? How should persisting risks be managed? Should the firm retain them or transfer them through the use of insurance, hedging, or some other device? Chapter Eight explores the problem.

Finally, Chapter Nine deals with performance evaluation and the concept of economic profit (or value added) by which you can monitor the success of a project over time, as well as evaluate the effectiveness of upper-level management.

Finance for Strategic Decision Making

What Non-Financial Managers Need to Know

M. P. Narayanan
Vikram K. Nanda

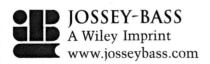 JOSSEY-BASS
A Wiley Imprint
www.josseybass.com

Published by Jossey-Bass
A Wiley Imprint
989 Market Street, San Francisco, CA 94103-1741   www.josseybass.com

Jossey-Bass books and products are available through most bookstores. To contact Jossey-Bass directly call our Customer Care Department within the U.S. at 800-956-7739, outside the U.S. at 317-572-3986 or fax 317-572-4002.

Jossey-Bass also publishes its books in a variety of electronic formats. Some content that appears in print may not be available in electronic books.

Library of Congress Cataloging-in-Publication Data

Narayanan, M. P., date
  Finance for strategic decision making : what non-financial managers
need to know / M. P. Narayanan, Vikram Nanda.—1. ed.
      p. cm.
Includes bibliographical references and index.
  ISBN 978-0-7879-6517-4
  1. Corporations—Finance. I. Nanda, Vikram K. II. Title.
  HG4026.N365 2004
  658.15—dc22

                                                        2003026449

FIRST EDITION
HB Printing   10 9 8 7 6 5 4 3 2 1

Contents

Series Foreword

Welcome to the University of Michigan Business School Management Series. The books in this series address the most urgent problems facing business today. The series is part of a larger initiative at the University of Michigan Business School (UMBS) that ties together a range of efforts to create and share knowledge through conferences, survey research, interactive and distance training, print publications, and news media.

It is just this type of broad-based initiative that sparked my love affair with UMBS in 1984. From the day I arrived I was enamored with the quality of the research, the quality of the MBA program, and the quality of the Executive Education Center. Here was a business school committed to new lines of research, new ways of teaching, and the practical application of ideas. It was a place where innovative thinking could result in tangible outcomes.

The UMBS Management Series is one very important outcome, and it has an interesting history. It turns out that every year five thousand participants in our executive program fill out a marketing survey in which they write statements indicating the most important problems they face. One day Lucy Chin, one of our administrators, handed me a document containing all these statements. A content analysis of the data resulted in a list of forty-five pressing problems. The topics ranged from growing a company to managing personal stress. The list covered a wide territory, and I started to see its potential. People in organizations tend to be driven by a very traditional set of problems, but the solutions evolve. I went to my friends at Jossey-Bass to discuss a publishing project. The discussion eventually grew into the University of Michigan Business School Management Series— Innovative Solutions to the Pressing Problems of Business.

The books are independent of each other, but collectively they create a comprehensive set of management tools that cut across all the functional areas of business—from strategy to human resources to finance, accounting, and operations. They draw on the interdisciplinary research of the Michigan faculty. Yet each book is written so a serious manager can read it quickly and act immediately. I think you will find that they are books that will make a significant difference to you and your organization.

Robert E. Quinn, Consulting Editor
M.E. Tracy Distinguished Professor
University of Michigan Business School

Preface

Central as finance is to strategic decision making, general managers are often unfamiliar with its principles. Those who try to inform themselves sometimes pick up a finance book but more often than not find themselves too bored to follow its discussion.

The problem they run into is that most finance books are not written for general managers; they're written for finance specialists or those who wish to specialize in finance. In addition, most finance books treat finance in isolation from other business functions. But general managers do not wish to learn finance (or marketing or human resource management, for that matter) for its own sake. They're looking for information to help them lead more effectively and make better corporate decisions. In this pursuit they need a comprehensive understanding of the financial model of the business but not of the computational details—they can delegate those to specialists. However, to delegate effectively and to comprehend the shareholder value implications of financial choices, general managers need a guiding framework not obscured by too much detail. This book provides that framework.

The inspiration to write this book grew out of our extensive interaction with general managers in the course of more than thirty years' collective experience as consultants and instructors in executive education programs. It grew out of the recognition that while general managers were adept at formulating strategy, they would welcome some help in assessing alternatives from a financial perspective—in the context of strategic decisions that the general manager faces.

We have aimed to present finance in an easily understandable fashion, demystifying and clarifying a subject that many general managers surrender to specialists to a counterproductive extent. The reality is that general managers' involvement in financial analysis is critical to sound decision making, and productive involvement depends on knowing more about finance than general managers often pick up through osmosis. Such partial knowledge without a clear understanding of the complete framework leaves them vulnerable to many misconceptions about financial decision making. A simplified presentation that clarifies the framework helps them avoid such misconceptions.

The book focuses on the goal of creating shareholder value and shows how every managerial decision can be linked to shareholder value. The content covers three broad but interrelated groups of topics. The first group has to do with internal resource allocation decisions that typically are regarded as the main province of the general manager. Chapter Two focuses on the cash flow drivers, a topic important in itself, and also one with implications for other topics such as mergers and acquisitions and performance evaluation. Chapter Three explores the cost of capital, which again is of great importance for other topics. Mergers, acquisitions, and divestitures, being important resource allocation decisions that change the scope of the firm, are dealt with separately in Chapter Six and Chapter Seven, respectively.

The second group of topics concerns the financial policies of the firm. Chapters Four and Five discuss financing and payout

policies, respectively, while Chapter Eight discusses risk management issues.

While the first two groups of topics are related to making decisions to enhance shareholder value, the third one deals with evaluating the outcomes of these decisions. We cover this part of the overall problem as performance evaluation, the topic of Chapter Nine.

■ Acknowledgments

Many people have contributed to this book. We would like to thank our colleagues at the University of Michigan Business School with whom we have discussed many of the ideas presented in the book over the course of several years. Thanks are also due to the many executives who discussed these ideas with us and helped us refine them. We have also benefited from comments on earlier chapters by anonymous reviewers.

We would like to thank the Jossey-Bass team, especially Kathe Sweeney and John Bergez, for helping us improve the writing style to make the book more accessible to the intended audience. Special thanks are due to Alan Venable for editing our original manuscript and for showing incredible patience with us.

Finally, we would like to thank our spouses, Lakshmi Narayanan and Nandini Nanda, for behind-the-scenes support and inspiration. Vikram would also like express his gratitude to Sudershan and Satayander for unflinching love and indulgence.

January 2004   M. P. Narayanan
Ann Arbor, Michigan   Vikram K. Nanda

Finance for Strategic Decision Making

Finance and Corporate Strategy

F inance is a mystery to many general managers. Nonfinancial executives often view finance (and accounting) as best left to experts. As a result they sometimes unquestioningly delegate the numbers aspects of decision making to their finance colleagues. Finance is, however, too important to be left to the experts!

When nonfinancial managers do not fully understand what the numbers represent and the assumptions behind the analysis, it is all too likely that they will make poor, value-destroying decisions. That same lack of understanding on general managers' part can also limit the usefulness of their financial managers' expertise, since the former may lack clear knowledge of the kind of information that the latter needs and may not be able to provide appropriate feedback about the operational aspects of the company. Contributing to this lack of information interchange is the fact that financial managers are often viewed as "numbers oriented," unable to comprehend the strategic implications of a decision. Unhappily, it is not uncommon to hear the refrain "though the numbers said otherwise, we decided to go ahead with the decision for strategic reasons," implying that finance and strategy are somehow independent of one another.

This arm's-length relationship that general managers have with finance often results in value-destroying decisions. For instance, it is well known that half of all acquisitions do not create shareholder value—and a major reason for this is overpayment by the acquirer. In other words, the acquisition has the potential to increase your firm's value, but not by as much as you paid for it, and therefore net value is actually lost. This unfortunate situation can easily be averted if the general manager can both recognize the value-creating potential of an acquisition and also quantify this value. In this book we discuss the pitfalls in acquisitions and how to avoid them, while also explaining how to evaluate an acquisition to avoid overpayment.

Another cause of value destruction is poor oversight of financial managers. General managers, often because of limited knowledge or outright ignorance, do not rein in financial managers who, in the guise of managing the risk of the company, indulge in speculative investments, sometimes even crossing the line into criminal activity. It is important for general managers to understand risk management tactics and their potential for value creation well enough to set risk management policy and place limits on what financial managers can do. For that reason, this book delineates exactly how risk management can create value, including a section on derivatives as a risk management tool. Such knowledge is essential to the general manager who oversees financial managers.

■ **Taking the Mystery Out of Finance**

The main objective of this book is to demystify finance for the general manager and show how to use economic reasoning to enhance the quality of strategic decision making. Finance is an integral part of evaluating decisions and monitoring their implementation. Without a complete understanding of how to evaluate the alternatives, it is impossible for the general manager to make the value-maximizing choice. Moreover, since most realistic decisions are complex, any financial analysis is likely to have limitations that the general manager must clearly understand so as to avoid taking it as more definitive than it really is. Similarly, the monitoring of past decisions is critical to ensure that future opportunities for shareholder value creation are not missed and that adequate resources are directed to promising investments while unpromising ones are reduced in scale or scope. Value-based performance evaluation can also reduce the mystery in the challenge of rewarding your value-creating managers and pruning your value-destroying ones. In general, a deeper understanding of the financial framework makes it possible for general managers to monitor the implementation of their strategic decisions and ensure that they create value.

Another important objective of the book is to dispel common misconceptions about financial decisions. Many general managers have just enough finance knowledge to be dangerous—enough knowledge to understand generally what is being said, but not enough to analyze or question the actions being proposed. Proposed actions, though erroneous, often sound quite plausible. For example, most general managers know that "debt is cheaper than equity." They instinctively understand that shareholder value is enhanced if capital is raised at the lowest cost. Therefore, a recommendation that the company increase debt in its capital structure might sound like a value-increasing decision. But in practice value creation is not simply a matter of substituting debt for equity, and the decision might well prove far too costly. Similarly, companies often throw good money after bad projects. The reasoning is that "we have so much invested in this project" that it would be a shame to waste what's already been spent, even though spending still more offers little hope of improving the results. To replace this sort of wishful thinking, we present a set of clearer frameworks for you to use in evaluating many different types of important decisions, guiding you through the right questions to ask.

Our approach differs from that of a standard finance textbook in three important ways. First, we recognize that managers are busy, so we focus on the essentials of finance without subjecting you to an overwhelming amount of detail. Second, we skip the technical details found in a typical finance textbook; you can delegate those details to finance professionals in your organization. Finally, we focus on decision making rather than on finance theory, presenting only those concepts necessary to reach a sound decision.

We assume that you already know the basics of accounting, the language of business, and that you have some familiarity with financial statements: balance sheets, income statements, and cash flow statements. We recognize that most likely you already have had some exposure to finance (perhaps you have taken a short executive education seminar or an internal company seminar, or have learnt it through osmosis!), but we do not presume that you have more prior finance knowledge than that.

■ It's All About Shareholder Value

This book champions shareholder value. It advocates that the \cus of all decisions be shareholder value maximization. Share-
\der value maximization is not "the flavor of the week" but
\ison d'être of a for-profit company. Shareholder value is

realized through cash dividends and share value appreciation. For a publicly traded company, shareholder value is therefore easily observable. For a private company it is still the central idea, though harder to ascertain because the lack of a market price makes it difficult to measure shareholder value unless the company is being sold.

There is some debate about the extent to which companies should focus on shareholder value. Some argue that shareholders are but one of the stakeholders of a company (the others being customers, employees, suppliers, lenders, and the community at large), and that the company should not ignore these stakeholders and focus exclusively on shareholder value. This argument is specious; there is no conflict between shareholder value and value to these other stakeholders. Shareholder value cannot be created without providing value to these stakeholders. By shortchanging customers or employees, for instance, the company might be able to boost short-term profit but only at the expense of future profits and hence, at the expense of shareholder value. However, this does not imply that value to these other stakeholders should be *maximized.* No one in their right mind would advocate that a company maximize customer value by supplying top-quality goods or services for free. (Or better still, paying customers to accept such goods or services!)

The key is to understand that shareholder value can be *maximized* only by *optimizing* the value to other stakeholders. Optimizing involves providing a fair value: for example, employees should be compensated on the basis of what they can earn elsewhere. Since shareholders are the residual claimants (they are paid only after all other stakeholders are paid) of a company's assets, it is fair that their value be maximized while other stakeholders' values are only optimized.

It is, therefore, important for the general manager to link every decision to measures of shareholder value. In principle this may seem easy and the "right thing to do," but general managers face problems when implementing this central idea. The first and foremost problem is that general managers are often unsure what the appropriate metric of shareholder value is for the particular decision at hand. Even for a publicly traded company with an observable share price, the share price cannot ordinarily be used directly for decision making. This is because the share price is the outcome of your decisions and the market's expectations regarding the firm's prospects. This means that the general manager needs internal measures that are correlated to shareholder value to help in the decision-making process. And the real problem is not the lack of such measures but the surfeit of them. The general manager is often presented with measures that appear to be related to shareholder value, such as net income or earnings per share. It is important to know which of these measures are most closely linked to shareholder value. In this book we show the appropriate metrics to use and link each decision to shareholder value through the use of these metrics.

■ The Role of Finance in Corporate Strategy

Figure 1.1 shows the role of finance in corporate decision making and its interaction with corporate strategy. As the figure shows, corporate managers choose value-creating strategies from a set of available choices. These strategies may involve operating decisions (where do we allocate our resources, which businesses do we divest, and the like) and financing decisions (what should be our capital structure, which risks do we need to manage and how, and so on).

The role of finance in operating decisions is primarily one of valuation and monitoring. Finance helps managers evaluate the operational alternatives available to them, and helps them monitor the decisions that are implemented. Such monitoring is

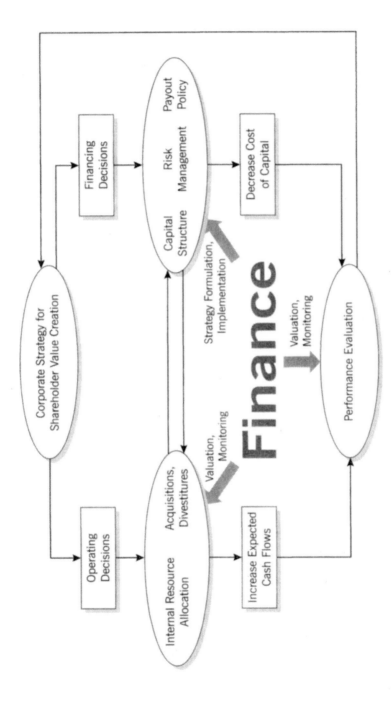

Figure 1.1. Role of Finance in Corporate Strategy

critical to the evolution of corporate strategy: it helps management change or adjust its strategy based on the outcomes of earlier strategies. The outcome of a well-thought-out and carefully monitored operating decision is higher future expected cash flow for the company. In addition to their impact on expected future cash flows, operating decisions can often have an impact on financing decisions. For example, if an energy company with generating plants decides to focus more on energy trading and less on generation, its tangible asset base will be depleted and so will its borrowing capacity. Such a company will need to invest more in risk management techniques and pay out less earnings as dividends.

The role of finance is obviously greater in financing decisions. Finance plays a major role in formulating the financing strategy, evaluating the alternatives, and monitoring the outcomes. The objective of the financing strategy is to raise capital at the lowest cost, which in turn increases shareholder value. At first glance, it might appear that these decisions are the purview of the CFO and others need not get involved in them. However, just as operating decisions have an impact on financing policies, so financing decisions can affect operating strategies. For example, a company whose financing decisions have led it into too much debt might not have the financial flexibility to raise capital quickly enough for needed growth. Or, on a positive note, a company whose financial policies include good risk management might be able to create a competitive advantage for itself by offering products that limit customer risk as well. Therefore, a general manager with a clear understanding of financial policies can leverage them to create value for shareholders. The role of finance in performance evaluation is identical to its role in operating decisions: valuation and monitoring.

The bottom of Figure 1.1 draws attention to performance evaluation. As mentioned earlier, general managers have two reasons for evaluating the performance of business units on a periodic basis. The first is to ensure that earlier decisions have yielded the predicted results and, if not, to decide the modifications needed: invest more, for instance, in outperforming projects and less in underperforming ones. The second reason is to provide the appropriate incentives to managers based on the performance of their units. It is critical, though, that the metric used to measure performance be congruent with shareholder value (as indicated by the feedback arrow in the figure from performance evaluation to shareholder value creation). If the evaluation metric and shareholder value diverge, it doesn't matter what other controls the decision-making process may include. Shareholder value creation will be unlikely, as the managers will maximize their own metric rather than shareholder value.

■ Handling a Range of Decisions

The book is organized in chapters that focus on a variety of strategic decisions designed to maximize shareholder value creation. Each chapter revolves around a case and gives you a conceptual framework with which to analyze decisions. Outside this systematic treatment, it also provides answers to additional questions that, in our experience, managers frequently ask.

Business strategy involves resource allocation, the subject of Chapter Two. By covering this central problem, the chapter lays the foundation for later chapters on topics such as mergers, acquisitions, and divestitures. The chapter provides decision rules congruent with shareholder value. It also explains the cash flow drivers and provides a template that can be used to estimate cash flows for resource allocation proposals.

Chapter Three deals with the cost of capital. This again is a central topic as the goal of any for-profit company is to provide a return in excess of the cost of capital. The chapter explains the drivers of the cost of capital: cost of debt, cost of equity, and the debt-equity ratio. It shows how to estimate costs of debt and equity.

Chapter Four deals with financing and capital structure (debt-equity ratio) choices. We explain how capital structure—and other corporate finance decisions such as payout policy—can be chosen to maximize firm value in the presence of market imperfections such as taxes, bankruptcy, and information problems. This imperfect market framework is used to understand the timing and the type of security sold when external financing is raised.

Chapter Five explores payout policy. It explains the significant differences between the two common methods of payout—dividends and share repurchases. It also explains the usefulness of payout in providing positive information about firm value and a commitment by managers to return shareholder money—despite the fact that payouts may require the firm to raise additional external financing.

Chapter Six deals with mergers and acquisitions. While many companies view acquisitions as an important vehicle for growth, research shows that acquisitions often do not create value for the acquirer. The chapter discusses the reasons for this dismal outcome and outlines steps that companies can take to ensure that their acquisitions not only increase revenue but also increase shareholder value. It explains how to value a prospective target, the most important step in ensuring a successful acquisition. Finally, it provides a brief discussion about bidding strategy and how to structure the payment.

Chapter Seven explains how divestitures can and should be part of a company's strategic tool kit. Even a growth company needs to constantly prune its underperforming units and use the resources to expand its core businesses. Several specific rationales for divestiture are discussed, such as increasing focus, raising capital, meeting regulatory requirements, and addressing liability concerns. The manner in which a divestiture should be structured—spin-off versus sell-off—is discussed as well.

Chapter Eight shows how a company can create value by managing its risk. While companies need to bear risks in areas in which they have expertise (an automobile manufacturer, for example, has to bear the demand and technological risks of the automobile business), they may be better off letting others bear external risks involving matters such as currency and interest rates. The chapter uses the framework for financial decisions developed in Chapter Four to explain the value drivers of risk management and briefly explains the tools for risk management.

Chapter Nine describes how to measure the performance of the company and its business units. It explains the notion of economic profit and how it relates to shareholder value. It shows a simple way to compute economic profit from the financial statements of the company or its business units. The chapter discusses why it is difficult to perfectly align managers' incentives with shareholders' interests. While economic profit is better than many performance measures, it too has limitations. The chapter describes these limitations, and discusses many other commonly used performance measures and their limitations as well.

SUMMARY

This book provides the general manager a financial framework that helps in strategic decision making for shareholder value creation. It explains the underlying financial concepts and provides tool kits for assessing corporate strategy. It demonstrates through case studies how to analyze strategic decisions from the point of view of shareholder value creation. Each chapter also augments the case study with a section of "frequently asked questions" addressing issues that could not be dealt with in the context of the case but are of interest or concern to general managers as they deal with the overall topic of the chapter.

After reading this book you will not only understand how to evaluate operating and financial policies from the point of view of shareholder value, you will also be able to apply prescriptions for creating value. The book achieves this by clearly delineating the value drivers for the various decisions and by showing the link between the driver and shareholder value, and also by providing check lists of action items at the appropriate times.

It is our hope that this book will convince general managers that finance is an integral part of corporate strategy and not a stand-alone function to be completely delegated to specialists.

The Resource
Allocation Decision

A s the newly promoted general manager of a premier chip
manufacturer's communications division, you are facing
your first major capital allocation decision. Your research
and development team has designed a high-speed communications microchip, code-named Mach O. Your financial analyst has
provided a preliminary analysis of the costs and benefits of con-
structing a new plant for its manufacture. Recently, you were at
a meeting of senior managers at which the CEO emphasized the
importance of shareholder value and the need to evaluate all decisions on that basis. The CEO said that the key measures of
shareholder value were a steady growth in the company's stock
price and maintenance of the dividend growth rate.

Formed in 1992, your company is the industry leader in microchips for many different applications—from computers and digital equipment to automobiles and other consumer goods. It was profitable from the very beginning and continues to make substantial profits. As the communications industry exploded, your company developed chips for communications equipment. Its current generation of communications chips, called Mach I, was the first that could handle substantial Internet audio and video communications. But projected increases in the demand for real-time streaming audio and video functions will stretch or surpass its capabilities. Your development engineers have been working on improving speed by using a very different technology. The new Mach O chip can transmit video images much faster. Now, at the end of 2005, the Mach O has been carefully tested. It's time for the company to decide whether to produce and sell it in place of Mach I.

In this chapter we walk you through two widely used methodologies for making such a decision: Net Present Value (NPV) and Internal Rate of Return (IRR). Both can provide objective criteria for allocating resources based on expected cash flows and the cost of capital. Here, we take the cost of capital as a given, postponing the discussion of ways to determine it until Chapter Three, but we go into some detail about expected cash flows. Understanding the components of expected cash flows is critical to identifying the key drivers of value, which in turn helps you manage or control these drivers to increase shareholder value. We show how the general manager can use resource allocation tools like NPV and IRR in the broader context of strategic decision making. Finally, we discuss ways risky business decisions can be viewed and evaluated as options.

Table 2.1, a summary report provided by your financial analyst, is a central tool for this chapter. (In fact, with minor modifications, Table 2.1 can be used as a template to evaluate *any* resource allocation problem.) The numbers labeled NPV and

IRR at the end of the table both indicate that investment in the new Mach O plant would increase shareholder value.

◪ Net Present Value

The Net Present Value method is widely used to make resource allocation decisions. The NPV of an investment measures the change in shareholders' current wealth that should result from the investment. In other words, it is the value, or wealth, created for shareholders if the investment is undertaken. Notice that the wealth is said to be "created" at the time of the decision, in anticipation of future benefits.

Calculating and Interpreting Net Present Value

The estimates for the Mach O project, provided in Table 2.1, allow us to calculate NPV. The calculation involves four steps:

1. Estimate all expected cash flows that the investment entails (Table 2.1, line 30). This includes all the inflows and outflows from the investment, reflected in the earlier part of the table and summarized in lines 26 through 29.
2. Estimate the risk of the project.
3. Estimate the annual rate of return that the investors can earn elsewhere at the same risk. This rate of return, expressed as a percentage, is called the cost of capital (Table 2.1, line 1) because it is what the investors give up by investing in the project instead of in alternative opportunities elsewhere at the same risk.
4. Discount the estimated cash flows at the cost of capital (Table 2.1, line 32) and sum them to find the NPV, shown as a rounded value in the third column.

Table 2.1. Financial Analysis of Mach O ($ and volume in millions, except per-unit figures)

Data

1. Cost of capital (percent) = 15
2. Tax rate (percent) = 35
3. Capital expenditure = $278
4. Salvage value (percent of capital expenditure) = 30

Year	2005	2006	2007	2008	2009	2010	2011	Notes
5 Price per unit		$250.00	$250.00	$230.00	$225.00	$225.00	$210.00	—
6 Volume		1.2	2.1	3.0	3.0	2.2	1.4	—
7 Cost of goods sold per unit		$80.00	$80.00	$70.00	$70.00	$70.00	$85.00	—
8 Selling, general, and administrative costs	$15.00	$15.75	$16.75	$18.00	$19.25	$20.50	$22.00	—
9 Depreciation schedule (percent)		20.00	32.00	19.20	11.52	11.52	5.76	—
10 Working capital/Forward revenue (percent)*	9	9	8	7	7	7		—
11 Annual depreciation		$55.60	$88.96	$53.38	$32.03	$32.03	$16.01	Depreciation schedule × Capital expenditure
12 Accumulated depreciation		$55.60	$144.56	$197.94	$229.96	$261.99	$278.00	Sum of all depreciation up to that year
13 Book value	$278.00	$222.40	$133.44	$80.06	$48.04	$16.01	$0.00	Capital expenditure – Accumulated depreciation
14 Working capital	$27.00	$47.25	$55.20	$47.25	$34.65	$20.58	$0.00	Working capital/Forward revenue × Next year revenue
15 Salvage value							$83.40	30 percent of capital expenditure

Cash flow template

	Year 0	Year 1	Year 2	Year 3	Year 4	Year 5	Year 6	Description
16 Revenue		$300.00	$525.00	$690.00	$675.00	$495.00	$294.00	Price per unit x Volume
17 Cost of goods sold		($96.00)	($168.00)	($210.00)	($210.00)	($154.00)	($119.00)	Variable cost per unit x Volume
18 Selling, general, and administrative costs	($15.00)	($15.75)	($16.75)	($18.00)	($19.25)	($20.50)	($22.00)	
19 Depreciation		($55.60)	($88.96)	($53.38)	($32.03)	($32.03)	($16.01)	—
20 Profit from asset sale							$83.40	Salvage value – Book value
21 Taxable income	($15.00)	$132.65	$251.29	$408.62	$413.72	$288.47	$220.39	Sum of lines above
22 Tax	$5.25	($46.43)	($87.95)	($143.02)	($144.80)	($100.97)	($77.14)	—
23 NOPAT	($9.75)	$86.22	$163.34	$265.61	$268.92	$187.51	$143.25	Taxable income – Tax
24 Depreciation		$55.60	$88.96	$53.38	$32.03	$32.03	$16.01	Add back depreciation (noncash)
25 Profit from asset sale		$0.00	$0.00	$0.00	$0.00	$0.00	($83.40)	Deduct profit from asset sale (noncash)
26 Operating cash flow	($9.75)	$141.82	$252.30	$318.98	$300.95	$219.53	$75.86	NOPAT + depreciation – profit from asset sale
27 Change in working capital	($27.00)	($20.25)	($7.95)	$7.95	$12.60	$14.07	$20.58	—
28 Capital expenditure	($278.00)							
29 Cash flow from asset sale							$83.40	Salvage value
30 Free cash flow	($314.75)	$121.57	$244.35	$326.93	$313.55	$233.60	$179.84	Operating CF + change in working capital – capital expenditure + cash from asset sale
31 Discount factor	1.0000	0.8696	0.7561	0.6575	0.5718	0.4972	0.4323	Discount factor: PV of $1 in Year n at 15 percent $= [1/(1+0.15)]^n$
32 Discounted value	(314.75)	105.72	184.76	214.96	179.27	116.14	77.75	Free cash flow x Discount factor

NPV = $564

IRR (percent) = 63.3

*This ratio provides the working capital needed at the beginning of a year as a percentage of the projected revenues for that year. This is the total amount of working capital needed for a year and not the incremental need for that year.

NPV is a measure of wealth created by the project, and the rule for its application is simple: if the NPV is a positive number (as it is for the Mach O chip), the project should be undertaken. The NPV tells us that producing Mach O will increase shareholder value.

Note that step 1 refers to expected cash flows rather than profits. We explain later why NPV uses cash flows rather than profits. We call the cash flows "expected" because the flows are typically risky, and the realized cash flows may be greater or less than expected.

Steps 2 and 3, how to estimate risk and the cost of capital, are discussed in Chapter Three. For now, just note that in step 3, "cost of capital" refers to the rate of return that investors can earn elsewhere at the same risk. In other words, we are not limiting the investors to opportunities within the company or even within the industry. Shareholders or investors have the option of investing anywhere, which means that the company competes for capital with all other companies in the world. Therefore, the Mach O investment must provide a rate of return that equals or exceeds that available anywhere in the world at the same risk.

Computing the NPV in step 4 requires multiplying the expected future cash flows on line 30 by the "Discount Factor" on line 31 (a process called "discounting"). Future cash flows are discounted for two reasons. One reason is the relation between value and time. The Mach O project's cash flows are spread over seven years, from 2005 to 2011, and future cash flows are worth less than current cash flows. The second reason is the risk of the cash flows. A guaranteed future cash flow is worth more today than a risky future cash flow with the same expected value. In the financial analysis of Mach O, the cost of capital is 15 percent (Table 2.1, line 1). This number includes a component for time value (equal to the risk-free rate) plus a premium for the risk of the project.

How does the discounting actually work? In other words, given a cost of capital, how do we arrive at the discount factors? In the Mach O example, the cost of capital is 15 percent, so to earn one dollar at the end of one year in an alternative investment at the same risk, one needs to invest $1 \div 1.15 = \$0.8696$ today (note that an investment of $0.8696 today is expected to return $0.8696 \times 1.15 = \$1$ one year later). This implies that a dollar expected at the end of one year at this risk is worth $0.8696 today. Therefore, the expected cash flow of $121.57 million in the year 2006 from the Mach O project (see line 30 of Table 2.1) is worth $121.57 \times 0.8696 = \$105.72$ million in 2005. (You can see this figure in Table 2.1, line 32, labeled "Discounted value"). Table 2.2 provides the details of the calculations for all the years. The discounted cash flows (Table 2.1, line 32) are then summed to obtain an NPV of $564 million for the Mach O project.

At this point, you have the basic idea behind NPV and a general notion of how it is calculated. Later in the chapter, under the heading "Expected Cash Flows," we return to the question of what exactly cash flows are and how they differ from profits or net income that companies report in their financial statements.

FAQs About NPV

Here are some questions frequently asked about NPV:

Suppose I have to evaluate two projects with different risks. For example, I have to choose between investing in research and development of more advanced microchips and investing in expansion of existing product lines. How do I use the NPV rule?

First you estimate the expected future cash flows and the investment needed today for each project. Then you estimate the cost of capital (more about this in Chapter Three) for each project based on the risk of the project. Finally you calculate the NPV of each project by discounting the cash flows of each project by the cost of capital of that project. Obviously, if one project's NPV is

Table 2.2. **Discounting Mach 0 Cash Flows**

Value of $1 invested at 15 percent after		
1 year	1.15	$= 1.1500$
2 years	1.15^2	$= 1.3225$
3 years	1.15^3	$= 1.5209$
4 years	1.15^4	$= 1.7490$
5 years	1.15^5	$= 2.0114$
6 years	1.15^6	$= 2.3131$

Value today of $1 received in the future if the annual rate of return is 15 percent	
Year received	**Value today**
1	$1/1.1500 = \$0.8696$
2	$1/1.3225 = \$0.7561$
3	$1/1.5209 = \$0.6575$
4	$1/1.7490 = \$0.5718$
5	$1/2.0114 = \$0.4972$
6	$1/2.3131 = \$0.4323$

Present value of Mach 0 cash flows in Table 2.1		
Year	**Cash flow**	**Present value**
0	($314.75)	($314.75) $\times$ 1.0000 = ($314.75)
1	$121.57	$121.57 $\times$ 0.8696 = $105.72
2	$244.35	$244.35 $\times$ 0.7561 = $184.76
3	$326.93	$326.93 $\times$ 0.6575 = $214.96
4	$313.55	$313.55 $\times$ 0.5718 = $179.27
5	$233.60	$233.60 $\times$ 0.4972 = $116.14
6	$179.84	$179.84 $\times$ 0.4323 = $77.75
		Total $563.86

positive and the other negative, you will invest in the positive one. As for other possibilities:

- If both NPVs are negative, reject both.
- If both NPVs are positive and the projects are mutually exclusive (that is, you can implement only one or the other), take the one with the greater NPV.
- If both NPVs are positive but you have enough capital only for one of them, take the one with the greater NPV.

- If both NPVs are positive, and the limitations in the previous two options do not exist, take both.

Does the NPV methodology imply that a company should not use a single company cost of capital for all resource allocation decisions?

In principle, yes, because every project has its own cost of capital based on its risk. However, as a practical convenience, a multidivisional company might use different costs of capital for projects from different divisions but the same cost of capital for projects from the same division. The assumption here is that projects from the same divisions have approximately the same risk and, therefore, approximately the same cost of capital. As noted in Chapter Three, the cost of capital cannot be calculated with great accuracy, so it does not make sense to differentiate between costs of capital that are very close to each other.

Doesn't the company face a single cost of capital in the market? After all, companies do not raise capital on a project-by-project basis.

It is true that companies do not raise capital on a project-by-project basis and, therefore, face a single cost of capital in the market. However, consider how the market arrives at this cost of capital. Suppose a company has two projects. Ideally, shareholders will attempt to estimate the expected future cash flows and investments of each project and, in addition, the risks of each project. Then for each project, shareholders estimate the cost of capital, that is, what they can earn elsewhere at the same risk. Shareholders will then charge in aggregate a blended average of the costs of capital of the two projects.

What would happen if we used the single company cost of capital for all projects?

Consider a company that has only two projects, one low risk and one high risk. Let the cost of capital of the low-risk project be 10 percent and that of the high-risk project be 20 percent, and say the blended average company cost of capital is 15 percent. If you use the blended cost to evaluate both projects, you will favor the high-risk project while penalizing the low-risk project. The high-risk project's cash flows, if discounted at the lower company cost of capital (15 percent), will yield a higher-than-deserved NPV. The low-risk project's cash flows, on the other hand, are being discounted at a higher cost of capital relative to their risk, resulting in a lower NPV than is appropriate. Such errors might result in serious misallocation of capital: accepting the high-risk project even if it destroys value while ignoring the low-risk project even if it adds value.

This explains why your division might be charged a higher cost of capital than some other divisions of the company. Clearly the company views your division as riskier than these other divisions.

What happens if I have a zero-NPV project or if the NPV is barely positive?

Theoretically, you should be indifferent between taking and not taking a zero-NPV project. In practice, most companies are unlikely to accept a project with a barely positive NPV as it is a lot of work for very little value added. Most companies use a positive (instead of a zero) threshold to accept a project. Sometimes though, companies realize that certain nonquantifiable benefits have been excluded from the NPV calculation. In this case, they might accept a zero-NPV project (or even a negative-NPV project) if the nonquantifiable benefits are significant enough.

My company imposes a hurdle rate on investment decisions. Is a hurdle rate the same as the cost of capital?

A hurdle rate is the minimum annual rate of return you are expected to earn from your investments. Therefore, conceptually, it is the same as the cost of capital. However, most companies add a premium to the cost of capital to obtain the hurdle rate. The idea is equivalent to having a positive acceptance threshold for NPV instead of a zero threshold. In other words, companies want to undertake only those projects that add a minimum positive value to shareholders, for any of several reasons. Most companies face resource constraints in terms of human resources and sometimes capital. Therefore, if they devote these scarce resources to marginal projects, they will miss the opportunity to invest them in potentially higher-valued future opportunities. Another reason the hurdle rate is often set higher than the cost of capital is that managers who propose the project are likely to be overoptimistic about the probability of the project's success.

Cash flows in the distant future are likely to be more risky than ones in the near future. Does the NPV rule factor this in?

In the quickly evolving microchip business, it is difficult to predict what will happen after a few years in terms of production technology, demand for products, and so on. Fortunately, the NPV rule does consider the greater risks that may be inherent in estimates of distant cash flows. It assumes that distant cash flows are likely to be riskier. In Mach O example, consider the discount factors used in Table 2.2. Note that the discount factor for the first year cash flow is 0.8696 while the discount factor for the second year cash flow is only 0.7561 (0.8696 × 0.8696). This shows that the cash flow in the second year is discounted twice, whereas the cash flow in the first year is discounted only once. Part of the additional discounting is to account for the time value of money, but part of it is also for additional risk. Net Present Value calculations assume that the risk of the cash flow increases at a constant rate over time. Only if you believe that the risk does not increase at a constant rate over time do you need to make adjustments to the standard NPV calculation. Consider the first-time launch of a new product such as Personal Organizer. Most of the risk is in the earlier years, when there is uncertainty about how the product will do in the marketplace (how well it meets customer needs, effect of competition, and so on). After this initial period, the subsequent cash flows are likely to be less risky. So it is reasonable to use a higher cost of capital for the initial years but a lower one for the later years.

NPV and Shareholder Value

Because your CEO emphasizes shareholder value, you wish to ensure that the decision criteria you use will result in increased shareholder value. While you understand that NPV measures the value created, you may be uncertain about how a project's positive NPV manifests as an increase in shareholder wealth.

Shareholder wealth can increase in two ways: the shareholder can either receive cash dividends or sell shares at a profit. When investors expect a positive-NPV project to increase a company's future cash flows (after adjusting for any needed future investment), they anticipate higher future cash dividends, in which shareholders who hold the company's shares for the long term will partake. The Mach O project has an NPV of $564 million. This means that, in present value terms, the company expects to generate $564 million more than it invests in the project, and this is the fund of future cash from which the company can pay the dividends.

In addition, the present value of the anticipated additional dividends will be reflected as an increase in stock price. Therefore, shareholders who wish to sell the shares in the near term will also benefit, as the stock price will have increased by the present value of the anticipated additional dividends. How much will the price increase? Say the company has 100 million outstanding shares. In this case, if the market obtains information about the NPV of the project (and agrees that it is $564 million), the stock price will increase by $5.64 ($564 million NPV ÷ 100 million shares).

However, keep in mind that an increase in share price equal to the per-share NPV will happen only if the stock price reflects the information about the project, and the market's assessment of the project is congruent with the managers' assessment. Many smaller companies, which are not widely followed by investment professionals, will find that the net present values of the projects they undertake are not quickly reflected in the stock price. Even bigger companies with a wider analyst following might find that the investment community often disagrees with their estimate of the value created by a decision. This highlights the importance of keeping credible communication channels open with the investment community.

If the company is not publicly traded and if it cannot spin off the project, then the wealth created by the discovery of the project can be realized only over time as the project cash flows are realized and paid out as dividends.

◼ Internal Rate of Return

When we use NPV, we evaluate a project based on the value it adds over what the investors could have earned elsewhere at the same risk. Thus, the NPV is a value measure. We can also evaluate a project in terms of its *rate of return*. To do this, we can compute the expected annual rate of return of the project and compare the rate to the cost of capital. Again, in effect, we are comparing the return on the project to what the investors could have earned elsewhere at the same risk. This methodology is called Internal Rate of Return (IRR).

IRR is intended to measure the expected "average" annual rate of return of an investment.[1] How do we use the IRR as a capital budgeting rule? Since IRR purports to measure the annual expected return of the project, we accept the project if the IRR exceeds the cost of capital, the rate of return investors can obtain from alternative investments of the same risk. Here is the IRR rule:

If IRR > Cost of capital, accept the project.

We can illustrate IRR using the same set of Mach O data that we used to illustrate NPV. First, however, it's useful to explore two other simple examples to illustrate the basic intuition.

Two Simple Examples

Consider Figure 2.1, which relates to a one-year project that requires an investment of $100 today and is expected to produce $110 in cash flow next year. In this case, the expected return next year is 10 percent ((110 – 100) ÷ 100). Since there is only one return, the average expected return is also 10 percent, which is the IRR of the project. Suppose the cost of capital is 8 percent. In that case, the IRR rule says that the company owner should accept the project.

Now consider Figure 2.2. Here, an investment of $4,000 today is expected to yield cash flows of $800 each year for the next five years plus the original $4,000 back at the end of the fifth year. Note that this cash flow pattern is similar to that of a certificate of deposit or a bond. You invest $4,000 now and, in return, expect to receive an interest of $800 each year for four years and the principal of $4,000 at the end of the fourth year. In this

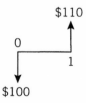

Figure 2.1. Cash Flows for a One-Year Project

case, the annual expected return is 20 percent ($800 \div 4{,}000$) each year. Therefore, the average annual expected return is also 20 percent, which is the IRR.

In these examples, the IRR calculations are simple because calculating the average is trivial: in the first example, there is only one year to consider; in the second example the expected returns are the same each year. In a more general example, however, the calculation becomes more complicated because the process of finding the average is more complex. In real-world financial calculations involving multiple years, we cannot take a simple average because the process of discounting makes the problem nonlinear. Therefore, the concept of an average expected annual rate of return is not well defined except for simple cases.

If the notion of average expected annual rate of return is not well defined in general, then what is IRR? To understand what IRR really represents, consider the first two examples again. Note that if we discount the future cash flows at a rate equal to IRR and subtract the initial investment, we get zero:

One-year example: $110 \div 1.1 - 100 = 0$.
Five-year example: $800 \div 1.2 + 800 \div 1.2^2 + 800 \div 1.2^3 +$
$$800 \div 1.2^4 + 4{,}800 \div 1.2^5 - 4{,}000 = 0.$$

This is not surprising. In these two simple cases, IRR *is* the average annual expected rate of return. Recall that, when we

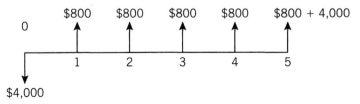

Figure 2.2. Cash Flows for Multiple Years

find a value using NPV, the rate used to discount cash flows is the rate of return investors can earn elsewhere at the same risk. Likewise, when we discount cash flows at the IRR, we are implicitly assuming that the rate of return investors can earn elsewhere equals the IRR. However, if the investors can earn elsewhere a rate of return equaling the average expected return from the project, the project adds no value to them. Therefore, the discounted cash flows net of initial investment will be zero if we use IRR as the discount rate.

To summarize, in these simple examples, the average annual expected rate of return is also the rate that yields zero as the NPV of the expected future cash flows. While average annual expected rate of return is generally not well defined, the rate that produces zero as the NPV of the expected future cash flows is much simpler to specify. In other words, in most cases you can calculate the rate that gives a present value of zero for the expected future cash flows net of the initial investment. Then you can simply assume that this rate is also the average annual expected rate of return, the IRR.[2] This is why we stated in our definition of IRR that it is "*intended* to measure the expected 'average' annual rate of return of an investment." In the case of the Mach O project, the IRR is 63.3 percent (if we discount the expected cash flows on line 30 at 63.3 percent, we get an NPV of zero), which exceeds the cost of capital of 15 percent. If we interpret the IRR as the average annual expected rate of return, then the IRR rule suggests that we should accept the project.

Comparing IRR and NPV

If shareholders expect to earn more from a project than from alternative investments at the same risk, the project will increase shareholders' wealth, and hence the NPV of the project will also be positive.[3] For instance, in the one-year IRR example, with a cost of capital of 8 percent, the NPV of the project is $1.85 (110

÷ 1.08 − 100). Thus, in that example, there is a correspondence between the IRR rule and the NPV rule: If NPV is positive, IRR > Cost of capital; if NPV is negative, IRR < Cost of capital; and, if NPV is zero, IRR = Cost of capital.

In most cases, decisions made by using IRR are consistent with those using the NPV rule—that is, both rules result in the same decision. However, in some instances the decisions will not match up. Such inconsistencies arise from the assumption that the rate that yields an NPV of zero for the expected future cash flows is also the average annual expected rate of return.[4] When the IRR and NPV methods give conflicting results, the decision should be based on the NPV rule. Overall, NPV is the cleaner measure of value creation. Thus, we recommend that you always calculate the NPV even if you like using the IRR rule.

FAQs About IRR

My company still uses IRR in addition to NPV, and you've told me that sometimes a decision based on the IRR rule may not result in increased shareholder value. Independent of comparing it with NPV, is there any way for me to tell when the IRR rule will result in decisions consistent with shareholder value maximization?

Yes, but not always. When the cash flow stream you are evaluating contains only one change in the sign of the cash flows, so negative cash flows in earlier periods are followed by positive cash flows in later periods, the IRR rule will result in decisions consistent with shareholder value maximization. If the signs of cash flows change more than once, decisions made using the IRR rule will not necessarily result in increased shareholder value.

The example in Figure 2.3 illustrates a situation in which the IRR rule provides a value-decreasing recommendation, in contrast to the NPV rule.

A pharmaceutical company plans to acquire the rights of a new drug developed by a biotech company. The cash flows from the commercialization of the drug are expected to be $450 per year for the next ten years, starting from next year. The biotech company has offered the pharmaceutical company two payment options for the rights to the drug:

- Make three installment payments of $1150 each in years 0, 4, and 8.
- Make a one-time payment of $2400 now.

Which of the two payment options should the pharmaceutical company take?

The following table summarizes the analysis. If one uses the NPV rule, it is clear that the one-time payment option creates more value for the pharmaceutical company than the installment option (NPV of $365.06 versus $293.11).

Since risk is not an issue between the choices (the cash inflows of $450 are the same for both choices and the payments have no risk associated with them), one might be tempted to pick the option with the greater IRR. This favors the installment option over the one-time payment option (IRR of 17.16 percent instead of 13.43 percent), even though the installment option is of lower value.

			Cost of capital = 10 percent		
Year	CF from Drug	Installment Payment	Net CF from Installment Option	One-Time Payment	Net CF from One-Time Payment Option
(1)	(2)	(3)	(2) + (3)	(4)	(2) + (4)
0		($1,150)	($1,150)	($2,400)	($2,400)
1	$450		$450		$450
2	$450		$450		$450
3	$450		$450		$450
4	$450	($1,150)	($700)		$450
5	$450		$450		$450
6	$450		$450		$450
7	$450		$450		$450
8	$450	($1,150)	($700)		$450
9	$450		$450		$450
10	$450		$450		$450
		NPV	$293.11		$365.06
		IRR (percent)	17.16		13.43

Figure 2.2. IRR Rule Is Not Always Consistent With Value Creation: Example

Suppose I have two projects that are competing for capital. Project A has an IRR of 18 percent while Project B has an IRR of 14 percent. Should I simply choose Project A?

Most people would do so, presumably based on the notion that they should pick the project with the higher return. But most people forget that IRR measures the *expected* average annual return, which implies that these projects are risky, and the information given thus far does not specify what the risks of the projects are. In other words, in comparing only the two IRRs, a company is trying to make a resource allocation decision without assessing the risks of the projects. Suppose Project B is less risky and has a cost of capital of 12 percent while Project A is riskier and therefore has a higher cost of capital of 20 percent. Using the IRR rule and comparing the IRR of each project with the respective cost of capital, it is obvious that Project B must be chosen.

The key issue to understand is that the IRR *measure* does not incorporate risk as it is based entirely on expected cash flows. The IRR *rule,* however, incorporates risk since it requires comparison of IRR to cost of capital, which is based on risk. The NPV *measure,* on the other hand, incorporates risk since NPV is obtained by discounting the expected cash flows by a risk-based cost of capital.

What is the difference between Return on Assets and IRR?

Return on Assets (ROA) is the ratio of net income to total assets. There are two fundamental differences between ROA and IRR. First, ROA is based on historical numbers from accounting statements and is an indicator of past performance; it is used to assess the performance in a single year. IRR, on the other hand, is forward-looking and is based on estimates of future cash flows; it is used to make resource allocation decisions. Second, measures such as ROA are not based on cash flows. As is obvious from its definition, ROA is based on net income (profit), which is not a cash number (a point we explain in detail later in the chapter).

The same differences exist between IRR and measures similar to ROA such as Return on Net Assets (RONA), Return on Investment (ROI), and Return on Capital Employed (ROCE).

Does IRR measure the expected return to stockholders?

This depends on the cash flows on which IRR is calculated. If we calculate IRR based on cash flows to stockholders, then we get the expected return to stockholders. If we calculate IRR based on cash flows generated by a project (before it is split into cash flows for various capital providers such as lenders and stockholders), then we get the expected return from the project. The cash flow template we use in Table 2.1, which is similar to the ones companies normally use, measures cash flows generated by the project.

What is the link between IRR and stock price?

The link between IRR and stock price is not as obvious as the link between NPV and stock price. All we can say is that if the IRR exceeds the cost of capital, the stock price will increase if the information about the project is conveyed to the market and the market agrees with the company's estimates.

■ Estimating Inputs: Expected Cash Flows

Now that you have a grasp of NPV and IRR as two common methods for project analysis and their implications for shareholder value, let's look more closely at the input data that they require. Both methods require two sets of inputs: the expected cash flows and the cost of capital. Understanding how each set of inputs is estimated will help you identify the value drivers of the project. That, in turn, will enable you to optimize those value drivers to maximize the value created.

All resource allocation decisions should be based on cash flows, because ultimately the value of a business is based on the amount of net cash (cash inflows less outflows) it generates. Before the advent of modern accounting systems, all businesses were run on a cash basis. The introduction of accounting measures such as profits (net income or earnings) and the importance given to these measures by the investment community has obscured the importance of cash flows. Profits, while correlated with cash flows, include several noncash items and therefore are different from cash flows.

Operating Cash Flows

Look back at Table 2.1. Lines 1 through 10 provide the data to evaluate the project. Per line 3, the project requires $278 million capital investment for fixed assets such as land, buildings, and machinery. This item is often called *capital expenditure*. The project also requires working capital (line 10), which is estimated as a percentage of forward revenue. Notice that the projected unit price declines over time in anticipation of competing products. Similarly, the volume (line 6) increases initially as the price falls, but declines in anticipation of better products. The per-unit Cost of Goods Sold (COGS) (line 7) includes direct production costs such as labor and material costs, energy costs, and so on. Selling, General, and Administrative costs, or SG&A (line 8), include costs that usually do not vary with the quantity produced. These typically include selling costs, administrative overhead, costs of information and accounting systems, and so on. The depreciation schedule (line 9) is based on the tax rules applicable to the items involved. The estimation period is six years because Mach O is expected to be obsolete by then. Since the capital equipment is expected to last more than six years, it is estimated that it can be sold for 30 percent of the original price (line 4). Table 2.3 provides a list of factors to be considered while making cash flow estimates.

Table 2.3. **Factors to Consider While Making Cash Flow Estimates**

Items	Factors to Consider	Questions to Ask
Price, volume	Competition from existing products	If we are facing a competitive marketplace for our product, what
	Competition from technological advances	is the volume we can sell?
		If we have a monopoly or quasi-monopoly, what is the demand for
	Value to customer	the product at various price levels (demand curve)?
		If we have a monopoly or quasi-monopoly, how long before competition enters the market?
		Can we use pricing strategy to deter competition for some time, if not forever?
		At the price we plan to sell, does the product add value to the customer?
		Is there cannibalization of an existing product?
Variable costs	Labor	Is labor cost truly variable or is
	Material	there rigidity due to labor contracts?
	Energy	Can we reduce material price risks through long-term contracts or price-hedging techniques?
		Do we have long-term contracts for energy costs or are we susceptible to market factors?
Fixed costs	Marketing (sales, advertising)	Are the fixed costs incremental? In other words, would we incur these
	Information technology	costs even if we did not make this product?
	Accounting	
	Management	
Capital expenditure	Property	Can we use existing capacity to
	Plant	make the product?

Table 2.3. Factors to Consider While Making Cash Flow Estimates, Cont'd

Items	Factors to Consider	Questions to Ask
	Equipment	If we can, are we using the market value of the existing capacity as a measure of the capital expenditure? Is it cheaper to outsource some or all the components?
Working capital	Inventory Accounts receivable Accounts payable	Have we minimized the inventory of raw material, finished goods? Can we reduce the cycle time, thereby reducing work-in-progress inventory? Have we checked the credit-worthiness of our customers? Are our collection systems efficient and do they minimize the time it takes to collect cash? Do we have payment systems in place that enable us to pay our suppliers on the last possible day?

Lines 11–15 of Table 2.1 are derived from the data in lines 1–10. Annual depreciation (line 11) is simply the depreciation schedule applied to the capital expenditure. Line 12 provides the accumulated depreciation to date. Line 13 provides the book value of the assets purchased and equals the difference between the capital expenditure and the accumulated depreciation. Line 14 provides the estimates of working capital required in each year while Line 15 provides the estimated salvage value.

A standard cash flow template can be used to estimate the cash flows of most resource allocation decisions with minor modifications. Lines 16–30 of Table 2.1 represent the cash flow template. In our cash flow template we use the following sign convention: inflows are positive; outflows are negative and shown in parentheses in the table. The cash flow template can be broadly divided into three parts. The first part is an operating income statement (lines 16 through 23). The operating income statement is very similar to the income statement found in a company's financial reports, except that the former considers only operational items and ignores financial items such as interest expense. The operating income statement contains four classes of items:

- Revenue items
- Cost items
- Depreciation items
- Profit or loss from asset sales

Everyone knows what revenue (line 16) is. Cost items (lines 17 and 18) include Cost of Goods Sold (COGS), Selling, General, and Administrative cost (SG&A) and any other out-of-pocket costs incurred for the project.

Depreciation (line 19) arises the following way. When you buy capital equipment (usually defined as equipment that lasts more than one year), you are not allowed to treat it as an expense for tax purposes in the year incurred. In other words, you cannot claim a tax deduction in 2005 for the entire $278 million you plan to spend for plant and equipment for Mach O. Tax laws require you to spread this amount over a specified number of years. The number of years over which you are required to spread the investment varies depending on the capital item involved. It is important to note that depreciation is not a cash expenditure.

Profit or loss from asset sales (line 20) is defined as follows for tax purposes. In the Mach O example, you expect to sell the plant and equipment after six years for 30 percent of the original purchase price of $278 million, or $83.4 million. The "profit" you make from this sale is the difference between what you sell it for and the book value of the assets at that point in time, that is, the value of the assets in the balance sheet. The book value of the assets at any given point in time is the difference between the original purchase price and the accumulated depreciation till that time. In this example, the original capital expenditure is fully depreciated at the end of six years. Since you expect to sell the plant and equipment after six years for $83.4 million, the taxable profit is also $83.4 million. Like depreciation, profit from asset sales is not a cash item because its calculation involves book values, which are not cash items.

Once the four components of the operating income statement are calculated, we can calculate the taxable income (line 21). Deducting taxes (line 22) at 35 percent, we get line 23, the after-tax operating income, which we call **Net Operating Profit After Taxes (NOPAT).**[5] Note that NOPAT in itself is not a cash flow because it includes noncash items. As discussed, depreciation (line 19) is not a cash flow since we do not actually spend this amount in the year indicated; rather, it is a way of spreading out the capital expenditure (incurred in an earlier year) over time for tax purposes. As long as we account for the capital expenditure that created the depreciation in the year in which it was incurred, the only cash effect of the depreciation is the reduction in taxes in the years in which it is deducted. Now that we have calculated the tax effect of the depreciation, we should add it back to the NOPAT as we have not actually spent it (line 24).

A second type of noncash item in the NOPAT statement is the profit or loss from asset sales (line 20). Again, the cash received from asset sale is the selling price or the salvage value of the asset. But an asset sale also triggers a tax event. The tax (or tax credit) is based on the so-called profit (or loss) from the asset sale. Once we account for the cash received from the asset sale and deduct the tax on the profit, the profit in itself should not play a role in estimating the cash flow. As with the depreciation, the profit should be subtracted from the NOPAT to calculate the cash flow (line 25).

Once these adjustments (or any other noncash adjustments) are made, we get line 26, the **operating cash flow**. All that remains is to take into account the capital required to generate this operating cash flow. The next part of the template deals with capital items. Note that the capital expenditure or the cash received from asset sales are not included in the operating cash flow as they are separately accounted for under capital items.

Capital Items

In general, a project needs two types of capital:

- Fixed capital, usually referred to as capital expenditure or *cap-ex*
- Working capital

Fixed capital is cash spent to acquire fixed assets such as land, buildings, plant, and equipment. On the balance sheet, fixed assets are sometimes referred to as Property, Plant, and Equipment, or PP&E. In our example (lines 28 and 29), $278 million is to be invested in plant and equipment in Year 2005 and $83.4 million of this investment is estimated to be recovered at the end of the project in Year 2011.

The motive for working capital is a bit more subtle. Working capital is required to enable the company to pay its suppliers and employees before collections from sales are realized. In other words, the need for working capital arises purely from the timing gap between when bills are due and when collections are realized. Therefore, if we make cash flow estimates on a day-by-day basis and book cash inflows and outflows precisely on the days they occur, we are automatically accounting for the timing gap and hence accounting for the working capital. However, when a company is evaluating a multiyear project, it is nearly impossible to estimate cash flows on a day-by-day basis. Most cash flow estimates for long-term projects are done on an annual basis, while short-term (one- to three-year) project estimates are done on a quarterly basis. It is the custom to assume that all revenues and costs occur at the end of the long-term year or the short-term quarter. Thus, the yearly or quarterly practice ignores the timing gap between collections and payments, thus ignoring the working capital requirement. Therefore, we do need to incorporate the working capital requirement separately into the analysis.

To estimate the working capital needs of a project, it is useful to understand the factors that drive those needs. Since most companies sell on credit, that is, offer interest-free loans to their customers, accounts receivable is an important component of working capital. The longer the collection period, the greater the accounts receivable per unit of sales and the greater the working capital. Companies that purchase materials and process them to create a product need working capital that allows them to acquire and hold inventory in various forms: raw materials, work-in-progress, and finished goods. Some of the working capital is also held as cash, called *operating cash* (for example, between collection and payments, the working capital could be held in cash). However, these working capital needs are often partially offset by the interest-free credit provided by suppliers (accounts payable), by employees, if some of their compensation (such as bonuses) could be deferred (accrued wages), and by the government, which permits taxes to be paid once a quarter (accrued taxes). Sometimes, though, suppliers insist on advance payments (prepaid expenses) which increase working capital needs. By the same token, any advances collected from customers (customer advances) reduce working capital needs.

In summary, working capital needs can be calculated as the difference between current operating assets (operating cash, accounts receivable, inventory, prepaid expenses) and current operating liabilities (accounts payable, accrued wages and taxes, customer advances). Note that current operating assets differ from current assets found in balance sheets; the latter include short-term financial assets such as excess cash (cash in excess of operating needs) and interest-bearing marketable securities. Similarly, current operating liabilities differ from current liabilities found in balance sheets; the latter include interest-bearing liabilities such as short-term debt. The simple rule is that all interest-bearing assets and liabilities and any excess cash should be excluded from the current assets and liabilities in the balance sheet to estimate current operating assets and current operating liabilities, and the difference between those totals provides an estimate of the working capital needs.

Since working capital is needed to bridge the gap between collections and payments, it will depend on both operational efficiency (how fast you collect, how little inventory you hold, and so on) and on the scale of operations. Thus, for a given operational efficiency, working capital requirements increase with the scale of the project or company and are often estimated as a percentage of revenues and costs. Since costs can be approximated as a percentage of revenues, it is also customary to estimate the components of working capital as a percentage of revenues. Working capital is clearly required at the beginning of each period and is estimated as a percentage of the expected revenues during that period.

For the Mach O project, the working capital requirement drops in the first four years from 9 percent of revenues to 7 percent of revenues (see Table 2.1, line 10). This drop can be attributed to the company's intention to carry excess inventory in the earlier years because it is more uncertain of the demand for the chip. As the project evolves and its scale changes, the dollar amount of working capital required (Table 2.1, line 14) changes as well. As the volume of sales increases between 2005 and 2007, the amount of working capital required also increases. The company, therefore, needs to invest additional working capital during these years. (Note that the working capital invested in earlier years continues to fund the operations and remains in the company in the form of its components.) In the final years of the project, the volume of sales declines and the working capital required also declines. During these years, therefore, the company can release some of the working capital, which results in a cash inflow. At the end of the project, it is assumed that the remaining working capital is recovered fully: the inventory is sold at full value, the receivables are collected fully, and payables are paid off. Thus, the cash flow impact of working capital is captured by the *changes* in working capital (line 27).

Finding Total Cash Flows

Look at Table 2.1, lines 26 through 30. By subtracting the capital required (capital expenditures net of cash flow from asset sales, and changes in working capital) to the operating cash flow, we obtain the total cash flows of the project. These are called **free cash flows** because this project does not have any need of the funds they represent. The company is free to use these cash flows for any other purpose it deems important: invest in other projects, reduce debt, pay additional dividends, or repurchase shares.

FAQs About Estimating Cash Flows

Why do we ignore interest payments in calculating cash flows? After all, interest payments are cash outflows.

When we estimate the free cash flows of a project, we are calculating the cash flows *generated* by the project before any payments to the capital providers. To calculate the NPV, we then discount these cash flows at the **Weighted Average Cost of Capital (WACC)**—more about this in Chapter Three—which is a blended average of what the investors (both lenders and stockholders) could have earned elsewhere at the same risk. A positive NPV implies that the project is expected to generate more than enough cash to satisfy both lenders and stockholders. One of the components of WACC is the cost of debt, which captures the interest payments. Therefore, the interest cost is incorporated in the NPV calculations as part of the WACC. To include it again in the free cash flows would be double counting.

If we deduct the interest payments from the free cash flows, the remainder (called the *cash flow to equity*) accrues to the stockholders. To calculate the NPV using these cash flows to equity, we should discount them at the cost of equity, not at the WACC. Discounting equity cash flows at the cost of equity will provide an identical NPV as our method of discounting the free cash flows of the project by the WACC.

If we ignore interest payments, isn't the tax used in the calculation of NOPAT different from the actual tax paid for projects partially financed by debt?

This is true. The actual tax would be lower, since you get a deduction for interest. This tax deduction is accounted for by using the after-tax cost of debt in the WACC calculation.

I notice that some of our existing equipment (which was idle) is being used for the microchip project. No cost was assigned to this equipment since it was fully depreciated. Is this approach correct?

No, it is incorrect. Whether there is a cost to the use of a resource should not be based on the book value of the equipment. The economic cost of a resource is what you can earn from that resource if you did not use it for the project. If this equipment can be sold, the cash you receive from the sale (minus any taxes you have to pay on profit from the sale) is the cost you should assign to the project.

How does one decide on the horizon over which to do the financial analysis of a project?

Some companies arbitrarily fix a horizon (say five to ten years) and estimate all projects over this horizon. The idea is that all projects must prove themselves over this horizon; effectively these companies assign no value to any cash flow that occurs beyond this horizon. A more reasoned way of choosing the estimating horizon is as follows. If the project being considered relates to a product (say, a microchip), estimate cash flows over the useful life of the product. However, not all products have an easily specified useful life. For example, if a chemical company is considering investing in a new facility to produce a basic chemical, it is not possible to assign a life to the product to be manufactured. In this case, cash flows can be estimated over the useful life of the facility being built. The useful life of a facility can be defined as the period after which major reinvestments in the facility will be required.

■ Value Drivers

Now that we know how expected cash flows are arrived at, we can use this information to identify the value drivers of a project. Knowing the value drivers and how they affect cash flows enables the managers to take actions to optimize the drivers to increase shareholder value. Figure 2.4 summarizes the typical value drivers in resource allocation decisions. Let's briefly discuss the factors that impact each of the key value drivers.

Revenues

Revenues are driven by the product price and volume, both of which are affected by how competitive the marketplace is. It is important to consider what the useful life of the product is and what effect the entry and exit of competition and technological innovations have on the price and volume during the life of the product.

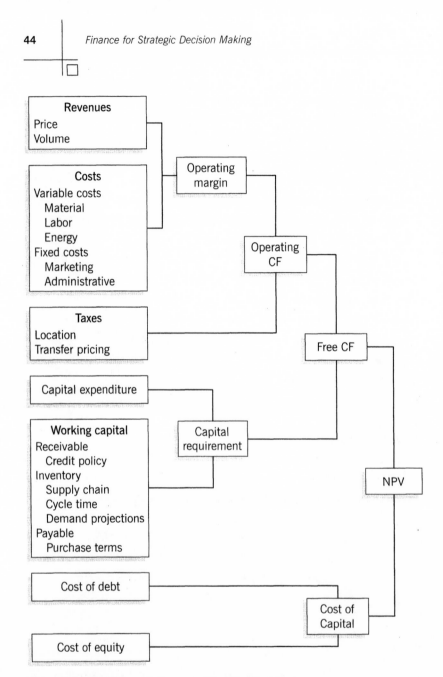

Figure 2.4. Value Drivers in Resource Allocation Decisions

Costs

Costs include the variable or direct costs (COGS) such as material, labor, and energy, and fixed costs such as marketing and administration (SG&A). It is important to include only incremental costs (costs affected by the decision being considered).

Taxes

Taxes have a significant impact on the value created. In the United States, the maximum federal corporate tax rate is 35 percent. In addition, states in the United States may charge a few percentage points in taxes. Therefore, taxes play an important role in deciding where (which country or state) to locate the facility. By locating high-profit centers in low-tax jurisdictions and low-profit centers in high-tax jurisdictions, a company can add value. In a company with some vertical integration, the profits of its units depend critically on the transfer price (the price charged between units of the company for internal transfers of goods and services). Companies with worldwide operations often follow transfer pricing policies to minimize taxes (high transfer prices if upstream units are located in low-tax regions and downstream units in high-tax regions, for example).

Capital Expenditures

Controlling capital expenditures adds value by lowering the capital charges. Capital expenditures can be lowered by fully utilizing excess capacity or by outsourcing production to companies with lower costs of capital.

Working Capital

As with capital expenditures, reducing the operating working capital required adds value by lowering capital charges. Reducing accounts receivable, inventory, or prepaid expenses, or increasing accounts payable or accrued expenses, will reduce the working capital needed. Accounts receivable can be reduced by offering tighter credit terms and screening out customers with poor credit. Inventory can be reduced by adopting just-in-time inventory practices, by reducing cycle time to reduce work-in-progress, and by more accurately forecasting demand to reduce finished goods inventory. Accounts payable and accrued expenses can be increased by lengthening payment periods to suppliers, employees, and the tax authority. Note that these suggestions assume that all other things are equal. In reality, though, there are trade-offs. For example, when you adopt a just-in-time inventory policy, you are transferring the inventory costs to your supplier, who in turn might compensate by charging you a higher price. Therefore, you reap a net benefit only if the benefit in capital costs offsets the increased price you have to pay.

■ Strategic Considerations

So far our focus has been on evaluating a project in isolation and identifying the drivers of its value. In this section, we place the resource allocation decision in the broader strategic context. Typically, you will always have more alternatives than a simple choice of implementing a project or not, based on the results of NPV or IRR. Since the NPV of the Mach O project is positive, the project clearly increases shareholder value, but does this mean that you should undertake the project? And what about the Mach I chip? Should that product be discontinued?

Considering All the Alternatives

The Mach O decision might seem obvious: If the project increases shareholder value, why not undertake it? Let's pause to consider. The analysis that is presented in Table 2.1 considers only the impact of introducing Mach O while discontinuing Mach I, but the Mach O case has three alternatives to consider (assuming that exiting the communication chip market altogether is not a viable option):

1. Introduce Mach O while discontinuing Mach I.
2. Introduce Mach O without discontinuing Mach I.
3. Do not introduce Mach O at all but continue to sell Mach I.

If you introduce Mach O while continuing to produce Mach I, you will sell fewer Mach O chips than you will in option 1. In addition, there will be some erosion or cannibalization of Mach I. Still, depending on the margins of each product and the demand for each, option 2 could very well be the most attractive one. Option 3, not introducing Mach O at all, is also worth strategic consideration. It is possible that the introduction of Mach O with its presumably higher price will result in some of your customer base (those who do not require the higher-speed chip) defecting to your competition. If the projected demand for the higher-speed communication chip does not fully materialize, continuing with Mach I might be the preferred option.

Effects of Competition

As the preceding paragraph implied, the effect of competition is another important strategic issue. If you expect the competition to introduce a high-speed communication chip similar to Mach O in the near future, the erosion of Mach I will occur anyway, the only question being how much of its erosion will be due to Mach O and how much due to the competition's product. Therefore, once we recognize that erosion of Mach I is inevitable, it follows that option 2 becomes more attractive (its NPV will be higher). In the presence of a new competing chip, the NPV of option 3 (do not introduce Mach O) decreases because sales of

□

Mach I will erode. Thus consideration of your competition's moves can have a significant impact on the NPV of your alternatives and, consequently, your strategy.

Treatment of Fixed Costs

The treatment of fixed costs is another issue that creates considerable debate in organizations. For example, in the Mach O case you notice that the financial analyst did not consider the salaries of the managers who were already in place (such as yourself) in the analysis in Table 2.1. The analysis was purely incremental; that is, it considered only additional costs to be incurred if you build the new plant for the production of Mach O, even though some of the senior managers of your team, including yourself, would be involved if the plant goes into production. The analyst supported this by pointing out that the managers' salaries will be paid whether Mach O is produced or not.

While you recognize this logic, you have two reservations. First, if every decision is made on an incremental basis, it is possible that the division will not make enough money to cover fixed costs. Second, if the new project gets a free ride with regard to fixed costs such as the entire salaries of the managers, existing operations of the division will be bearing these costs. The first reservation is indeed legitimate. Assume that the decision facing you is whether or not to invest in Mach O today and that there are no other alternatives. If the NPV of the Mach O project is positive on an incremental basis (as calculated by the analyst), it is better to produce Mach O than not produce it. However, if every project were decided on this basis, soon you could have a portfolio of projects that collectively do not recover your fixed costs. To protect against this possibility, you should periodically conduct a net present value analysis of the whole division, including these fixed costs. In other words, you conduct an incremental analysis for the whole division, assuming that these fixed costs will be incurred only if the division is profitable; if it is not, the managers will be laid off and the company will not incur these fixed costs.

The second reservation (about giving a free ride) is more a cost allocation issue than a resource allocation issue, but it is important from the perspective of incentive compensation. Allocation of costs between different operations does not affect shareholder wealth because the total costs are unaffected. However, shareholders can afford to ignore cost allocation only if managers will act to maximize shareholder wealth without any incentive compensation. In reality, this is unlikely—as the prevalence of incentive compensation practices proves. Shareholders and senior management representing them need to be cognizant of this issue. Unfortunately, it is not an easy one to resolve. If all managers of a division were compensated based only on overall divisional performance, then the cost allocation within divisional units would not affect their compensation, and hence would not affect their performance, either. Such a compensation system would create incentives to free-ride to some extent since individual units' performance would play no role in the compensation of the respective unit managers. If, on the other hand, unit managers' compensation were based solely on unit performance, cost allocation across units would become a contentious issue. The important thing to note is that cost allocation has no direct bearing on the resource allocation decision from the shareholders' perspective.

Resource Allocation as a Series of Embedded Options

So far, we have considered resource allocation decisions as a series of irreversible expected cash flows. A more appropriate way is to think of each investment as a series of options. For example, consider the strategy of introducing Mach O while continuing to produce Mach I. It may be possible to use existing facilities to introduce Mach O first on an experimental basis to gauge the demand. After that, if the demand for high-speed communications chips takes off as expected, a new full-scale production facility could be built. The investment in the pilot production provides the option of building a full-scale facility if the demand for the product is high. If not, you can choose not to build the full-scale facility and even consider shutting down the pilot production. Thus, the first investment should be evaluated not only on the basis of the NPV of the pilot production but also on the basis of the two options it provides: the option to build a full-scale facility and the option to shut down the pilot production. To see the value of viewing investments as options, consider Figure 2.5.

Suppose the NPV of the pilot production is negative: −$100 million. This might indicate that the pilot production in itself is a value-destroying decision. However, you recognize that the pilot production is a "loss leader" whose value lies in positioning the company to take advantage of a potential growth in demand with a full-scale production facility. You believe that, within a year, the uncertainty in demand will be largely resolved. You estimate a 50 percent probability that demand a year from now will be high, and if so, the NPV of the full-scale facil-

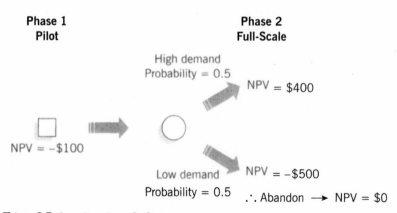

Figure 2.5. Investments as Options

ity will be positive: $400 million (in next-year dollars). Likewise, you estimate a 50 percent probability that demand will be low, in which case the NPV will be negative: $-$500 million. Assuming that you will inevitably go ahead with full-scale production, therefore, the expected NPV (before the demand is known) is $0.5 \times 400 + 0.5 \times (-500) = -$50 million. Since even the expansion phase has a negative NPV, the standard NPV analysis suggests there is no reason to invest in pilot production.

However, the standard analysis implicitly assumes that you make all your decisions today. Specifically, by using the net present values of the full-scale facility in both high- and low-demand states to arrive at the decision, you are effectively committing today to build the full-scale facility regardless of what the demand turns out to be a year later. Of course, you do not need to do so. In reality, you have the option of deciding whether to invest in the full-scale facility after observing the demand for the product during the first year. If the demand is low, you will not invest in the full-scale facility and, therefore, in that case, the NPV of next year's decision will be zero (not $-$500 million). This means that the expected NPV now (before the demand is known) of next year's decision is $0.5 \times 400 + 0.5 \times 0 = $200 million. Thus, it is worthwhile investing in pilot production today. This decision costs you $100 million today but buys you the option of building a full-scale plant a year later with an expected value of $200 million. Thus, viewing investments as options recognizes that decisions are made sequentially based on information available at the time of the decision, and improves the resource allocation process.

Similarly, if you decide not to introduce Mach O now, you still have the option of introducing it later. Therefore, the third strategy (do not introduce Mach O now) is really an option to introduce Mach O *later*, at an optimal future date. This strategy is more valuable than a simple NPV analysis would indicate. To correctly evaluate this strategy, we must evaluate the option to introduce Mach O at a future date and add it to the NPV of continuing with Mach I today.

In practice, every decision you make buys you several options for the future: expand, contract, abandon, switch, and so on. However, the analysis can get very complex very quickly if you wish to consider all the embedded options. You must decide which of the options are the important ones and limit the analysis to them. In general, the greater the uncertainty surrounding the variable underlying the option, the greater the value of the options. In Figure 2.5, for example, the greater the demand uncertainty, the greater the value of the option to wait to build a full-scale plant.

The fact that investment decisions involve options has been recognized for a long time. Recent advances in option pricing technology and the availability of cheap computing power and prepackaged option analysis software has made it possible for managers to incorporate options easily into their analysis.

SUMMARY

In this chapter we discuss the economics of resource allocation decisions in relation to shareholder value. Net present value (NPV) is the recommended method for evaluating resource allocation requests. It measures the value created. Internal Rate of Return (IRR) is a second method that gives recommendations consistent with NPV most but not all of the time.

To use either method, we need to estimate the expected cash flows of the project and its cost of capital, which is defined as the rate of return investors can earn from alternative investments (outside the company) with the same risk as the project. This suggests that, in principle at least, every project has its own cost of capital. In the case of the NPV methodology, we discount the expected cash flows at the cost of capital to compute the net present value and accept the project if the value is positive. In the IRR methodology, we calculate the internal rate of return based on the expected cash flows and accept the project if it exceeds the cost of capital.

This chapter discussed the estimation of cash flows, leaving the discussion on the cost of capital to Chapter Three. The cash flow template provided can be used to estimate the cash flows of any resource allocation decision with minor modifications. Five value drivers determine the cash flows: revenues, costs, taxes, and fixed and working capital.

Major resource allocation decisions involve more than a simple NPV calculation. Strategic alternatives must be considered, keeping in mind the effect of competition on the various alternatives available. If there is considerable uncertainty regarding the value drivers of the project, the major options embedded in the resource allocation decision must be explicitly considered and evaluated.

The next chapter completes the discussion on the resource allocation decision. In that chapter, we discuss the determination of the cost of capital. The content of both these chapters lays a framework that will be useful for later chapters such as mergers and acquisitions and performance evaluation.

Cost of Capital

C hapter Two presents the basics of NPV and IRR, two methods for resource allocation decisions. To implement either method, we need the cost of capital of the specific resource allocation decision (that is, the project under consideration). This chapter follows up by explaining how cost of capital can be determined for use in those methods. In discussing the cost of capital, we also address another related issue still pending from Chapter Two, namely, the estimation of risk. Let's begin once again with a case.

Suppose that, as head of strategic planning and business development for a conglomerate with interests in a wide range of consumer and industrial businesses, you are responsible for making recommendations to the CEO about all strategic capital investments. These decisions include proposing acquisitions and major capital expenditures of the various divisions in line with the firm's strategy. The proposal that you are currently evaluating concerns the purchase of a factory manufacturing basic chemicals from another company. As you evaluate the financial analysis, you notice that the cost of capital used to value the factory is different from your conglomerate's cost of capital and from that of the chemical division of your conglomerate. While you are able to critically evaluate the estimation of cash flows provided to you by your team, given your prior experience in manufacturing and marketing, you are unsure about how cost of capital is estimated. You recognize the need to understand how the cost of capital is determined to make effective resource allocation recommendations to the CEO.

■ WACC: A General Approach to Estimating Cost of Capital

Since the cost of capital of a project is determined by what investors expect to earn elsewhere at the same risk as the project, the cost of capital depends in part on the risk of the project. Therefore, one way of estimating the cost of capital of a project would be to estimate the risk of the project and use that estimate to compute its cost of capital. However, in practice, it is quite difficult to estimate the risk of an individual project.

In practice, typically, the cost of capital of a project is estimated by benchmarking it to a company that is publicly traded and whose risk is similar to that of the project under consideration. Since the benchmark company is publicly traded, we can obtain data to estimate its cost of capital; we then plausibly assume that this is the cost of capital of the project under consideration. The benchmark company is called a **pure play** of the project. In many cases, the pure play might be the same company that is considering the project. For example, if a cement company is considering opening another cement plant in a different location, then it can use its own cost of capital to evaluate the project. On the other hand, if a company that has produced only software is planning to produce a line of handheld organizers, it might wish to use the cost of capital of other companies that produce similar devices to evaluate the project.

In your case, your company's cost of capital is a blended average of the costs of capital of all its divisions. This cost of capital cannot be taken as the cost of capital of any single project from any of the divisions. Even the chemical division's cost of capital may be inappropriate because the division might be making products with different risk profiles. For example, specialty chemicals usually have a higher risk profile than basic chemicals.

The foregoing comments bring us to the central question of this chapter: How do we estimate the cost of capital of a pure play? By either observing or inferring the rate of return required by the investors. In general, a company has two types of investors: debtholders or lenders (who provide debt capital) and stockholders (who provide equity capital). The risk that these investors bear is primarily driven by the risk of the investments financed by their capital. Collectively, they bear the entire risk of the company and, therefore, collectively they demand a cost of capital that is related to the risk of the company. However, the two types of investors bear different risks. Specifically, debtholders bear less risk than stockholders by virtue of the seniority of their claims (they must be paid first before shareholders can be paid). This insight provides us a way to estimate the cost of capital of the pure play company: estimate its cost of debt capital and its cost of equity capital, and then find the weighted average of both, the weights being the proportions of debt and equity in the pure-play company's capital structure. Since this is a weighted average, it is often referred to as the **weighted average cost of capital (WACC)**. To find the WACC, we need three items:

- Cost of debt
- Cost of equity
- Proportions of debt and equity

For a pure play, these data either are available or can be estimated from publicly available data.

Estimating Cost of Debt

The cost of debt is the interest rate the company effectively pays on its debt. Clearly the cost of debt is easier to estimate than the cost of equity because the rate of interest is specified in the debt contract. The cost of debt of a project is, therefore, easy to obtain if your own company is the pure play for the project. If the pure play for the project is another company, a simple way to estimate the cost of debt of the pure-play company is to find the bond rating of that company and the yield (the effective rate of interest charged by investors) of similarly rated bonds. Such information is now easily available on the Internet.

It is important to note that the interest rate a company effectively pays is likely to be lower than the rate charged by investors because of the tax-deductibility of interest payments. For example, if a company pays 8 percent interest on its debt and is in the 35 percent tax bracket, its after-tax cost of debt is only 8 percent $\times (1 - 0.35) = 5.2$ percent. Note equity payouts such as dividends have no similar tax break in the United States. Also, a company cannot take advantage of this tax-deductibility of interest in years in which the company does not earn an operating profit. In such years, the cost of debt will equal the rate charged by investors.

Estimating Cost of Equity

Unlike the cost of debt, the cost of equity is not specified contractually, for the simple reason that there cannot be a contract between the company and its legal owners. The owners simply receive what is left over after paying all claimants. With no contract, we have to estimate the cost of equity.

We know that the cost of equity is essentially what the stockholders can expect to earn from alternative investments of the same risk. The lower bound on the cost of equity is clearly the risk-free rate, which would apply to a company with no risk at all. Therefore, the cost of equity of a company can be written as:

Cost of equity = Risk-free rate + Risk premium.

It is customary to use the ten-year Treasury bond yield as a proxy for the risk-free rate.

What about the risk premium? One can view a stock's risk as made up of two components: one due to factors idiosyncratic to the company and another due to economy-wide factors. Examples of factors that contribute to **idiosyncratic risk** include variations in management skills, risk of labor disputes, and risks due to inadequate operating systems (involving manufacturing, customer service, information technology, and so on). Risks due to economy-wide factors include things such as customer confidence or recession that affect the demand for a company's product. This type of risk is also called the **market risk.**

One might reasonably assume that stockholders would want a premium for bearing both idiosyncratic and market risks. While this is true in general, it is not true for stockholders who are well diversified. These stockholders do not bear the idiosyncratic risks of the companies whose stocks they own because they can diversify away these risks. The only risk that they bear is the market risk. Therefore, well-diversified investors demand a premium only for bearing the market risk. It is reasonable to assume that investors have diversified their portfolios by investing their savings in mutual funds and through the holdings of their pension funds.

The fact that a risk is a market risk does not mean that the level is the same for every company in the market. Here is an example that will illustrate this from an investor's perspective and reinforce the distinction between idiosyncratic risk and market risk.

Consider a well-diversified investor whose portfolio includes GM shares. If a labor dispute involves GM, the company faces a risk of disruption of production with the associated risk of lower cash flows due to permanent loss of market share. This risk is idiosyncratic to GM. The well-diversified investor, however, is not concerned about this risk because the investor's portfolio also includes shares of GM's competitors: Ford, Toyota, and others. So a disruption in GM production will be bad news for GM but good news for its competition, whose stock prices will rise. For the diversified investor, a disruption in GM production is merely a transfer of value from one asset to another, with no net gain or loss. Therefore, such idiosyncratic risks cause little concern. However, if the economy goes into a recession, all auto stocks will be affected so the investor has to bear this risk; but at the same time, some stocks will be affected more than others. For example, suppose Ford manufactures more of its components in-house while GM outsources more of its components. In that case, Ford has more fixed costs than GM and its stock will be more affected by a recession, whereas GM shares the market risk with its suppliers and will be less affected by a recession. In this example, diversified investors will deem Ford stock riskier than GM stock.

A measure of the market risk of a stock is the sensitivity of the stock to market movements. This sensitivity is measured by a number represented by the Greek letter β, which is the average percentage movement in the stock price for a 1 percent movement in a broad market index such as the S&P 500. The beta of the market is defined as having the value +1. If a stock has a beta of 2, it means that the stock moves, on average, twice as much as the market. Similarly, if a stock has a beta of 0.5, it means that the stock moves, on average, half as much as the market. Several companies provide estimates of stock betas (Value Line Investment Survey and Ibbotson Associates are two examples). Table 3.1 shows the betas of several companies.

Suppose we know the risk premium investors would demand for holding a portfolio that mimics a broad market index such as the S&P 500 (such a portfolio is called the market portfolio). This risk premium is called the **market risk premium.** Using beta and the market risk premium, we can derive a value for the risk premium of a stock:

Risk premium of stock = Beta of the stock
× Market risk premium.

In other words, the risk premium of a stock is the market risk premium scaled by the beta of the stock. For example, if a stock had a beta of 1, investors would demand a risk premium equal to the market risk premium. If a stock had a beta of 1.5, they would want a 50 percent increase in the risk premium; if the beta were 0.5 they would accept a risk premium half as much as the market risk premium. Earlier, we wrote the cost of equity of a company's stock as follows:

Cost of equity = Risk-free rate + Risk premium.

Now we can rewrite it thus:

Cost of equity = Risk-free rate
+ (Beta of the stock × Market risk premium).

Table 3.1. Stock Betas of a Sample of Companies

Company	Beta
Alcoa	1.00
Anheuser Busch	0.80
Bank of America	1.40
Bell South	0.75
Boeing	1.10
Cisco	1.55
Citigroup	1.55
Coca-Cola	0.90
Consolidated Edison	0.50
Dell Computers	1.50
Dow Chemical	0.95
Duke Energy	0.55
Dupont	1.00
Eastman Kodak	0.85
ExxonMobil	0.80
General Dynamics	0.70
General Mills	0.55
General Motors	1.10
Goldman Sachs	1.50
Heinz	0.60
Hewlett-Packard	1.20
Intel	1.30
Kroger	0.80
McDonald's	0.80
Merck	1.00
Merrill Lynch	1.85
Microsoft	1.20
Motorola	1.30
Newmont Mining	0.40
Oracle	1.40
Pfizer	1.05
Philip Morris	0.65
Procter & Gamble	0.70
Revlon	1.05
Sears	1.15
Southwest Airlines	1.10
Texas Instruments	1.65
UAL, Inc.	1.15
Union Pacific	0.90
Wal-Mart	1.15
Whirlpool	1.10

This relationship between the cost of equity and the beta of the equity is called the **Capital Asset Pricing Model (CAPM).** As the formula tells us, the CAPM requires three data items: the risk-free rate, the beta of the stock, and the market risk premium.

Each of these items can be determined. As noted earlier, the risk-free rate is a value common to all stocks, and the rate that is commonly used is the ten-year U.S. Treasury bond rate prevailing at the time of the decision. Also as noted, the beta of a stock can be obtained from several sources. As for the risk premium of the market, the market is usually proxied by a broad market index, such as the S&P 500 index or the Russell 2000 index. The market risk premium is a topic of some debate among experts, but currently most finance professionals use a number between 6 percent and 7 percent. Note that the market risk premium ultimately depends on the risk tolerance of the investors and is therefore not likely to change frequently.

Proportions of Debt and Equity

Now that we know how to find the cost of debt and estimate the cost of equity of a company, the only parameter that remains to be estimated is the proportion of debt (or equity) in the company's capital structure.

When calculating the proportions of debt and equity, think in terms of market values rather than book or accounting values, because market values represent the true value of capital invested in the company. It is useful at this point to distinguish between book and market values of debt and equity. The book values represent the *amount* of debt and equity capital invested in the company at any given point in time, while market values represent the *value* (as assessed in the marketplace) of debt and equity capital invested in the company at that point in time. In other words, book values represent the amounts of capital *provided to* the company in the form of debt or equity while market values represent what these investors *can take out of* the company at the time under consideration. What investors can take out of a company is in effect their opportunity capital invested in the company and it is on this amount that they expect a rate of return, not the amount they originally provided to the company.

For publicly traded companies, the market value of equity is easy to find: it is simply the market capitalization, which is the stock price multiplied by the number of shares outstanding. Market value of debt is more difficult to calculate because part of the total consists of bank debt or privately held debt, and even publicly held debt does not trade as frequently as equity. However, since market values of debt of healthy companies do not usually deviate significantly from book values, it is common practice to use the book value of debt as a proxy for market value of debt. The book value of debt can be estimated from the company's balance sheet. It is simply the sum of all interest-bearing debt (short- and long-term) plus the capitalized value (that is, the present value) of all lease payments.

Example: Calculating WACC

For the basic chemical factory that your company is considering acquiring, calculating the Weighted Average Cost of Capital (WACC) will proceed as follows. First, you will identify one or more pure-play companies that make solely the basic chemical under consideration. Let us say that Alpha Chemicals is one such company. The next step is to estimate the WACC of Alpha Chemicals. To do so, you collect the following data about that company:

- Cost of debt: 8 percent
- Book value of debt: $400 million
- Current stock price: $30

- Number of shares outstanding: 20 million
- Stock beta: 1.2
- Corporate tax rate: 35 percent

In addition, you find out that the current risk-free rate (ten-year Treasury bond yield) is 5 percent. Also, you take current expert advice that the market risk premium is 6 percent.

With this information, you calculate the WACC of Alpha Chemicals as follows:

1. After-tax cost of debt = 8 percent $\times$ (1 − 0.35) = 5.2 percent.
2. Cost of equity = 5 percent + (1.2 $\times$ 6 percent) = 12.2 percent.
3. Market value of equity = $30 $\times$ 20 million = $600 million.
4. Market value of debt is assumed to be equal to the book value of debt = $400 million.
5. Proportion of debt = $400 million ÷ ($400 million + $600 million) = 40 percent.
6. Proportion of equity = 60 percent.
7. WACC of Alpha Chemical = 5.2 percent $\times$ 0.4 + 12.2 percent $\times$ 0.6 = 9.4 percent.

If you assume that the basic chemical factory that you are planning to acquire has the same business risk as Alpha Chemical and can be financed with the same proportion of debt and equity, then 9.4 percent is the cost of capital that should be used to value the future expected cash flows of the factory. If multiple pure plays can be found, often their WACC values are averaged to estimate the WACC of the factory. This calculation, of course, would assume that the risk of your factory was the average of the risks of the pure plays.

In the chemical factory example, a WACC of 9.4 percent means that, if the factory earned $9.40 a year from its operations after tax (before any payments to capital providers are considered) for every $100 of market value of capital, it would be able to just satisfy both its lenders (who demand 8 percent) and stockholders (who demand at least 12.2 percent). Figure 3.1 summarizes the situation.

Let's follow the figure, beginning at its upper-left corner:

- For every $100 of market value of invested capital, lenders' share is 0.4 × 100 = $40. In return for this capital each year they require a return of 0.08 × 40 = $3.20.
- For every $100 of market value of invested capital, stockholders' share is 0.6 × 100 = $60. In return for this capital each year they require a return of 0.122 × 60 = $7.32.
- Therefore, the company needs to pay a total of 3.20 + 7.32 = $10.52 each year to its capital providers from the cash flows generated by the factory. However, the company receives a tax deduction because of the interest payment it makes. The annual tax deduction is worth 0.35 × 3.20 = $1.12. Therefore, the company needs to earn from the factory only 10.52 − 1.12 = $9.40 annually, or 9.4 percent of the market value of invested capital, to satisfy both lenders and stockholders.

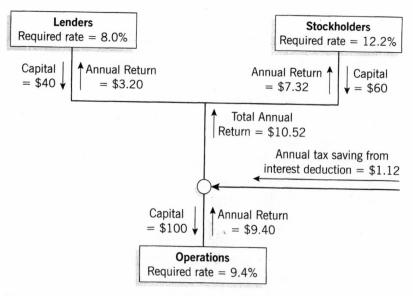

Figure 3.1. Illustration of Flows in the Chemical Factory Example

FAQs About Cost of Capital

I am told that the cost of capital of an entity depends on the risk of the cash flows of that entity. Since my company is a conglomerate, the different divisions could potentially have different costs of capital. However, we cannot measure the beta of a division. How can we then estimate divisional cost of capital?

Whenever we have to estimate the cost of capital of an entity that is not traded publicly (such as company divisions, specific projects with risk profiles different from the company, or private companies), we resort to using pure plays. Recall that pure plays are publicly traded companies whose operational risk is similar to that of the entity whose cost of capital you are seeking. If we assume that the project will have approximately the same business risk and capital structure as the pure play, we can use the WACC of the pure play as the WACC of the project. We can use this pure-play technique for finding the cost of capital of individual projects or divisions.

Is the technique identical if we wish to estimate the cost of capital of a private company?

Mostly, yes, except that the cost of capital of the pure play is only the starting point in calculating the cost of capital of a private company. Two fundamental differences between a private company and a publicly traded pure-play company make the private company's cost of capital potentially greater than that of a publicly traded company. First, there is no liquid market for the shares of a private company, so its stockholders might demand a premium for the lack of liquidity. Second, private companies are typically owned by families, whose members are less likely to be well diversified. Unlike diversified investors, therefore, these investors may not have fully diversified away the idiosyncratic component of the risk. They are likely to bear both market risk and idiosyncratic risk, and for this reason as well might demand a higher premium, pushing the cost of capital of a private company above the pure-play cost of capital.

Is there a way to estimate these premiums for liquidity and lack of diversification?

Adjusting the pure-play cost of capital for liquidity and lack of diversification is tedious. Instead, we can incorporate the impact of these two issues on the private company's cost of capital indirectly in our resource allocation decisions. First, we estimate the future cash flows of the private company as described in Chapter Two. Next, we calculate the value of the private company by using the cost of capital of the pure play. We recognize that the value so calculated will overstate the value of the private company since the cost of capital of the private company is greater than that of the pure play. To adjust for the difference in cost of capital, we then apply a discount to this value. Researchers have used different techniques to estimate the magnitude of this discount. For example, it has been found that private companies are acquired at a discount of about 30–35 percent compared with similar public companies. We can therefore apply this discount to the value calculated using the cost of capital of the pure play as a reflection of the increased cost of capital of private companies.

If I raise the entire investment through borrowing, can I use the borrowing rate as the cost of capital, simply disregarding the cost of equity?

It might seem logical that the cost of capital is the borrowing rate if the entire investment is borrowed. However, one must ask why it is possible to borrow the entire investment of a project. If the project is a stand-alone company, it will be impossible to finance the entire project through borrowing. Lenders will insist on some equity capital. Your conglomerate, on the other hand, is able to borrow the entire investment on one project because it has other assets that were partially or wholly financed by equity capital to support the loan. Therefore, the borrowing rate of the project does not truly reflect the risk of the project. The appropriate cost of capital of the project is its weighted average cost of capital, based on how much of the project would have been financed by debt if it had been a stand-alone company. This would be similar to the cost of capital of the project's pure play.

I find that the cost of capital (of a division, for example) changes through time even though I don't see any changes in the risk profile of the division. How can this be?

The risk of a division's operations is not the sole determinant of its cost of capital. Recall that the cost of capital of an entity is the sum of the risk-free rate and the risk premium of the entity. The risk premium is driven by the risk of the entity, but the risk-free rate is driven by economy-wide factors. The risk-free rate can be divided into two components:

Risk-free rate = Real rate of interest + Expected rate of inflation.

The first component—the real rate of interest—is the pure "cost of money." It is what lenders in a competitive market would charge if they had no concerns about default risk or inflation. It depends on the supply of and demand for money in the economy, both of which vary over time. When the savings rate is high or the demand for money is low, the real rate of interest will be low. Conversely, when the savings rate is low or the demand for money is high, the real rate will be high.

The second component of the risk-free rate, expected rate of inflation, varies over time as well. Therefore, the risk-free rate varies over time and so does the division's cost of capital, even if the division's risk has not changed.

What are some of the factors that affect the real rate of interest?

The investment climate plays a big role. An economy that is expanding, all other things being equal, will increase the real rate. Conversely, the real rate will be low in a recessive economy for two reasons. Since consumption is low in such an economy, saving is high and so is the supply of money. At the same time, in a recession companies are paring down their capital investments, so the demand for money is low.

Another factor that affects the real rate is government fiscal policy. If a government decides to balance its budget (instead of running a deficit budget) the real rate will decrease because of the lower demand for money by the government. Similarly, budget deficits increase the real rate as the government demand for capital increases.

The size of the pure play differs from the size of the project being evaluated. Should I take that into account?

It has been found that the cost of capital of smaller companies is higher, all else remaining the same. Therefore, it is customary to make an adjustment for size. Most finance texts explain how to make this adjustment.[1]

When you tell me to use the pure-play technique to estimate the cost of capital of a division, you are assuming that the pure play and the division have the same risk. However, doesn't my division, being part of a multisegment firm, have a lower risk because of its synergy with other divisions within the firm?

That is possible. And the pure-play technique does not account for that. It works better for estimating the divisional cost of capital of conglomerates such as General Electric where the divisions are in very different types of businesses and there is not much synergy between them. It might not work as well for a company such as DuPont, whose Nylon and Polyester segments might benefit from being under one umbrella and might be less risky than similar stand-alone firms. Unfortunately, there is no accepted methodology that allows us to adjust for the risk-reduction resulting from being part of a multisegment firm.

My conglomerate acquires many companies. What cost of capital should we use in estimating the value of the acquisition?

It depends. Let us first consider the easier case: a true conglomerate acquisition in which there is no synergy between the target firm and any of your divisions. If the target is a publicly held company, you can use its own WACC to value it. If is privately held or is a division of another company, you will use the pure-play technique to value the target. Note that the value so calculated is the value of the target after it is taken over by you.

If the target company is similar to one of your divisions, the situation is more complex, but you can still use the pure-play technique. In this case, you might reasonably expect some synergy between your target company and the division of your company with which it is similar. You can use the division's cost of capital to evaluate the target company. As described earlier, there might be a reduction in risk when you combine the two; however, no simple formal procedure will help in quantifying the value due to this risk reduction.

The important thing to note is that you do not use your own company's WACC to value the acquisition unless your company is the pure play for the target.

One of our divisions makes unique automobile components—that is, no publicly held companies are making these components. What should we do for a pure play?

Finding a pure play is a mix of science and art. If you cannot find a pure play in the same line of business, try to find a business that is affected by market conditions in more or less the same way as your business. For example, the fortunes of the

automobile components business are closely tied to the automobile business itself. You can therefore use companies that
make other types of automobile components; in the absence of
such companies, you can use the automobile manufacturers
themselves as pure plays and make adjustments for the larger
size of automobile manufacturers, as explained earlier.

*It appears that my own company's capital structure plays no role in
the estimation of the WACC. Can that be correct?*

When you use a pure play's WACC for a project or a division, you are implicitly assuming that the business risk of the
pure play and its capital structure are similar to that of the project
or division under consideration. In other words, the assumption
is that if the project or division were a stand-alone firm, it would
have the same business risk and capital structure as the pure
play. If you believe that the target capital structure of the project
or division on a stand-alone basis is different from that of the
pure play, you can adjust the WACC of the project or division to
reflect this difference. Most finance textbooks explain how to
make the adjustment.

*Since the cost of debt is lower than the cost of equity, can I reduce the
cost of capital by increasing the proportion of debt in the capital
employed?*

Unfortunately, reducing the cost of capital is not that simple. If we increase the proportion of debt, the risk to stockholders increases. This is because the probability that the stockholders
get paid is lower with the increased debt commitment. Stockholders will demand a higher rate of return to compensate them
for the increased risk, increasing the cost of equity. How the cost
of capital changes depends on the amount of debt relative to the
optimal level of debt. If debt is too low, the increase in debt will
lower the cost of capital. If debt is too high, the increase in debt
will increase the cost of capital. Chapter Four discusses how to
determine the optimal proportion of debt financing.

SUMMARY

In this chapter, we provide a brief overview of the estimation of cost of capital for a project. The estimation of cost of capital is important as it has a significant effect on valuation. The key idea is that, ideally, every investment decision must have its own cost of capital, based on the prevailing risk-free rate and the risk of the expected cash flows from that decision. Since the risk of a project is not directly observable, the standard method involves estimating the risk of a *pure play*—a publicly traded company whose risk should be similar to the project under consideration. The cost of capital of the pure play can be estimated using publicly available market data.

The cost of capital of the pure play is a weighted average of the costs of debt and equity of the pure play, the weights being the proportions of debt and equity, respectively, based on market values. The market value of equity is easily obtained as the product of the share price and the number of shares outstanding. The market value of debt is often approximated by the book value of all interest-bearing debt, which can be obtained from the company's balance sheet.

The cost of debt is the current after-tax rate of interest that company pays on its debt. The cost of equity is the sum of the risk-free rate and a risk premium. The latter is estimated as the product of the sensitivity of the pure play stock's movement with a broad market index (that is, beta of the stock) and the market risk premium as a whole (about 6–7 percent for U.S. companies). The stock beta is an appropriate measure of risk if investors are well diversified. The cost of equity of a company is computed as:

Cost of equity = Risk-free rate
+ (Beta of the company's stock × Market risk premium).

The weighted average cost of capital is then computed as:

WACC = After-tax cost of debt × Proportion of debt +
Cost of equity × Proportion of equity.

The discussion in this chapter focuses on obtaining the cost of capital of a pure-play company (and hence the cost of capital of the project under consideration), given the company's capital structure (proportions of debt and equity). The next chapter lays the foundations for the determination of the capital structure.

Capital Structure and Financing

As discussed in Chapter Three, a firm's cost of capital can be obtained by blending the returns that investors require on the firm's debt and equity capital. Left unanswered was the question of what **capital structure**—that is, what mix of debt and equity capital—should be chosen to minimize cost of capital and thereby maximize firm value. As usual, we begin with a case.

Let's say you are responsible for a strategy and planning group at Amgear, a midsized manufacturing firm with publicly traded equity. Amgear's revenue is largely derived from multi-year contracts for the supply of specialized components to a small group of clients. Although finance is not your forte, you have been asked by the CEO to take a close look at the issue of the firm's capital structure. Amgear has always been reluctant to borrow funds and has relied mainly on equity financing and retained earnings for its financing needs, but other firms in the industry, the CEO notes, have tended to obtain 30–35 percent of their capital from borrowing. The CEO wants to know whether replacing some of its equity by debt capital would lower Amgear's cost of capital.

Amgear's current earnings before interest and taxes (its EBIT) are about $100 million. These are expected to continue for the foreseeable future. The market value of the firm is $850 million. Your investment bankers indicate that the cost of debt, if your company wants to have 30–35 percent of your capital as debt, would be about 8 percent. The corporate tax rate is 40 percent.

You see two main issues related to Amgear and its competitive environment that you believe should probably be considered in making a capital structure decision. The first is that if the economy turns sour, one or more competing firms in the industry are likely to be driven out of business. If Amgear has maintained a low level of debt financing, it might be in a position to pick up the assets of the financially troubled competitor at heavily discounted prices, possibly 30–50 percent below what they might be worth to Amgear in the long run.

The second issue concerns the impact of financial distress on the firm's customers, reputation, and workforce. Amgear has developed a relatively skilled and motivated workforce—but would the firm be able to retain its critical employees if it ran into serious financial trouble? How would relationships with existing clients affect and be affected by the prospect of financial distress? To investigate these issues with some care, you assign your team to obtain estimates of likely scenarios, tax issues, and the like.

In the course of this chapter, we develop a simple framework that underscores the importance of market frictions—such as taxes and bankruptcy costs—and their impact on corporate finance decision making. The framework is used to address the issues raised in the case. The framework also provides a basis for tackling issues in later chapters, such as firm payout policy in Chapter Five. Toward the end of the present chapter we also talk about different types of equity offerings and the pros and cons of public versus private financing.

The choice of capital structure is all about attempting to maximize firm value in the presence of market frictions. However, to reach this understanding, it's necessary to begin somewhat paradoxically with the supposition that markets are frictionless or **perfect**. A perfect capital market is an idealization of a capital market, presumed to have none of the frictions of real-world markets such as taxes, bankruptcy costs, or **information asymmetry** (that is, no one has superior or inside information).

■ Capital Structure When the Market Is Perfect

Would decisions about capital structure add value to a firm if markets were perfect? **Firm value** is the market value of all the firm's outstanding financial securities or, equivalently, the sum total of its debt and equity capital. The claim—first made by Modigliani and Miller[1]—is that if there are no frictions in the capital market, then capital structure has no effect on firm value. The argument is that what matters for firm value is the total set of cash flows distributed by the firm to its investors—and not whether investors receive the cash flows in the form of debt or equity flows.

Why doesn't choice of capital structure matter for firm value in a perfect market? An analogy is sometimes made between firm value and a pie: the size of slices into which the pie is cut does not change the total quantity of pie available, so long as nothing is lost in the cutting process. The manner in which the firm originally distributes these cash flows to various investors is of little consequence, since investors can repackage their cash flows in any way they choose.

Here is an example to illustrate why capital structure will not affect firm value in a perfect capital market. Suppose that the market value of an all-equity firm is $100 million. Miller and Modigliani claim that any alternative capital structure will still be such that

Equity value of leveraged firm + Debt value of leveraged firm = Value of all-equity firm = $100 million.

To make the argument, let us suppose that this were not the case and that the firm could issue some optimal combination of debt and equity capital such that firm value would increase to, say, $105 million. Such a situation could not prevail in a perfect market. Here's why: in a perfect market any investor could buy all the equity of the firm for $100 million. The investor could then sell new debt and equity securities that were to be paid from all the cash flows from the acquired firm. Note that all the investor would be doing is buying equity cash flows and then repackaging them so that, depending on the amount of debt and equity securities sold, some cash flows would be paid to new debtholders and the rest to the new shareholders. Were it possible to sell a debt and equity combination that the market values at $105 million, the investor would have made a quick and riskless (arbitrage) profit of $5 million. But in a perfect market of no costs and no private information, no one could hold this special advantage to generate large profits. Hence, competition among investors would drive up the price of the firm's original securities to the highest possible value that the investors could hope to obtain from refashioning the cash flows and selling the securities. This means that the firm's original capital structure choice would be irrelevant—since, if the firm did not issue the best combination of securities, someone would buy the firm's cash flows and issue the securities at zero cost.

But capital structure can matter in the real world—and this can happen only if the market is imperfect. We move, therefore, to a discussion of market imperfections that are important to the capital structure decision.

■ An Overview of Market Imperfections

Despite their increasing efficiency, actual capital markets suffer from significant imperfections. In the presence of such market frictions, capital structure choice and other corporate financial decisions will have a significant effect on firm value.

The problem with analyzing a market that is less than perfect is that there are many more ways to be imperfect than to be perfect! Over the years a consensus has emerged among observers of financial markets regarding the most important and widely encountered market frictions. They are taxes, costs of financial distress, information asymmetry, and other transaction costs.

Taxes

Income is taxed differently depending on its source and on the tax status of the individual or entity. There are, for instance, differences in the tax treatment of interest income and dividends (which are largely excluded from corporate taxation). Regulatory burdens matter as well and can be loosely regarded as a form of tax.

Cost of Financial Distress

The costs of financial distress are the various costs that tend to occur when a firm defaults or is close to defaulting on its debt obligations. They can be direct (such as legal costs) or indirect (such as loss of a firm's reputation capital). Many of the costs of financial distress tend to be driven by market imperfections such as the asymmetry of information among the various participants—as between the better-informed management and various creditors. Also, there tend to be significant problems and delays in settling claims on account of the conflicting objectives of various parties such as shareholders, management, and senior and junior debtholders.

Information Asymmetry

One facet of information asymmetry involves moral hazard. The term **moral hazard** comes from the insurance business, where it refers to the notion that once insurance has been obtained, individuals tend to behave more riskily. For instance, if you have very good insurance coverage against theft or collision of your car, you may be less careful about how you drive and where you park and whether you install an expensive security system. The reason, of course, is that if a loss occurs, it comes out of the pocket of another entity and not your own pocket. Moral hazard also includes the notion of agency problems. **Agency problems** are the types of problems that arise when an agent (say the manager of a firm) acts to further personal goals rather than those of the owners (shareholders) or principals.

Adverse selection is another facet of information asymmetry. It is commonly known as the "lemons problem" or the "winner's curse." The notion is that if you are trying to buy a used car, the probability of getting a lemon is substantial. After all, owners who know their cars to be lemons may be anxious to get rid of them. On the other hand, the owners of good cars may be more inclined to hold onto them, at least in part because they may not receive a good price for the used car—since the number of lemons on the market tends to drive down prices. Many situations involving such adverse selection problems are evident in financial transactions.

Other Transaction Costs

This is a catch-all category for frictions that are not easily assigned elsewhere. Among transaction costs important to financial decisions are the costs of issuing securities, collecting information, and writing and enforcing contracts.

◼ A Trade-Off Approach to Capital Structure

In the presence of capital market imperfections, the capital structure choice is one of maximizing firm value (equivalently, minimizing the firm's WACC) by trading off the various costs and benefits of financial leverage. A well-recognized trade-off is that between the benefit from the tax deductibility of interest and the potential costs of financial distress. Mainly because it is more quantifiable than some other costs and benefits of leverage, we discuss this trade-off first in detail—and then go on to consider the effect of other frictions such as information asymmetry on capital structure choice.

A Positive Side of the Trade-Off: Tax Shield Benefits from Leverage

In the presence of corporate taxes, the cash flow generated by a firm is divided among equity-holders, debtholders, and the government (which receives tax payments). Since interest payments are normally treated as an expense, adding debt into the capital structure can reduce tax payments, leaving more after-tax income for investors. The increase in firm value from reducing tax payments accrues to equity-holders, as in the following example.

Table 4.1 summarizes information regarding a firm that earns $10 million before interest and taxes, of which $3 million is paid out in interest. The firm is expected to generate this cash flow in perpetuity, and the corporate tax rate is 40 percent. The table shows the effect of increasing debt, supposing that the firm decides to recapitalize by issuing $10 million in 10 percent notes (increasing its annual interest payments by $1 million) and distributing the proceeds from the debt offering to shareholders. As a result the firm is required to pay out $4 million in annual interest payments.

The resulting increase in cash flow ($.4 million) to investors accrues to equity-holders—since this is the increase in cash flow after taxes and interest payments. Using a discount rate of 10 percent (the same as the required rate of return on the interest payments on debt that gives rise to the tax shield in the first place), you can value the stream of tax savings as a perpetuity:

PVTS (PV of tax shield) = 0.4 ÷ 0.1 = $4 million.

Table 4.1. Tax Effects of Increased Leverage

Item	Computation	Value
Earnings before interest and taxes (EBIT)		$10 million
Taxable income before recap	$10 million – $3 million (interest payment)	$7 million
Taxable income after recap	$10 million – $4 million	$6 million
Taxes before recap	.4 × $7 million	$2.8 million
Taxes after recap	.4 × $6 million	$2.4 million
Reduction in taxes paid	$2.8 million – $2.4 million	$.4 million

The $4 million represents the increase in equity value from the higher leverage. Of course, since $10 million was paid out to equity-holders and replaced by $10 million of debt financing, the net drop in equity value after the recapitalization is $6 million ($4 million gain from tax shield less $10 million paid out in dividends). The firm's value increases by the tax shield of $4 million.

Let's generalize the example. Consider a firm that maintains a debt level D (debt maturity is not an issue because the debt can be regularly refinanced). Denote the corporate income tax rate by T and the interest rate on the debt by r_D. The annual interest payment by the firm equals $r_D D$. The annual tax saving (brought about by the reduction in taxable income) is given by $r_D TD$. Maintaining our earlier assumption that the interest rate on the debt provides an appropriate discount rate for the tax savings, we arrive at the following present value of the perpetuity of tax savings (that is, the PV of the tax shield):

$$PVTS = Tr_D D \div r_D = TD.$$

Hence, TD, the present value of the tax shield, is the value difference between a leveraged and an unleveraged firm. In other words, in the presence of corporate taxes (but no other market imperfections), with risk-free perpetual debt:

Value of leveraged firm = Value of unleveraged firm + TD.

From this expression it appears that a firm's value can keep increasing with debt level. However, for firm value to increase with leverage, the firm must have sufficiently high taxable earnings to take advantage of the interest tax shields. The equation also ignores the potential increase in bankruptcy costs with leverage.

A Negative Side of the Trade-Off: Costs of Financial Distress

On the negative side of the leverage trade-off are the potential costs of bankruptcy (a term we use interchangeably with "financial distress") when a firm is unable to service its debt obligations. A bankruptcy results in the transfer, sale, or reorganization of the assets of the firm. The assets (at least the tangible ones) continue to exist, of course, though their ownership may change. The actual bankruptcy procedure varies across countries and has undergone substantial changes in the United States over time as well. U.S. bankruptcies are usually conducted under Chapter 11 of the bankruptcy code—a procedure that gives considerable discretion to management to propose a plan for reorganizing the firm.

The actual costs of legal proceedings (such as the costs of lawyers and court time) have been recognized as being only a small portion of the total losses from bankruptcy. There are many other, less direct, sources of loss from financial distress as well. A potentially significant cost, unless the firm's assets are highly marketable, is that the firm may be forced to liquidate its assets at fire-sale prices. Part of the reason for such prices is that there may be low demand for the firm's assets at the time, if the firm's poor performance is related to generally poor industry conditions. Important factors affecting the loss in the value of the firm's assets are their tangibility and liquidity. For instance, the bankruptcy of a gold mining company may not substantially affect the value of its mining properties—after all, the mines could, presumably, be operated just as well by another gold mining firm. On the other hand, if a firm's primary assets are intangibles such as its brand image or its human capital (for example, if the firm is R&D intensive) a bankruptcy may be very costly— the brand image may be damaged; skilled individuals may move to greener pastures.

Contributing to bankruptcy costs is the fact that firms in financial distress may no longer be able to obtain favorable trade credit from their suppliers, their longer-term contracts or guarantees may have diminished value, and executive time may be largely consumed in dealing with the bankruptcy. Other sources of loss are the actions of various claimholders seeking to maximize their own value rather than firm value—leading to conflicts between debt- and equity-holders. For instance, senior debtholders may prefer to liquidate the firm if they can get their claims paid off, even if liquidation does not serve the interests of other claimholders.

To incorporate the costs of financial leverage into the capital structure decision, we need a measure of expected bankruptcy costs associated with specific capital structure choices. As noted, the loss in the event that the firm becomes bankrupt differs across firms and depends on factors such as the tangibility and liquidity of the firm's assets. The other component in expected costs is the likelihood of becoming bankrupt in the first place. The probability that a particular firm will actually become bankrupt is determined by the leverage in the firm's capital structure and by the variability of its cash flows. Expected cost of bankruptcy is given by the following:

Expected cost of bankruptcy =
(Probability of bankruptcy) × (Loss from bankruptcy).

How do you obtain information on the likelihood of financial distress? For a publicly traded bond that has been rated by rating agencies such as Standard and Poor or Moody's, the probability of bankruptcy can be estimated from the historical evidence on defaults on bonds with different ratings (see Table 4.2).

If the bond has not been rated, the cost of financing associated with the bond (that is, bond yield) can be used to determine

Table 4.2. Average Cumulative Default Rates, 1985–2001

Moody's Ratings	One-Year Horizon (percent)	Five-Year Horizon (percent)
Aaa	0.00	0.00
Aa	0.00	0.34
A	0.02	0.72
Baa	0.19	2.10
Ba	1.54	14.38
B	7.06	33.76
Caa–C	21.57	56.71

the rating category that is appropriate for the bond. You may want to use the rating information about the bonds issued by firms in the same industry that have comparable capital structures. Another way to proceed is to obtain the probability of bankruptcy directly by inputting various accounting measures such as your firm's (anticipated) interest coverage ratio, its (anticipated) debt-equity ratio, and others. (A well-known model of this type is the one developed by Altman.)[2]

The Trade-Off Between Tax Benefits and Expected Costs of Bankruptcy

The trade-off between tax benefits and expected bankruptcy costs can also be expressed in equation form. Earlier we saw that

Leveraged firm value = Unleveraged firm value + TD,

where TD represented the value of the tax shield. Now, taking the expected bankruptcy costs into account, we can express the trade-off between the tax shield and expected bankruptcy costs:

Leveraged firm value = Unleveraged firm value + Tax benefits of debt − Expected bankruptcy cost from the debt.

As a numerical illustration of the trade-off, consider an unleveraged firm with a market value of $50 million. The firm faces a corporate tax rate of 40 percent. The firm's managers consider the possibility of recapitalizing the firm, issuing debt and paying the proceeds in the form of a dividend to current shareholders. The firm estimates its default probability (based on historical experience of similarly situated firms) for the relevant time period. It estimates that if it defaults on its debt, this will result in direct and indirect losses of about 40 percent of firm value in terms of current present value, that is, a loss with a PV of $20 million—a high number reflecting the nature of the firm's assets.

For this example, the probability numbers and estimates of expected bankruptcy costs for different debt levels are shown in Table 4.3. The value of the tax shield is estimated as *Tax rate* × *Debt level*, which is appropriate when the tax savings are taken to be in perpetuity; it is a fair approximation if the period under consideration is quite long.

Among the four *Debt levels* shown in the table, the optimal dollar debt level is the one that maximizes firm value per the trade-off formula.

Column 5 in the table provides the expected net gain (tax benefits less expected bankruptcy costs) for different debt levels. As indicated, firm value is maximized for a debt level of $10 million. The leveraged firm value is $50 million + $3.1 = $53.1.

Table 4.3. Costs and Benefits from Debt ($ millions)

(1) Debt Level	(2) Default Probability (percent)	(3) Expected Bankruptcy Cost: (2) × $20	(4) Tax Shield = .4 × Debt	(5) Net Gain from Leverage = (4) − (3)
$5	3	$.6	$2	$1.4
$10	4.5	$.9	$4	$3.1
$12.5	10	$2	$5	$3
$15	20	$4	$6	$2

Applying the Trade-Off Approach to Amgear

Recall the case of Amgear from the beginning of the chapter. You were assigned the task of determining the potential costs and benefits from leverage and coming up with recommendations for capital structure choice. The firm generates an EBIT of $100 million currently or an after-tax cash flow of $100(1 − .4) = $60 million each year.

Your objective is to replace some of the firm's equity by debt so that the firm value is increased by the tax savings that the debt financing brings about. But how much to replace? The answer to this maximization problem will depend on the trade-off with potential financial distress as well as other considerations for various amounts of debt that you could choose. Most of what you are about to do is summarized in Table 4.4, which proposes six different hypothetical amounts of debt in Column 1, and then compares the benefits and costs of each amount.

The benefit side, as we know, is represented mainly by the increased value of the firm that results from the tax shield created by debt:

$$\text{Firm value (after recapitalization)} = \text{Value of equity} + \text{PVTS}.$$

Table 4.4. Cost-Benefit Analysis of Debt Levels ($ millions)

(1) Debt Value	(2) Probability of Default (percent)	(3) Expected Tax Benefit: Debt × Tax Rate	(4) Expected Cost of Default	(5) Net Benefit	(6) Adjusted Net Benefit
$50	0.00	$26.60	$0.00	$26.60	$26.60
$100	2.00	$52.67	$10.00	$43.20	$42.67
$150	4.00	$78.204	$24.00	$55.80	$54.20
$200	6.00	$103.21	$42.00	$64.40	$61.21
$250	9.00	$127.02	$72.00	$61.00	$55.02
$300	12.00	$150.02	$108.00	$51.60	$42.02

PVTS, the expected tax benefit, will equal the Debt times the tax rate (40 percent). Column 3 of the table shows that amount.

Let us now consider the downside associated with financial distress. To determine the probability of bankruptcy associated with various levels of debt financing, you consult rating agencies to obtain a preliminary assessment of the likely ratings of the firm's bonds and the related default risks associated with various debt levels over a twenty-year horizon.

Column 2 of the table shows your estimate of the probability of financial distress associated with each level of debt. Column 4, expected losses from bankruptcy, will depend on factors such as the tangibility and liquidity of the firm's assets. In the case of your firm, you know that a significant amount of value comes from intangibles such as the firm's reputation, its relationship to its customers, and the quality of its employees. You would, therefore, expect financial distress to have severe consequences. A guide to the amount of losses from bankruptcy is the *recovery rate*—that is, the fraction of the promised amount that debtholders have received in the event of a default—for different classes of bonds and types of firms. Based on your analysis of the loss of business and value, you estimate that a bankruptcy would reduce the value of the firm by about 50 percent. These losses may also depend on the amount of the debt outstanding, since the costs of resolving bankruptcy proceedings are affected by factors such as the number of investors and the variety of debt instruments that have been issued. The estimated expected loss figures in Table 4.4, column 4, are obtained by multiplying the default probability (column 2) times the loss in the event of bankruptcy.

The values in column 5, the net benefit from taking on the various levels of debt, are given by this formula:

$$\text{Net benefit} =$$
Expected tax benefit − Expected cost of financial distress.

As the table shows, the net benefit is maximized for a debt level of $200 million. The associated net benefit is $64.4 million. Now let's consider some possible adjustments. In estimating the expected benefit from tax reduction, we have neglected the fact that the firm will not have taxable income in the event of a default. A simple adjustment for this fact is to reduce the expected tax benefit by the probability of default. If the likelihood of a default is similar across the twenty-year horizon, it is reasonable to expect that by the time a default occurs, something on the order of half the average of the anticipated tax shield benefits will be realized. Hence, to account for lost tax shield benefits when default occurs, you can adjust the anticipated tax benefits as follows:

Adjustment for loss of tax shield in the event of default =
.5 × Default probability × Expected tax benefit.

The figures in column 6 of Table 4.4 are the adjusted net benefits. As we might expect, for the debt value of $200 million there is a relatively small change to the expected net benefit; the adjusted figure is $61.2 million. The highest firm value is still being achieved with a debt value of $200 million.

Here is another possible adjustment. In our earlier description of the industry environment that Amgear faces, we mentioned that other firms in the industry tend to obtain 30–35 percent of their capital from debt financing. Hence, a $200 million level of debt financing will result in Amgear's having a similar fraction (roughly 30 percent) of its capital financed with debt. However, if the industry does poorly, it might become possible to buy competitor assets at a significant discount. This suggests that having a lower-than-average level of debt financing may enable your firm to take advantage of such a situation.

Now suppose you try to quantify the possible benefit from a lower debt level, say $150 million relative to $200 million. Note that the lower level of debt financing reduces your overall probability of default by about 2 percent. If the performance of firms in the industry is affected by similar economic and industry factors, then, by reducing your debt and by reducing your odds of being financially distressed, you have increased your chance to buy the assets of another competitor by about 2 percent as well.

What would be the dollar value of this 2 percent chance? Let us say that the value obtained by buying assets from a financially distressed competitor is about $100 million. Then the decrease in debt to $150 million and a 2 percent chance of buying assets cheaply generates expected benefits of the order of 2 percent $\times$ 100 million, or about $2 million. This is, however, much smaller than the drop in adjusted net benefit indicated in the table, which is about $7 million. Hence, in this case, despite the significant benefits from acquiring a competitor's assets on the cheap, the benefits are not large enough to affect the firm's capital structure choice of $200 million. It is clear that if the benefits were larger—for instance, if a number of competitors could be acquired by your firm—the benefit from reducing the probability of financial distress may be much larger. A benefit of $400 million from being solvent while your competitors are in trouble would suggest that a lower level of debt financing of $150 million would be the best choice.

Another issue that may be relevant to Amgear's capital structure choice is the fact that Amgear manufactures specialized components for a few large clients. This can affect the capital structure decision in two ways that tend to offset each other. On one hand, clients have placed multiyear orders for specialized components, and it may not be easy for them to obtain the same components from other manufacturers. This suggests that the clients may be willing to enter into arrangements—such as providing advance payments or helping arrange for financing—to avoid a disruption in the supply of their orders. This would indicate that the firm might face lower default costs than it may have supposed. On the other hand, such arrangements have a downside: if the firm has invested heavily in specialized equipment, it may find it relatively difficult to sell these assets if it does face liquidation.

▉ Debt Equity Conflicts: Another Cost of Financial Leverage

Leverage has other costs and benefits for a firm, in addition to those related to taxes and financial distress. The main benefit has to do with reducing managerial (agency) discretion over the cash flows of the firm, an issue we explore a bit later. First, however, let's look at the major cost, which has to do with debt-equity conflicts.

Underlying the conflict between equity-holders and debtholders is the fact that maximizing the value of equity is not always the same as maximizing the value of the firm (or maximizing the value of debt):

Value of firm = Value of equity + Value of debt.

Indeed, for a given value of the firm, shareholders can *maximize* their value by *minimizing* the value of debt—implying that debtholders and shareholders will often not agree on best investment and financing decisions. Three common manifestations of the problem are described in the following sections.

The Debt Overhang Problem

The notion of the *debt overhang problem* (sometimes also called the *underinvestment problem*) is that shareholders may prefer not to invest in otherwise good projects if much of the value created goes to pay existing debtholders, rather than coming to shareholders. This is a problem if the firm has a substantial amount of debt outstanding and is in danger of defaulting on the debt—so that an increase in the firm's value is captured primarily by debtholders.

The Asset Substitution Problem

The nature of the *asset substitution* or *risk-shifting problem* is that equity-holders will tend to prefer investments that are riskier, even if they are worse than other investments in terms of NPV. The problem is exacerbated when a firm is in danger of defaulting. The reason is that shareholders receive their payoff only after debtholders are fully paid off. Hence, if equity-holders expect the firm to default and to receive little if anything from bankruptcy proceedings, they may want the firm to take on greater risk. Consider, for instance, a firm that has assets worth $75 million but has a $100 million debt obligation due in a few months. The firm's equity-holders will want it to invest in risky projects, even ones that are the equivalent of a double-or-nothing gamble. This is since, if things go well, equity-holders benefit. On the other hand, if things go badly, equity-holders have little to lose and the downside losses are largely borne by debtholders.

Reluctance to Liquidate

Another manifestation of the debt-equity conflict is that equity-holders prefer to keep a firm going rather than liquidate it. Often, even in default, since managers have considerable discretion in the bankruptcy process (Chapter 11 of U.S. bankruptcy code), a firm is not liquidated even when the proceeds from liquidation would exceed its value as a going concern. The reason is that equity-holders and managers have no incentive to liquidate if they are to receive little after the liquidation—and there is some chance of receiving a positive payoff if the firm is kept alive.

Minimizing Debtholder-Shareholder Conflicts

How can a firm minimize the conflict between debtholders and shareholders? The simplest solution is to eliminate the debtholders by eliminating debt. But because there are offsetting advantages associated with debt financing (for example, the tax advantage), firms have an incentive to include debt in their capital structure and to engineer their debt instruments in ways that minimize the potential conflicts between borrowers and lenders.

Even though the conflict between shareholders and debtholders frequently results in the interests of debtholders being harmed, *it is the equity-holders who ultimately pay the costs of these conflicts!* Why? Because debtholders are presumably going to deny capital or charge high rates if they are concerned about future expropriation. Hence, equity-holders have an incentive to convince debtholders that the latter face a minimal possibility of future expropriation risk. Following are some useful strategies.

Use Short-Term or Puttable Debt
Holders of short-term debt are generally less concerned about expropriation risk because they know that managers will have little incentive to increase the risk of the underlying investments—given the short maturity of existing debt, the firm will soon need to go back to the market for refinancing. At that point, if the firm has indeed increased its risk, it will be forced to pay a higher cost for its new debt. The fact that it is harder to expropriate value with short-term debt reduces debt-equity conflict. A downside, of course, is the fact that short-term debt means a firm will have to bear the cost of raising capital more frequently.

There are variations of the debt contract, such as puttable debt, that can be used in place of short term debt. *Puttable debt* has the benefit of short-term debt in that it gives investors the right to *put* the debt (that is, to shorten the debt maturity by forcing the firm to buy it back). Issuing puttable debt can, therefore, assure investors that the firm has no desire to increase risk. This allows the firm to issue puttable debt with longer maturity, reducing the frequency with which the debt needs to be refinanced.

Use Convertible Debt
Hybrid securities (those with both debt- and equity-like features) such as convertible debt (usually convertible from debt to equity at the discretion of the investors) can be used to resolve debt-equity conflicts and allow a firm to obtain financing that it is unable to raise through nonconvertible debt. Convertible debt is particularly useful to deal with concerns that relatively risky projects may be undertaken at the expense of bond investors, who suffer if the investment fails but do not get to participate on the upside if the outcome is good. Convertible debt can help if it convinces investors that the manager gains no advantage from choosing the risky project (to try to expropriate value from debtholders) since, in the end, a good bit of the upside payoff from a risky project ends up with the debtholders.

Use Protective Covenants
Covenants can be written into debt contracts to explicitly prohibit certain actions, such as the issuance of additional senior debt, or to restrict action such as cash payout to shareholders without prior approval of the debtholders. Debt covenants commonly require the firm to redeem the debt in the event of change of control. The downside of protective covenants is that they reduce managerial discretion, in some cases restricting the manager's ability to respond to new opportunities.

Place Debts with Banks or Private Lenders
Banks and private lenders are better able to monitor the investment decisions of firms and to enforce protective covenants. This is particularly useful when the incentives to increase risk are most severe. Renegotiation of terms and information sharing are

easier to accomplish in such a setting as well. Offsetting such advantages are the loss of the better liquidity and risk-sharing (and the associated lower cost of financing) that result from issuing debt in public markets.

Improve the Information Flow

To deal with investor concerns, it may be valuable to increase firm transparency to the extent possible without placing the firm at a competitive disadvantage. Increasing information flow is by no means an easy task given the difficulty in verifying the accuracy of information provided by firms. Many of the reporting requirements imposed on publicly traded firms by the SEC and exchanges are designed precisely to increase the flow of reliable information to investors.

■ Reduction in Agency and Expropriation Costs: Another Benefit of Financial Leverage

Other than tax advantages, the major benefit of financial leverage for shareholder value is a reduction in agency and expropriation costs. Debt reduces managerial discretion over firm cash flows and this may be beneficial when managers are perceived to be hoarding too much free cash flow.[3] Also, the *senior nature* (greater priority) of debt contracts can be used to reduce exposure of firm value to expropriation by third parties in cases such as litigation (for example, tobacco lawsuits), wage increases (strikes less likely if firm is constrained financially), and reduction in rates for regulated utilities (rate reduction by public utility commission is less likely if this can result in default).

The separation between a firm's ownership (equity) and its agent or control (management) gives rise to potential conflicts of interest. These conflicts are especially severe when the firm generates substantial "free cash flow"—cash flow in excess of that required to fund positive-NPV projects. The notion is that, lacking good investment opportunities and possessing excessive amounts of free cash flow, managers may be free to pursue their pet projects or engage in unprofitable growth and acquisition activity. These problems are likely to be worse if the firm is largely equity financed. In such a setting, debt can provide a means—imperfect though it may be—of reducing the amount of free cash flow that the manager has access to. In other words, keeping the manager alert since the burden of making regular, contractually enforceable debt service payments provides effective discipline for managers. It is argued that dividends can serve a similar function, except that companies have considerably greater discretion in making dividend payments compared to debt payments.

As with any financial decision, the context is important. Constraints on managerial discretion can be costly if the manager is deprived of the ability to respond effectively to competition or to take advantage of new opportunities. Free cash flow is likely to be a problem in firms in which technology is well established and offers few growth opportunities, while at the same time the firm produces a steady flow of cash from existing operations (in other words, has one or more "cash cows" it can rely on).

■ Check Your Intuition

Take some time here to review the sections about the costs and benefits of leverage and the uses of different capital structures. Then try to describe briefly the level of leverage and types of financing participants that would best serve the interests of shareholder value for some different types of firms. Think about such things as the firm's competitive and regulatory environment, the size and nature of its assets, risk, and ability to accommodate debt versus its cost of financial distress, potential for growth, and so on. Give answers for each of the following:

- A small biotech company
- A U.S. tobacco company
- A boutique investment banking firm
- A defense firm
- A mining company

Compare your answers with the ones given in the following sections.

A Small Biotech Company

For a firm that is small and risky, with many intangibles, low or no leverage appears appropriate. Such firms are typically financed by venture capital, with the venture capitalists being closely involved in both financing—using a variety of hybrid contracts such as convertible debt—and close monitoring to protect their investment.

A U.S. Tobacco Company

For a firm that is large and has historically had very stable cash flows, high debt can be accommodated easily. Higher leverage may also reduce investor concern about wastage of free cash flow as well as the risk of expropriation stemming from lawsuits.

A Boutique Investment Banking Firm

Low leverage is probably appropriate given the intangible nature of the assets (human capital, reputation, bank-client relationships) and high cost of financial distress. The bank is also likely to have volatile earnings and is likely to want to have flexibility to respond quickly to investment opportunities—which would also suggest low leverage.

A Defense Firm

Because it is likely that the Defense Department will support this firm if it runs into financial trouble, the firm might be able to take on moderate or even higher leverage, although decisions on which weapon systems are finally ordered can have a huge impact on firm value. If the firm has ongoing defense contracts, this will usually be associated with highly predictable earnings. The tangibility of some of the assets would suggest the ability to take on some debt as well.

A Mining Company

In general you would expect the firm to have low growth (though some mining companies will not fit the pattern) and highly tangible assets—suggesting that such firms could support significant leverage. The ability of the firm to support debt will be higher if it has entered into longer-term supply contracts or engages in managing the price risk of output.

■ Raising Capital

Having decided on a capital structure for your firm, how quickly should you try to achieve it and, in general, how closely should the firm try to adhere to it? In most cases, the desired capital structure is best viewed as a long-term goal rather than as a precise objective that needs to be maintained at all times. An important reason why your firm might be willing to deviate from its target capital structure is that there are times when a firm is significantly better (or worse) off financing by equity rather than debt.

Established firms tend to finance their investments largely through the use of internal funds generated by retaining past profits. Firms also raise external financing by selling securities in the public market—such as debt, equity, preferred stock, convertible debt, or more exotic securities. They can also turn to nonpublic sources of financing as well. Among them, banks are an important alternative to the issuance of publicly traded securities and can be especially critical to small and midsized firms. Financing is often also raised through private placements with large investors. Very young firms may get much of their financing through venture capital funds.

In our discussion of external financing we focus specifically on the issue of selling firm equity. The issues we encounter are present to a degree in the selling of other types of securities as well. We also look at market imperfections that afflict the raising of external capital, and at ways market institutions can help reduce these frictions.

As we mentioned earlier, maximizing shareholder value can involve balancing among market imperfections: taxes, bankruptcy costs, agency, and information problems. In the context of issuing new securities and firm payout policies, the salient market imperfection is asymmetric information. Investors are concerned that a firm's managers and other insiders, with superior information about the firm's value and prospects, might seek to benefit at their expense.

Raising Equity Capital: Seasoned Equity Offerings

A Seasoned Equity Offering (SEO), as the name indicates, is the selling of new equity by a publicly traded firm (the equity is *seasoned* relative to, say, that of a firm going public for the first time). The selling of any security—and especially equity—is plagued by information concerns of potential buyers since managers of the firm selling equity tend to have superior information about its value.[4] Furthermore, managers have the incentive to sell equity when the firm's stock price is relatively high (that is, overvalued) compared to the manager's own assessment. An indication that such information problems are present is the negative stock market response to announcement of equity offerings. The negative response is in line with the perception that since equity is to be sold, managers probably consider the firm to be overvalued. The typical announcement of a stock offering results in a 3 percent drop in the stock price.

Given investor concern about the timing of equity offerings, underwriters play an important role by certifying the quality and value of the securities being sold. An underwriter guides a firm through the various steps, such as the SEC registration process, and employs its sales network and that of its syndicate partners to sell the offering. Securities are usually sold via the *firm commitment* method, in which the underwriter sells the issue in the market at a fixed offer price. The underwriter purchases the securities from the issuer at a price a little below—reflecting the underwriter's spread—the offer price. For obvious reasons, this offering price is usually finalized only a few hours before the selling is to begin. By accepting the spread, the underwriter assumes the risk that the demand for the firm's securities will be lower than expected. The compensation to underwriters is the money they make because of the spread when they resell to investors. For an SEO the spread is about 3.5 percent of the total proceeds.

The reason to use investment banks to underwrite the offering is that they have experience in evaluating market conditions and have established connections to institutional and retail investors. These attributes are valuable in allowing an underwriter to bridge information and other problems between the firm and investors in the market. Important to the process is the fact that, in underwriting the offering, the investment bank is in effect providing a certification of the value of securities. The underwriter has the necessary skills and a significant reputation at risk, which enhances investor confidence that proper care has been taken to ensure that the shares are fairly priced (similarly, venture capitalists' reputations may be at stake when a firm is taken public in an Initial Public Offering). The fact that the firm commitment process exposes the underwriter to some risk by requiring it to buy and then resell the securities in the market adds to the credibility of the underwriter. Underwriters are also exposed to the risk of lawsuits if investors believe that they did not exercise due diligence in valuing the securities and the firm before the offering.

Pecking Order and Information Asymmetry

Firms tend to follow a certain hierarchy (often referred to as a *pecking order*) in their financing choices. The first preference of firms is for internal financing, followed by senior debt, subordinated debt, and finally equity. The rationale for this order of preference can be understood in terms of the information sensitivity of the securities being sold. The more information-sensitive a security, the greater the problems with asymmetric information and the greater the potential concern of investors. This suggests that firms will prefer to finance using securities where investor concern with information asymmetry is least, using more information-sensitive securities only when other forms of financing are not readily available.

Timing of Equity and Debt Offerings

As noted, firms have a greater incentive to sell equity when they believe their equity is overpriced by the market, and this leads the market to negatively reassess a firm's value when an equity offering is announced. Although there is no clear consensus, some experts claim that firms can take advantage of being overvalued. The evidence for this claim is that in the months following SEOs (and IPOs), the stock price performance of issuers is relatively poor compared with the performance of other firms in similar industries and of roughly the same size.[5] Another indication that timing may be an important factor in issuing equity is that equity offers (SEOs and IPOs) tend to be associated with an increase in stock prices in the months prior to the offering.

In contrast to equity offerings, debt offerings show little evidence of timing. The volume of debt offerings does not go through the significant swings associated with equity offerings and Initial Public Offerings that are related to movements in the stock market and to stock price increases in industries of firms selling equity. There is, however, evidence of some increase in corporate bonds being sold when interest rates are low. The stock market largely ignores announcements of debt offerings—though announcements of bank financing are associated with positive market reactions, suggesting that markets view the news that banks are willing to extend additional loans to a firm as a positive sign. Overall, the level of information problems associated with debt are substantially less. To an extent the information problems are reduced by the rating agencies, which serve a valuable function by tracking the quality and risk of the liabilities of various firms.

Raising Capital from Public or Nonpublic Sources

The Initial Public Offering process allows privately held firms to sell some of their equity in public capital markets. A successful IPO results in the firm's raising equity capital and, by becoming publicly traded, establishing access to stock markets for future rounds of financing. The IPO, thereby, allows firms to access greater amounts of capital than they may have been able to obtain from sources such as venture capital, banks, or personal funds.

When a firm becomes publicly traded, the benefits for financing go beyond the potential for future equity capital. Because of analyst following (since investors are now interested in valuations of the firm), a publicly traded firm is more transparent and visible. Also, the publicly traded firm is required to make a significant amount of income and balance sheet information available to the public through the SEC and by the stock exchange on which it is listed. The rationale for the laws requiring public disclosure of information is that they provide smaller investors with better access to information about the firm and, presumably, a more even playing field vis-à-vis larger investors. With their greater visibility and transparency, publicly traded firms are able to access nonpublic forms of financing (such as banks and private placements) more easily as well.

Among other reasons for firms to become public corporations is to allow founders of the firm to diversify their assets and cash out partially after the firm becomes publicly traded (rather than have their wealth entirely tied up in the same enterprise).

For numerous reasons, some large and successful firms such as Cargill and Bechtel choose not to be publicly traded. One reason is that the increased disclosure required of a public firm may leave them more vulnerable to competition. A second reason is that a public firm is more vulnerable to loss of control and contests for control. Becoming a publicly traded firm also has the effect of diluting the owner-manager's incentives because of the increased separation between ownership and control. A third general reason is cost. For example, the underwriting costs of going public are 7 percent or so of the offer proceeds.

Bank Financing and Private Placements

In contrast to the arm's-length arrangements of public debt markets, bank debt is more intimate in the sense that banks and their clients share much more information. Hence, bank debt has the advantage of greater flexibility in response to unexpected developments—since the debt can be renegotiated and expanded or contracted, with the bank's being able to monitor developments and the performance of the firm. But there are also disadvantages, one being the reluctance of banks to extend loans beyond a certain size to limit their risk; also, banks may be in a position to exploit the relationship and charge excessive rates if the firm is regarded as locked in, with few options in terms of other sources of capital. The latter reason explains why it is advisable for firms that rely heavily on bank borrowing to develop borrowing relationships with multiple banks.

In a private placement market the investors are typically large institutional investors such as insurance companies. Because these investors are regarded as more sophisticated, private placements do not have to satisfy the information disclosure and registration requirements of publicly issued securities. The benefit is that, unlike public offerings, the firm can share considerable information with investors without concern about alerting competitors. Contracts in the private placement market often have special features to meet the needs of the investors and the firm. Another advantage of private financing is that the securities can be sold quickly (no SEC registration, for instance) and information can be shared with a small number of sophisticated investors to deal with their concerns and to communicate the firm's plans.

The big disadvantage, of course, is that privately placed securities have little liquidity (though there have been some legal and market developments to enhance the ability of investors to trade these securities). The lower liquidity of these securities and, possibly, the market power of institutional investors results in less attractive prices for the securities being sold.

Capital Structure and Financing Choice: A Checklist

Here is a sequence of activities and questions that can guide your firm through the main decisions regarding capital structure and financing options.

1. Assess the current cash flow and capital structure position in light of your business plan. In evaluating your cash position, ask

   - Is the firm in a stable, mature industry where the generation of cash flow exceeds investment needs? In a lower-growth industry, a higher leverage could be accommodated.
   - Or is the firm in a growth industry where the cash flow generation is low relative to investment needs? In this case the firm should minimize its fixed obligations.
   - Is the firm facing competitive threats that may require it to make significant investments if the competition intensifies?
   - In terms of capital structure and cash flow position, how does the firm compare with its competitors?

2. For various levels of debt financing, create a careful scenario or conduct a simulation analysis of the firm's cash flow position three to five years out, using historical industry data if possible.

   - What is the level of cash in various contexts, especially in the bad years?
   - Will the firm have enough resources in the worst cases?
   - What's the interest coverage ratio in the worst-case scenario?

3. If the simulations indicate that the firm will face cash flow problems in the worst cases, can it be confident of being able to access banks or capital markets to raise external financing? If the answer is no, can the firm enter into contingent contracts now with banks that might enable it to borrow in such an eventuality? Does the firm have enough assets that could be liquidated to enable the firm to get out of a liquidity crunch?

4. In the simulations, estimate the potential tax savings from using different levels of debt. Keep in mind that the tax saving from debt will be more significant if the firm has fewer

other items such as depreciation credits to deduct from taxable earnings.

5. Can the risk of fluctuation in the firm's cash flows be reduced through the use of long-term contracts or financial instruments? (Chapter Eight discusses risk management.) If so, then the firm would be able to take on greater leverage.

6. Once you have determined your cash flow needs and a desirable capital structure, ask to what extent you are relying on external financing. Consider the fact that you may be forced to raise debt financing since it might be undesirable for you to sell equity at a particular time in the future (its price may be too low compared to your estimate of fair value).

7. Consider alternatives to standard debt and equity. If debtholders have concerns about the risk of future projects, consider the use of convertible debt financing.

8. Finally, how flexible is your business plan? If there are significant deviations from what is expected, can the firm survive? What are the worst-case losses? Are you likely to lose reputation or skilled employees? The more intangible the firm's assets, the greater the margin of safety you should have.

FAQs About Capital Structure

What role do taxes at the personal level play in determining capital structure?

Investors, not surprisingly, care about the after-tax return on their investments. Hence, the (pretax) rates of return required on firm debt and equity will be driven up to compensate investors for the taxes they expect to pay. We note, for instance, the substantially lower (about 30 percent) rate of return investors require on tax-exempt municipal bonds. The issue is of particular interest when a firm can sell new securities that are intended to lower the overall taxes paid by the firm and its investors combined, since this will allow the firm to raise capital at lower cost.

Examples of this occurred prior to changes in the tax law in the 1980s. Before the changes, a number of issuers were selling zero-coupon (a single principal payment at maturity) that were tax-advantaged relative to regular bonds (with regular coupon interest payments).

Can firms actually use bankruptcy to their advantage?

Yes, even though bankruptcy is an outcome usually triggered by the firm's defaulting on its debt payments. Under Chapter 11 of the bankruptcy code, firms can declare bankruptcy as a way to reorganize the firm and its debt, even if there is no actual bankruptcy. There have been instances in which firms—especially in the airline industry—have functioned for long periods in Chapter 11. The reason firms may choose to go into bankruptcy preemptively is that Chapter 11 confers certain advantages to a firm that is in a tight financial position: the firm's management has the exclusive right to propose a reorganization plan in the hundred days after filing, a time period that is often extended. Also, the firm is no longer required to make payments on existing debt, and the firm can raise new debt financing that is senior to all existing claims.

Why are debt contracts not contingent on a firm's earnings, since this would reduce the costs associated with bankruptcy?

The so-called income bond—in which the bond payments were contingent on the firm's earnings—was tried but quickly and sadly abandoned because accounting rules provided firm managements with sufficient flexibility that investors in income bonds might not be paid even when firms were actually doing well. Apparently, in every case in which such bonds were issued, investors did poorly and had to take the issuers to court to try to get paid.

It is, however, quite easy to structure bonds in which the coupon payments depend on some well-defined economic numbers. Oil firms have, for instance, successfully issued bonds in which the coupon payments are linked to oil prices, in line with their anticipated income.

Are there securities other than debt that would be regarded as not being information-sensitive?

The pecking order argument (that less information-sensitive securities are preferred as a way to raise funds) is one of the reasons for the popularity of relatively new types such as asset-backed securities (ABS). Drawing upon the ideas underlying mortgage-backed securities, these claims are issued by firms, backed by a variety of receivables on the asset side of the balance sheet. Unlike conventional debt or equity securities, which are usually claims on the cash flows of the entire firm, asset-backed securities are collateralized by well-delineated assets such as lease receivables, auto loan receivables, and credit card receivables.

Among the advantages of raising financing with ABS is that, to begin with, there is often little information asymmetry associated with the underlying receivables. Then, by creating structures that are sufficiently transparent and have appropriate safeguards, the firm can even further reduce investor concerns about information asymmetry and agency problems. For instance, the receivables are invariably separated from the rest of a firm's assets by creating a trust that issues the ABS claims and then uses the proceeds raised to purchase the receivables from the firm. In addition, the ABS are usually credit enhanced so as to be rated Aaa. To obtain such a rating there may need to be an overcollateralization—that is, an excess of receivables in the trust to provide a safety margin. Once the ABS claims are paid off, any excess assets in the trust—the residual—are usually owned by and revert to the firm issuing the ABS.

To the extent possible, ABS offerings are structured in line with the preferences of various investor clienteles and their maturity and risk preferences. The net result is that by lowering information problems, reducing agency problems by limiting discretion of the issuer, and trying to match investor preferences, ABS can allow a firm to raise financing at relatively attractive rates while cleaning up its balance sheet at the same time.

SUMMARY

Capital structure and other corporate financing decisions matter only because of market imperfections such as taxes, bankruptcy costs, and information asymmetry. In choosing the firm's capital structure you are trading off the costs and benefits of leverage. Among the benefits of debt are the tax savings from the deductibility of the interest payments from taxable income. Debt can also enhance firm value by reducing the risk of expropriation by third parties and by signaling managerial commitment to not waste free cash flow.

On the other side of the trade-off, default on debt payments can lead to bankruptcy-related costs. The presence of debt-equity conflicts can result in the firm's being unable or unwilling to fund positive-NPV projects or to take on risky or low- or negative-NPV projects. Some of these potential problems may be mitigated by actions such as the use of short-term or convertible debt, by the use of debt covenants, through the use of bank or privately placed debt, and by greater information disclosure.

The capital structure choice should be viewed as being a long-term goal—since a firm can often be opportunistic in its choice of financing, raising external debt or equity capital depending on how it is perceived by the market. In general, firms appear to follow a pecking order in which they issue less information-sensitive securities such as debt in preference to equity—with much of the equity capital being the result of retained earnings rather than external financing.

Firms can raise external capital in public markets or from sources such as banks or private placements. While firms may have greater ability to share information and negotiate the terms in bank loans and private placements, the resulting debt is also illiquid and can be more expensive.

Chapter Five turns to another important facet of corporate finance policy: that of payments made to the firm's equity-holders in the form of dividends and stock repurchases. The decision interacts closely with the financing and capital structure decisions discussed in this chapter. In particular, the case in Chapter Five is chosen to emphasize the close connection between financing and payout decisions. Our approach to payout policy relies on the perspective developed in this chapter, that is, one that recognizes the existence of market frictions and views corporate finance decision making as an attempt to maximize shareholder value in the presence of such frictions.

Payout Policy

The flip side of equity financing—discussed in Chapter Four—is the distribution of cash by the firm to its shareholders. Such payouts are common and take the form of dividend payments and share repurchases. Firm payout and financing policies are inextricably linked since, for instance, larger payouts will tend to increase the external financing that a firm needs to raise. The framework developed in the context of financing—that of corporate decision making in the context of imperfect markets—also makes it easier to understand the role and impact of payout policy.

Managers have considerable discretion in paying out cash to shareholders, since equity, unlike debt, comes with no explicit payment obligations. As a consequence, the factors that influence a firm's payout policy can be quite subtle. In this chapter, our objective is to understand the nature and trade-offs involved in the choice of a cash payout policy. After discussing the two forms of payout and the general purposes that they serve, we provide a brief guide to creating and maintaining a payout policy. After that we present a case in which financing decisions and payout decisions are crucially connected, illustrating what happens when a firm in need of capital faces an unattractive choice between raising equity capital or cutting back on dividend payments.

■ Payouts and Their Rationale

First, here is a closer look at the two forms of payout. Then we discuss why payouts in general matter.

Dividends and Share Repurchases

Firms distribute cash in two ways: by dividends and by share repurchases. Historically dividends have been the predominant form of corporate cash payout to shareholders. However, as part of a trend starting in the mid-1980s, share repurchases have become comparable to dividends in terms of total cash flow from firms to shareholders. At the same time, the fraction of listed firms paying dividends has fallen from historical standards.[1]

From a tax perspective dividends and share repurchases are different. Dividends received by individuals are taxable income, although, as of this writing, changes in the tax code in 2003 are expected to lower individual taxation of dividend income and could thereby boost dividend payout. Dividends received by corporations, however, are largely exempt from taxes. Share repurchases, for both individuals and corporations, are taxed as capital gains. Since capital gains tax rates are lower than income tax rates for individuals, individual investors will normally prefer to receive firm payout in the form of share repurchases. These tax issues thus affect the choice between the two forms of cash payout.

The commonest types of dividends are cash dividends paid regularly at quarterly or semiannual intervals. Barring unusual circumstances, investors expect dividend payments to be sustained in the future. Besides regular dividends, companies sometimes issue special dividends that are designated as such and are not expected to be repeated. They also occasionally issue *liquidating dividends*—which, as the name indicates, involve the payment of cash obtained by liquidating some or all of the firm.

Surveys suggest that managers are generally conservative in setting dividend policy.[2] They are reluctant to increase dividends unless they expect to be able to maintain the dividend increase. They are even more reluctant to decrease dividend payout. As a result, corporations tend to smooth their dividend payments, and changes follow shifts in long-run sustainable earnings. In addition to being smoothed, dividends tend to be somewhat lagged compared to reported earnings.

Whereas dividends are equal payments on each outstanding share, share repurchases are payments that the firm makes for whatever specific shares are acquired. The firm can either repurchase shares through **tender-offer repurchase** (making a tender offer to shareholders) or through **open-market repurchase** (gradually buying back shares in the open market). In a tender offer repurchase, firms will typically offer to buy the shares at a price somewhat above the prevailing market price, presumably to ensure a sufficient response from shareholders who may otherwise be disinclined to sell shares because of capital gains taxes and other transaction costs. In an open-market repurchase, the firm usually declares its intention to repurchase a certain amount of outstanding shares over a period of time.

Compared to open-market repurchases, tender-offer repurchases usually involve repurchasing a larger fraction of the firm's shares. They also tend to have a larger positive impact on stock prices when announced, as we discuss later. Repurchases can also be structured in the form of a Dutch auction, in which investors submit information on the prices at which they are willing to sell back their shares. In this instance, the price at which the shares are repurchased is the lowest price at which the firm can buy the desired number of shares. Dutch auction repurchases are discussed in somewhat more detail in the FAQs.

Why Payout Policy Matters

Why should payout policy matter at all? As discussed in Chapter Four, in the real world of imperfect markets, the choice of capital structure has an effect on the ultimate value of the firm. The same is true for payouts. In both cases, if markets were perfect, the choices would not, in fact, make any difference.

If there were no frictions in financial markets then, as with capital structure, shareholders should be indifferent as to whether a firm retains or pays out cash and whether it does so in the form of dividends or by repurchases (assuming that the firm's investment policy remains unchanged).

Consider, for instance, a setting of perfect markets in which a firm decides to distribute dividends to its shareholders and finances the dividends by issuing equity. Suppose that, before the dividend payout, the following data apply:

Outstanding shares: 2 million
Share price: $10
Outstanding debt: $10 million

Then suppose that the firm plans to pay $2 million in dividends by issuing additional equity. What are the wealth consequences of this dividend payment on the firm's security-holders?

In fact, there are no wealth consequences in the absence of market frictions. The total amount to be raised in outside equity is $2 million to finance the dividend payment. If this amount of equity is to be sold, 200,000 additional shares at a price of $10/share (the current share price) will need to be issued. By raising $2 million, the total equity of the firm increases to $22 million, as shown in Table 5.1, which is based on the firm's balance sheet. While the number of shares increases to 2.2 million, the stock price stays at $10/share and can be sold by the firm at this price.

The assumption of market perfection is important here since the balance sheet numbers shown in the table would not hold true if, for instance, there were costs to raising funds or if there were information problems.

What happens *after* the $2 million dividend is paid out to the 2.2 million shareholders? We revert to the left ("Before raising equity") side of the table. The total equity of the firm will again be $20 million, though there are 2.2 million shares outstanding. The new share price after the dividends are paid out is (rounded out): $20 ÷ 2.2 = $9.09/share. This is the ex-dividend stock price. Shareholders, having received $2 ÷ 2.2 = $.91/share neither benefit nor lose as a result of the dividend payment and its financing.

What would happen in this example if we substituted share repurchases for the dividend? If we were to pay the cash out in the form of share repurchase, it would simply involve reversing the process by which $2 million had been raised in the first place. If .2 million shares are repurchased at $10/share, we have distributed $2 million in cash. The total payout is the same as with the dividend payout, but the number of shares is different

Table 5.1. Firm Balance Sheet ($ millions)

Before Raising Equity		After Raising Equity	
Cash	Debt	Cash	Debt
$0	$10	$2	$10
Other assets	Equity	Other assets	Equity
$30	$20	$30	$22

and share price stays at $10/share. This is a matter of indifference to shareholders as in neither case is their wealth affected.

The point of this example is to emphasize that the form and policy of payouts is relevant to the value of the firm only because of market imperfections such as taxes, information problems, and transaction costs. In practice, a significant benefit of an appropriate payout policy is that it can help reduce some of the costs associated with market imperfections.

Why Not Keep the Cash in the Firm?

As noted in Chapter Four, in the presence of transaction costs and asymmetric information, raising external financing can be expensive. But doesn't this suggest that firms should not pay dividends or repurchase shares unless they never expect to raise external financing? Why not hoard all the cash one can, in order to reduce costs of external financing in the future?

There are four important reasons why dividends and share repurchases are in the interest of shareholders, despite the fact that this may raise the amount of external financing required.[3]

Agency Problems and Cash Payout
Managers who regularly pay out cash are, in effect, reducing the amount of free cash flow or discretionary funds available to them. Even if this has the effect of forcing the firm to raise more external funds than otherwise, it can prove beneficial in two ways. First, by having to access external capital markets more frequently, managers indicate their willingness to subject the firm more frequently to the scrutiny of investors and investment banks. Second, excessive cash retained inside a firm is an invitation to some managers to waste resources in the pursuit of unprofitable pet projects or acquisition strategies; it may also be an invitation to lawsuits and takeover attempts. In economies with weaker investor protection a reputation for dividend payments can be especially valuable.

Signal Information to Outside Investors

If there are significant differences between the information available to firm managers and insiders relative to outside investors, cash payout decisions may provide a credible way to communicate information about firm value to outsiders. Unlike accounting numbers (which are more easily abused), a firm must actually have the cash resources if it is to pay dividends or repurchase shares.

Capital Structure

If the firm wants to move toward a more leveraged capital structure (for instance, to obtain greater debt tax shields), it can issue debt and distribute the cash to shareholders in the form of a special dividend or share repurchase. In general, a firm that generates positive income steadily (after interest and capital investments) will inevitably become less leveraged over time, unless it pays cash out to its shareholders.

Transaction Costs

For investors who need a steady stream of cash, it may be cheaper for the firm to pay them regular dividends than to have them frequently sell a fraction of their shares to raise cash, thereby incurring significant transaction costs. Some institutional investors are required by law or their own policy to hold stocks that pay a regular dividend.

▣ Share Repurchases, Dividends, and the Interests of Various Investors

We have noted that dividends received by individual investors in the United States have usually been taxed at the personal income tax rates, although in many countries dividends are taxed more favorably and recent tax changes tend to move U.S. law in the same direction. Share repurchases, on the other hand, are usually taxed at the capital gains tax rate—usually somewhat lower than the income tax rate. An exception to this occurs when share repurchases are used explicitly as dividends, in which case the IRS treats them as such. Hence, a share repurchase that results in a proportional buyback from all shareholders will be treated as a dividend for tax purposes—because there is little change in the ownership pattern of the firm.

Earlier, we noted that in recent years there has been a market shift toward share repurchases, and yet dividends remain important. The basic tax-related difference between dividends and share repurchases raises the so-called dividend puzzle: Why is cash payout not *primarily* in the form of share repurchases instead of dividends?

As an explanation of the puzzle it has been argued that if managers or some classes of investors have superior information, share repurchases will have the effect of benefiting some informed investors or managers at the expense of other firm owners. Therefore, despite a tax disadvantage, many small investors with little access to insider information will prefer dividend payout—and favor firms that pay more dividends.[4]

A second possible explanation is that the tax treatment of dividends and share repurchases is quite different for corporations, which are largely able to exclude dividends from taxes but face the corporate tax rate on capital gains. Other investors that benefit from dividend payments are tax-exempt institutions. To the extent that the stock price of dividend-paying firms is lowered by the taxation of dividends, it works to the benefit of these investors. It has been suggested that a benefit of paying dividends is that it attracts large institutional investors who monitor the firm and, thereby, improve corporate governance.

A third explanation is that while share repurchases are regarded as an occasional, special cash payout, regular corporate dividends, as we observed, are regarded as a commitment by the firm managers to pay out regular amounts over the long haul.

The fact that some investors prefer higher dividends while others prefer share repurchases and low or no dividends suggests that firms with different payout policies are likely to be held by investors with different preferences. What this means for payout policy is that, unless it has compelling reasons to change, a firm should follow a consistent payout policy. If the firm does intend to change its dividend policy, for instance, it needs to provide plenty of advance notice to investors so that they are not forced to liquidate their holdings in a hurry—in the process, causing a temporary drop in the firm's stock price.

■ The Information Content of Cash Payouts

Announcements of changes in dividend payment policy and share repurchases tend to have a significant effect on a firm's market value. How significant are the effects on stock price for announcements of the two different forms of payout? And how might we use this information in choosing payout policies?

According to studies, *dividend* initiations or omissions can produce especially extreme market stock price reactions. These reactions are a rational response to the information that these changes in payout policy communicate about the current and subsequent financial condition of the firm. For example, in a 1988 study of companies that initiate dividends or stop paying dividends, Healy and Palepu found that the announcement of a dividend initiation was greeted by an average 4 percent abnormal stock return.[5] Average earnings jumped 43 percent in the year that companies paid a dividend for the first time. The study found also that the announcement of the dividend cessation was greeted by an average negative 9.5 percent abnormal stock return. Average earnings fell in the year following a stopped dividend.

As we mentioned, the reason for these strong reactions is that changes in dividend policy appear to provide investors with significant information about the financial position of the firm.

From past experience with the dividend policies of most corpora-tions, investors know that an increase is usually made only if the firm expects to be able to sustain the increased payout; a decrease is usually made only when the firm is in a very tight financial con-dition. (In our case we take up a somewhat unusual—but not un-realistic—situation in which a firm that is not in financial straits may deliberately choose to make a dividend cut to save on exter-nal financing costs.)

The announcement of stock repurchases also produces strong positive market reactions. As in the case of dividends, the cash payout is viewed favorably by the market in part because it communicates the manager's willingness to limit the amount of available free cash flow. A second reason for the positive mar-ket reaction, from an information perspective, is that a stock re-purchase signals that firm managers consider their stock to be undervalued. The rationale for this is precisely the reverse of the argument that we made in Chapter Four regarding the issue of shares in a Seasoned Equity Offering (SEO).

Announcement of a stock repurchase via a tender offer re-sults in firms' experiencing large positive stock price reactions. Smaller positive stock price reactions result from an announce-ment that a firm will repurchase shares in the open market. Why the difference in stock-price reactions? Tender offers to repur-chase shares are made, on average, for about 15 percent of out-standing shares, whereas open market share repurchases are typically for a much smaller amount of outstanding shares. Moreover, unlike tender offers, an announcement to repurchase shares in the open market is not binding—though companies will usually follow through.

■ A Guide to Payout Policy

Based on what we have said so far, here is a short checklist to guide you in the selection of an appropriate payout policy.

1. Has the firm been paying regular dividends? If so, maintain the policy.
   a. Increase cautiously and only if you believe that the growth in earnings is likely to be maintained by the firm in the long run.
   b. Decrease only if the firm faces a serious financing crunch. If there is only a short-term financing problem, compare the alternative of raising some external financing, or announce a delay in dividend payments and be willing to take a decrease in stock price. The drop will be mitigated if the firm is clearly able to explain the temporary nature of the cash shortfall.
2. If the firm is considering initiating dividends, again be cautious. Ascertain the firm's ability to sustain its dividend payments. If you do not expect to be able to sustain the dividend payments, announce a special dividend, or better still, use the cash to repurchase shares.
3. If the firm has significant amounts of cash from a one-time infusion from, say, the sale of some assets, consider doing a share repurchase.

■ The Case: A Financing Problem

As we have pointed out, financing and payout policies are closely related. In fact, a significant rationale for paying dividends is that it reduces the information and agency concerns that outside investors have about the firm, thereby facilitating the raising of future financing. In the case that follows, the question is essentially one of comparing the potential costs of obtaining cash through external financing with the cost of obtaining the same amount by eliminating dividend payouts.

Fitzgerald Measuring Tools (FMT), a company producing industrial gauges and measuring devices, is planning to set up a new plant for manufacturing industrial instrumentation systems.

As the CFO of the firm, you have been assigned the task of comparing and recommending among alternative methods by which FMT can raise financing for the project. The investment required for the new plant is estimated to be about $700 million, to be made over the course of two years. The new plant will enable the firm to offer a more complete line of instrumentation devices to its clients, thereby strengthening the overall appeal of the firm's products. Estimates based on a variety of future scenarios indicate that the project is likely to have a substantial positive NPV.

The Basic Choices

You have developed estimates of the free cash flow or internally available funds that could be made available for financing the project. These figures were developed assuming no drastic changes in the firm's sales and profitability over the period and that the firm maintains its existing financing and dividend policies. The total internally available funding over the course of the two years is about $400 million, well below the estimated investment requirement.

About the only way in which the project can be entirely funded by internal financing is if the firm drastically cuts back on the level of its dividend payments. The firm has been paying regular quarterly dividends for the last twenty years. Last year the quarterly dividend paid was $.50/share, or $2.00 on an annual basis. Eliminating the dividend could lead to an additional saving of $200 million each year. The problem, of course, is that investors usually regard elimination or even cutting back on dividend payments as a very negative signal of a firm's prospects. You know only too well that cutting back on dividends could lead to a sharp drop in the firm's stock price. The management is also likely to get an earful from unhappy investors since, in a survey conducted by the firm, about a third of the investors have indicated their preference for generous dividends. The management and board members hold about 15 percent of the firm's equity. This ownership may be reassuring to investors who might otherwise be concerned about the motives of the management.

If internal financing poses problems, so does external financing. You are of the opinion that raising funds through debt financing is not really an option at this stage. In your view the firm already has substantial debt obligations and any significant amount of new debt financing could trigger a drop in the rating of the firm's debt from an investment-grade rating of Baa to a lower, non-investment-grade rating. This concern is based on discussions the firm has had with bond rating agencies such as Moody's. You believe that a non-investment-grade rating implies significantly greater borrowing costs, even if the firm seeks financing from banks or places its debt privately. Another reason to stay within the investment grade is your concern that, in a liquidity crunch, firms with non-investment-grade debt can easily find themselves shut out of the corporate bond market altogether.

Another external possibility is to raise the funds through equity financing. This will move the firm toward a lower debt-to-equity ratio. There are, however, some drawbacks to selling equity to raise financing. The first is that underwriting fees are relatively high (about 3–4 percent of the proceeds) and other costs are involved as well. Another problem is that you and other managers believe that FMT's stock is significantly underpriced. In your opinion, the stock price does not reflect the improvements the firm has made in terms of increasing production efficiency; nor does it reflect the value of the expansion plans that will give the firm a greater ability to compete with rivals. In your view a stock price of $12/share would have been a better reflection of firm value than the current stock price of $10/share. What makes the matter more galling, in your view, is that there tends to be a negative stock market reaction to offerings of equity. Such a market reaction would only worsen the price at which equity could be sold. Therefore, instead of a public equity offering, you wonder whether it might not be better to place the equity privately with a few large investors, thus avoiding the fanfare and publicity of a public equity offering.

As you grapple with the costs and benefits of alternative methods financing, you know that this is an important decision that could have a large impact on the firm's bottom line—not to mention your career and the value of your holdings of the firm's equity.

To compare the alternatives, let us begin with an analysis of the anticipated costs of raising equity capital.

Anticipated Costs of External Financing

The first task is to estimate the costs to FMT shareholders of raising $300 million in external equity financing. Combined with an internal financing of $400 million, this amount would be enough to allow FMT to pursue the project. Raising equity financing with an SEO has two significant costs: the cost on account of the firm's equity being mispriced (as perceived by you and other managers), and the underwriting and other costs associated with the offering process. Note that the cost of mispricing is implicitly tied to the fact that the project cannot be delayed without significant cost. If there are only small costs associated with delaying a project, then a firm may choose to postpone raising external financing until a time when its equity is not undervalued.

In your view, a fair valuation of the firm would be a stock price around $12/share, about 20 percent higher than the current stock price of $10/share. With 100 million shares outstanding, this would put the firm's equity value at about $1.2 billion. You guess that if the firm announced an equity offering of $300 million, this could cause a further decline in the firm's stock price. For estimation purposes, you assume that the announcement of the equity offering drops the stock price by another 5 percent (a bit higher than the average stock price drop of 3–4 percent) bringing it down to about $9.50 per share.

The underwriting and associated costs of an SEO (such as cost of legal services, SEC registration) are usually in the ballpark of 3–4 percent of the proceeds raised in the offering. You choose the figure 4 percent. Since the firm needs to raise $300 million for the project's investment, the proceeds will need to be about $312 million to cover costs.

With an anticipated stock price P of $9.50/share, we can find the total number N of new shares to be sold:

$$\text{Required Proceeds} = N \times P$$

$$N \times 9.5 = \$312 \times 10^6$$

$$N = \frac{312 \times 10^6}{9.5} \approx 33 \times 10^6 \; Shares$$

Hence, the cost to the firm's existing shareholders (as a group) is that their ownership of the firm will have been diluted so that, after the equity offering, they will own 100 million of the 133 million shares outstanding. What dollar cost is implied by that dilution? That figure will be the difference between the loss of value in the current shareholder group's shares and the proceeds of the offering. To find the loss of value we need to know the total equity value of the firm after the equity offering, which is $1.5 billion (your assessment of $1.2 billion plus the $300 million proceeds from the equity offering).

That total equity value implies a post-SEO stock price P = (1.5 billion ÷ 133 million) = $11.28. Note that since the existing shareholders will now own only 100 million of the 133 million shares outstanding, they will therefore have given up 33/133 of the total equity value of the firm in order to raise the $300 million.

$$\$1.5 \times 10^9 \times \frac{33}{133} = \$372m$$

Since the existing shareholders are giving up equity worth $372 million to raise $300 million, they have paid a cost of $72 million. Of this cost about $12 million stems from underwriting and associated costs. The rest, $60 million, is on account of the mispricing of the firm's equity. This is clearly not a cost-effective way to raise the financing, and you will want to seriously consider the alternative of financing by cutting back on dividends.

Before proceeding further, you might want to see the numbers that would apply under the assumption of no mispricing. Figure 5.1 works them out to illustrate the difference that mispricing makes not only in the net amount but also in the stock price and consequently in the number of shares that would need to be sold.

Accounting for the Effects of Timing

So far, we have ignored the timing of the investment requirements. But the fact that the investment is to be made over the course of two years can affect the costs because we do not necessarily need to raise $300 million for investment in the first year. Let us consider this scenario:

- Of the $700 million investment, $400 million is required in the first year and $300 million in the second year.
- Of the $400 million anticipated from internal sources, $300 million is available in the first year and $100 million in the second year. This leaves $100 million and $200 million to be generated from external financing in the first and second years, respectively.
- There is a high probability that investors will obtain reliable information about the value of the firm (from, say, analysts, auditors, information releases from the firm, and possibly

What if there were no mispricing—that is, if managers and outside investors were placing the same value on firm equity? We want to find the value of P (the post-SEO stock price) and the value of N (the total number of shares that would need to be sold) in that event.

The market value of new equity to be sold (the proceeds of the offering) would still need to be $P \times N = \$312$ million, and the firm equity value after the sale of stocks would still be $1.5 billion. Since, after the equity offering, the total number of shares outstanding will be 100 million + N, after the sale of the equity:

$P \times (100 \text{ million} + N) = \$1.5$ billion

Since $P \times N = \$312$ million (proceeds from equity offering):

$\$P \times 100$ million + $\$312$ million = $\$1.5$ billion

From this expression we can calculate a stock price $P = \$11.88$, and from that price the number $N = 26.26$ million shares.

Notice how, without mispricing, the post-SEO stock price is higher and the number of shares to be sold is much less.

Note: If there are no costs of underwriting the offering, that is, precisely $300 million of new equity is to be sold, then you can check that the stock price remains at $12 and N = 25 million shares.

Figure 5.1. The Offering Calculation With No Mispricing

from its rivals) over the course of the first year. As a consequence, we might expect the firm's stock to be fairly priced in the second year of the investment.

Under this scenario (maintaining the assumption of 4 percent underwriting and other costs), only $104 million of equity will be sold in the first year. If, as before, equity is sold at $9.50/share, this is the number of shares that the firm will need to sell:

$$N = \frac{104}{9.5}\, m = 10.95m \approx 11m \text{ shares (approximately)}$$

Proceeding in a similar fashion as before, this number would allow us to calculate that the existing shareholders have given up about $129 million in the first round to raise $100 million. Since only $4 million of the former amount is required by various expenses, the cost on account of the mispricing must be about $25 million. In the *second* round, if the firm can raise $200 million at a *fair* price, its cost will be only the $8 million it has to pay in fees. Hence, it will be able to generate the external funding for a total cost of about $37 million. That is still expensive, but not as bad as the cost when the full $300 million is raised in the first year.

Thus, one benefit of having two rounds of financing is that prior to the second round of equity financing, at the end of one year, the management's view of the firm's higher value may indeed be supported by new information and firm performance. The result should be to reduce or eliminate the misvaluation. There is also a second benefit that we did not explicitly consider. It comes from the fact that potential investor concern about the firm's attempting to time the stock market (that is, to take advantage of the firm's being overvalued) will be less as well since the firm is raising equity in two rounds a year apart. This might be expected to reduce the negative price impact of the equity offering.

The likely downside of having to go to the market twice is greater underwriting costs—the costs of issuing have a fixed component as well. However, the issuing costs of two rounds of financing may be lowered by the use of a so-called *shelf offering*, which simplifies the SEC registration process and allows a firm to register its equity offering only once, even though the new shares may be sold in more than one round.

The Option of Cutting Back on the Dividend

External financing through an equity offering thus appears to be an expensive option. The question now is whether the alternative of cutting dividends to obtain funds is the better way to proceed.

With little doubt, cutting dividends will produce a strongly negative market reaction. The reason is simple: managers do not usually cut dividends unless they must, and dividend cuts are often precursors to poor earnings and financial trouble. The question is whether FMT should be willing to suffer a stock price drop even if, as management believes, the price impact would be temporary.

Let's maintain the same timing scenario assumptions: funds required in the first and second years are $100 million and $200 million, respectively. The rest of the funds, $300 million and $100 million in the first and second years, are expected to be available from internal sources.

To raise $100 million in the first year the firm will need to reduce its annual dividend to $1/share from its current level of $2/share. We expect the dividend reduction to bring down the stock price, at least until investors are persuaded that the firm is indeed using the dividends for a productive investment—and that the dividend cut was not forced upon the firm by a decline in earnings. One factor that may mitigate the negative stock price impact is that a significant amount of the firm's equity (15 percent) is controlled by the firm's insiders, which should lower investor concern about agency issues and wastage of free cash flow.

The cost of a stock price drop would be of great concern if the firm planned to issue securities such as equity. But that is not a concern here since cutting the dividend allows the firm to do without an equity offering.

Now the question turns to the reactions of the firm's current shareholders. You have ascertained that about a third of them apparently attach value to receiving investment return in the form of dividends. The dividend cutback is likely, therefore, to trigger the loudest complaints from this class of investors. Your approach to dealing with their displeasure will be to point out that by cutting dividends, the firm will be avoiding the need to issue equity. By avoiding the equity offerings, the firm is saving between $37 million (the best-case scenario, with multiple rounds of equity financing and mispricing disappearing after a year) and $72 million (the worst case, with unrelenting mispricing). Naturally, management should act in ways that save the firm substantial money in the long run—rather than letting a minority of shareholders determine the policy for long-term shareholders that benefit from a policy of internal financing.

If all goes well, the stock price should recover in a year or less as information filters down to shareholders about firm value and the mispricing disappears. The quicker the stock price recovers, the sooner the firm may be able to use alternative modes of financing to restore its dividend policy. For instance, if the stock is properly priced by the second year, it may not be necessary for the firm to miss out on the second year's dividend. At that stage, the firm could issue sufficient equity to raise the $200 million in funding required. If the mispricing remains significant in the second year, the firm may have to miss paying the second-year dividend; or it could choose to pay $1/share dividend for another year and raise $100 million in equity.

Putting the various elements together, it appears that despite the potential for short-run pain, the dividend cut is the way to go in longer-term shareholder interest. Clearly, investors should be provided with as much information as possible about the rationale for the dividend cut and your expectation that the firm will be able to restore its dividend payments in one or, at most, two years.

FAQs About Payout Policy

How is price determined in a Dutch-auction repurchase?

As noted, a Dutch auction is an alternative to the fixed-price tender offer method of repurchasing shares. It has been used since the 1980s in U.S. markets. In this method interested shareholders submit offers of the quantities of shares they are willing to sell back to the firm at specified prices. The corporation aggregates these sell orders and determines the lowest price at which it would be able to repurchase the desired quantity of shares. The shares are then purchased at this price from shareholders who had offered to sell at this or at a lower price. The average premium paid in Dutch-auction repurchases tends to be lower than the premium paid in fixed-price tender offer share repurchases.

What are targeted stock repurchases?

These are share repurchase offers directed at only a specific segment of shareholders—and are usually seen in the context of struggles for corporate control. Targeted repurchases are typically used to buy out the holdings of a large shareholder, who might be a potential acquirer of the firm. The prices of the repurchase are negotiated and, as one might expect, tend to be well above the prevailing market price of the stock.

Should debtholders be concerned about dividend payments?

Debtholders have every reason to be concerned about dividend payments. By making dividend payments a firm is directly distributing its assets to shareholders—potentially at the expense of its debtholders. This potential conflict between debt- and equity-holders is usually resolved through the use of covenants in debt contracts (see Chapter Four). These covenants might be used, for instance, to restrict the firm's ability to make significant increases in dividend payout without prior approval of bondholders.

Doesn't a firm's dividend policy have an effect on its investment policy?

If dividend policy is regarded as being of high priority by management, it can affect the investment decisions of the firm. In practice, however, dividend policies do not appear to have a significant effect on investment decisions of U.S. firms. Evidence suggests that, in general, firms appear to be able to finance profitable investments through the use of external financing when necessary, while maintaining their dividend policies.

SUMMARY

Distributions of cash by firms to their shareholders are common and take the form of dividend payments and share repurchases. Investors differ in terms of their preference for the level and form of cash payout. For instance, while dividends received by individual investors are taxed as income, dividends received by corporations are largely exempt from taxes. Share repurchases, for both individuals and corporations, are taxed as capital gains. As a consequence, individual investors prefer share repurchases while corporations favor dividend payments.

The fact that some investors prefer higher dividends while others prefer share repurchases and low or no dividends suggests that firms with different payout policies are likely to be held by investors with different preferences. As a result, absent compelling reasons to change, a firm should follow a consistent payout policy. If the firm does intend to change its payout policy, it needs to provide plenty of advance notice to investors so that they are not forced to liquidate their holdings in a hurry—in the process, causing a temporary drop in the firm's stock price.

Cash payout can enhance firm value by communicating information about the firm's prospects and by assuring investors that firm management is willing to reduce the amount of available free cash flow. These benefits can be large enough to offset the increase in transaction costs from the firm's having to resort more frequently to costly external financing on account of significant payouts.

Because payouts represent actual cash—as opposed to accounting earnings—changes in payout policies are regarded as very important indicators of the firm's present and prospective performance. There are significant differences in the way firms act—and investors *react*—with regard to the payment of dividends compared to share repurchases. Firms are extremely reluctant to cut their regular dividend payment—which results in firms' also being cautious about *increasing* their dividends unless they are confident about being able to maintain them in the future. Evidence indicates that firms tend to omit dividends only when their financial situation is quite poor. Dividend omissions are associated with a significant drop in the firm's stock price and poor earnings performance. This suggests that, at least as far as regular dividends are concerned, a firm needs to be cautious in either decreasing or increasing the dividends—unless the change reflects a long-term change in its capacity to sustain the dividend payments.

The case suggests that, in certain situations, a firm may choose to cut its dividend payments temporarily; it does, however, have to deal with the market's concern that the dividend cut might signal poor long-term prospects. This can be mitigated by providing as much information as the firm can, while explaining why the dividend cut is a form of lower-cost financing instead of an indication of poor prospects. The most convincing evidence for the market, of course, comes when the firm is actually able to generate higher earnings and, eventually, restore dividend payments.

Unlike regular dividend payments, share repurchases allow firms to exercise substantial flexibility. The repurchase of shares is greeted with a positive increase in stock price as well. The repurchase has the benefit of reducing free cash flow, while indicating the manager's willingness to limit the free cash flow in the firm. It can also be used effectively as a signal that the firm's managers consider the firm's stock to be undervalued.

Mergers and Acquisitions

Y ou are the new CEO of GreatDrill, a major player in the hand tools industry. You've just taken over the reins when your strategic planning group recommends that GreatDrill acquire TimTools, a family-controlled hand tool manufacturer whose founding family holds 20 percent of TimTools shares. Both companies are publicly traded. This being the first acquisition since you became CEO, you wish to thoroughly review the GreatDrill acquisition strategy and how TimTools fits into that strategy. Having experience in acquisitions at other firms, you are aware that such efforts often fail. You want to ensure that this acquisition produces the intended results and in particular that it creates shareholder value. If you decide to acquire

TimTools, you also have to decide how much to pay for it and in what form to pay.

■ Acquisitions Strategy and Shareholder Value

Every company wishes to grow, but many are unclear about the appropriate metric for growth. Many focus solely on revenue or asset size growth. But in keeping with the objective of maximizing shareholder value, we contend that growth in share price is the most appropriate metric for evaluating the efficacy of a company's growth strategy. A growth strategy will increase the share price if the aggregated future benefits of implementing the strategy exceed the aggregated future costs of implementation. It is important to evaluate growth strategies from this perspective to ensure share price growth.

Companies should also realize that acquisitions are but one way to grow, and not necessarily always the best way. It is therefore important to compare acquisitions with other growth strategies such as organic or internal growth, joint ventures, and contractual agreements such as licensing.

Do acquisitions increase shareholder value? At the time of an acquisition, managers of acquiring companies must believe (or at least profess to believe) that the acquisition will do so. However, after the acquisition, managers very often revise their opinion about its success in this regard. In fact, in a survey of managers involved in acquisitions, only 58 percent felt that their own acquisitions created value and only 51 percent felt that their deals achieved their strategic goals.[1] The scientific evidence on the success of acquisitions (from the acquiring company's perspective) supports this dismal survey result. The post-acquisition performance of acquiring companies indicates that about half of them failed to deliver expected results.[2] Such post-acquisition performance has made investors leery of acquisitions. Upon announcement of acquisitions, acquirer stock prices drop (adjusted for market movements) in about half the cases.[3] In other words, the market correctly views the success of acquisitions on the whole as no better than a coin toss. Why the poor record for acquisitions?

■ Why Many Acquisitions Fail to Create Shareholder Value

Why does such a major decision as an acquisition of another company end up failing to create shareholder value in about half the cases? The failures generally have one of six major reasons.

Acquisitions That Do Not Fit the Firm's Corporate Capabilities

Many corporate acquisitions stray far from the capabilities of the management. Research has repeatedly shown that conglomerate acquisitions involving unrelated businesses are viewed most negatively by the market whereas acquisitions involving related businesses are viewed positively. A recent study by Booz-Allen Hamilton found that only about half as many acquisitions with the stated objective of adding capabilities, developing new business models, or moving upstream or downstream in the value chain met expectations as did acquisitions intended to grow existing business.[4] While this result indicates that companies should be cautious about overstretching their capabilities, it does not imply that companies should not diversify at all. Research has shown that companies that diversified moderately (67 percent of the revenues from two lines of business) have provided a greater shareholder return than either companies that are too focused or companies that are too highly diversified.[5]

Overestimation of the Growth from Acquisitions

Frequently managers seem to overestimate the value to be derived from acquisitions. A recent study found that 53 percent of the deals failed to deliver their expected results. The most commonly cited expectation is accelerated growth. However, research has shown that only 12 percent of the merged firms managed to significantly accelerate their growth.[6] Many companies expect that acquisitions will lead to growth through the creation of market power. However, research shows that efforts to enhance market position have not resulted in value creation.[7]

Overestimation of the Value of Cost Reductions

Cost reductions are often cited as the main reason for mergers. However, fully 40 percent of mergers fail to capture the expected cost savings.[8] And in many cases, management, under pressure to show results, starts cutting costs at inappropriate places or cuts costs excessively, which only worsens the problem.

Underestimation of the Difficulty and Costs of Extracting Value

Both revenue growth and cost reduction require planning and effective implementation. Two-thirds of the companies in the Booz-Allen Hamilton study cited earlier attributed implementation issues (loss of key personnel, delays in communication, poor due diligence) as reasons for the failure of acquisitions. This shows how difficult it is to extract value even from acquisitions with clearly identified sources of value.

Why is it so difficult? For instance, to achieve cost reductions, some systems or units will have to be integrated, some units might have to be eliminated, some best practices transferred. All these activities are unlikely to be implemented without disruption, and are likely to cause employee anxiety resulting in reduced efficiency and, in some cases, departure of key personnel. The resulting value destruction could sometimes overwhelm any anticipated value gains. And cost savings are relatively *easy* to achieve compared to building new industry models or growing existing businesses. In acquisitions motivated by such other objectives, the cost and difficulty of extracting value are concomitantly greater.

Underestimation of the Difficulties of Post-Acquisition Integration

In general, the closer in size the acquirer and the target are, the more critical post-acquisition integration issues tend to be. Since integration is a key value driver (synergies created and costs reduced through integration) the integration work needs to start at the planning stage. An integration team needs to be in place even before the deal is consummated, and changes resulting from the acquisition need to be communicated constantly to employees, investors, and customers. Many companies tend to be too internally focused during the early stages of integration and lose sight of customer concerns.[9] Companies that are not used to doing acquisitions systematically underestimate the importance of these issues.

Overpayment

Even in acquisitions that truly create value, the acquirer may not reap any of the benefits if it overpays for the acquisition. Almost all academic studies report that the combined gains to acquirer and target shareholders are positive (based on the market adjusted returns on announcement of the acquisition).[10] This indicates that acquisitions are not a zero-sum game; they are a value-creating activity in the aggregate. On the other hand, as noted earlier, there is strong evidence that the shareholders of acquiring companies generally lose out in acquisitions; the share prices of acquiring companies drop on average when they announce acquisitions. This indicates that acquirers are often overpaying even in acquisitions that make economic sense.

■ Avoiding the Pitfalls in Acquisitions

Given the rather dismal evidence on the success of acquisitions, how does an acquiring company improve its chances of success? Here are several precautions that a company can take.

Don't Confuse the Objective

Most companies say they wish to maximize shareholder value. However, when it comes to decision making, they use metrics that are not necessarily congruent with shareholder value. For example, in the context of acquisitions, companies often use the increase in immediate earnings per share (EPS) as a criterion. It is true that increasing current *and* future EPS will increase shareholder value. However, companies often focus myopically on increasing current EPS without considering the acquisition's effect on future EPS. The example in Figure 6.1 illustrates how current EPS can be boosted by an acquisition without creating any value. When you buy a company that has a lower price-earnings (P/E) multiple than your company's, you trigger a sort of "pyramid" scheme in which the only way to keep the investors from realizing that future growth has been compromised is to keep making similar acquisitions.

A similar confusion of objective occurs when companies use diversification as a motive for acquisitions. Many conglomerates are built in this fashion. However, it is well established that, on average, conglomerates sell at a discount relative to a matched portfolio of single-segment firms.[11] It might appear at first glance that, by diversifying, companies create value for their shareholders, since diversification is a sound portfolio strategy

In this example, we show how one can increase the current EPS of a firm by acquiring another firm with a lower P/E multiple even if the acquisition does not add any value to shareholders.

Consider this data, especially the shaded cells:

	Acquirer	Target	Combined Firm
Share price	$25	$16	$25
Number of shares	200	300	392
EPS	$2	$4	4.08
P/E multiple	12.5	4	6.13
Market capitalization	$5000	$4800	$9800
Total earnings	$400	$1200	$1600

A company with a share price of $25, 200 shares outstanding, and a current EPS of $2, acquires another company with a share price of $16, 300 shares outstanding, and a current EPS of $4. Let us assume that

- The acquisition creates no value.
- The acquirer pays market price for target. In other words, the acquirer does not overpay. Since the acquisition creates no value, anything exceeding the target's share price will result in overpayment.
- The acquirer issues new shares to finance the acquisition.

The P/E multiple for each company is computed by dividing the share price by the EPS. The market capitalization of each company is computed by multiplying the share price by the number of shares. The total current earnings are computed by multiplying the EPS by the number of shares.

The share price of the combined company should be $25 (same as that of the acquiring company) since no value was created by the acquisition and there was no overpayment to the target company. The market capitalization and the total current earnings of the combined company will be the sum of the respective numbers for the target and the acquirer. The total payment to the target company is its market capitalization of $4800 since we assumed that the target is paid the market price. At $25, the acquiring company needs to issue $4800 ÷ 25 = 192$ shares to the target company. After the acquisition, the acquiring company will have 200 + 192 = 392 shares outstanding. The current earnings per share of the combined company will be $1600 ÷ 392 = \$4.08$, which exceeds the pre-acquisition EPS of the acquiring company.

This example shows that it is possible to increase current EPS through an acquisition without creating value. The acquirer has boosted its current EPS by buying a company with a low P/E multiple. This enables the acquirer to buy high current earnings for a low price (relative to its own), thus boosting its own current EPS. Yet since no value is added, it must be true that the growth in EPS of the combined firm will be lower because of the acquisition.

An acquisition such as this is likely to lower the future earnings growth of the acquirer. Essentially, the acquirer trades off future EPS for current EPS.

Figure 6.1. Boosting Current EPS Without Creating Value: Example

for investors. However, these companies fail to recognize that investors can diversify themselves very easily nowadays. With the availability of hundreds of mutual funds and exchange-traded funds, extensive diversification can be achieved at a very low cost. The only benefit of pure diversification (that is, diversification with no synergy or cost benefits) is that it reduces the probability of financial distress with its associated costs, because during times in which any one segment passes through a downturn in its business, it can be supported by other segments that are doing better. However, the steep premiums companies pay for acquisitions (the average premium in the United States is about 30–35 percent) can easily offset this benefit, destroying value by doing something at a higher cost that its investors can do themselves cheaply. The only people who benefit from pure diversifying acquisitions are the managers, who thus protect themselves from business downturns.

A third confusion of objective occurs when companies use lowered borrowing costs as the motive for acquisitions. It is possible that the target company was finding it difficult to raise capital at a fair cost because its potential was not fully realized by the market and the financial institutions. In this case, an acquirer, well regarded by investors and financial institutions, can add value by taking over the target and raising capital for the target's projects at a lower rate. However, in many cases the combined company is able to raise capital at a lower rate than the target only because the acquirer will stand behind the loans for the target's projects. In this case, the acquirer is subsidizing the target, and so the acquirer's borrowing rate is likely to increase. This is what happened when American Airlines acquired a significant interest in TWA. One of the benefits cited was that American could renegotiate lower lease rates on TWA jets. The new lease rates were indeed lower by $207 million per year. However, Moody's downgraded several American debt issues, raising American's borrowing costs.[12]

Evaluating acquisitions from the perspective of shareholder value creation will allow you to avoid many of the pitfalls in acquisitions.

Have a Clear Growth Strategy

It is important to define your growth strategy clearly and then ensure that the target company fits that strategy (for example, eliminating overcapacity in the industry while providing the acquirer with a distribution system in a country or region where the acquirer didn't already have one). The checklist in Figure 6.2 is a good place to start. It is also important to investigate whether the same growth objective can be achieved through means other than an outright acquisition (for example, by building your own distribution system). By doing so, you will get a clearer understanding of the incremental value created by the acquisition. This will then play a major role in determining the maximum price that you can afford to pay the target, thus avoiding overpayment.

Identify Value Drivers and the Process of Extracting Value

When evaluating the target, it is important to identify the value drivers of this specific acquisition clearly. In other words, how does the combination of a specific acquirer and a specific target create value? What are sources of increase in revenue and decrease in costs? Are there specific targets for growth and cost reductions, and how exactly does the acquiring company plan to achieve them? Using a discounted cash flow (DCF) analysis for this purpose enables the acquirer to clearly identify the value drivers and set targets to be achieved after the acquisition.

Fully Understand the Costs of Integrating the Target

Most often when a company acquires another company, it integrates the operations of both companies. It is important to

Value-Creating Potential of the Acquisition

Use the correct metric: Shareholder value, not current EPS or diversification.

Be clear about our growth strategy.

- Product extensions?
- Product market extensions?
- Geographic roll-ups?
- Elimination of overcapacity in the industry?
- Knowledge acquisition (R&D)?
- Industry convergence?

Ensure that the acquisition fits with our growth strategy.

Identify the value drivers.

- Eliminate overcapacity in the industry?
- Introduce new products for open segments?
- Create new distribution in open areas?
- Create new markets?
- Bring desired manufacturing capabilities?
- Provide desired R&D capabilities?
- Provide economies of scale?
- Position us for future industry convergence?

Specify targets for each value driver and evaluate the acquisition based on the targets.

Investigate viable alternatives to the acquisition (organic growth, joint venture, partnership, collaboration, and so on).

Integration Issues

Human Resources

Is target's culture compatible with our own?

- Are the corporate governance and management styles of both companies similar?
- Are both companies at the same stage of business life cycle?
- Are values and principles of both companies the same or similar?
- Will the cultures of the two companies allow information to flow easily? If not, can we manage the differences?

Figure 6.2. Creating Shareholder Value from Acquisitions:
A General Manager's Checklist

Do the organizational capabilities of the target match those demanded by the market? If not, do we have the capabilities in our organization? Have we identified the key employees at the target (value creators) and locked them in?

Are there people issues at the target?

- Is the general morale positive?
- Does the target seek to create valuable and challenging work for its employees?
- Do target HR practices (promotions, reward systems) motivate employees?

Production, Operations, and Marketing

Are the target's production capabilities compatible with ours?

Is the target's IT system compatible with ours?

Is the target's distribution network complementary to ours?

Is the target's sales force complementary to ours?

- Can the target's capabilities in these areas be leveraged to reduce costs?

Legal Issues

Are there pending legal liabilities at the target?

Are there any regulatory or tax issues that could threaten future returns?

Are we required to disclose merger intentions to existing allies, partners, or stakeholders?

Does the target conduct business in any new international markets? If so, have all legal and operational issues in those countries been considered?

Are there any contractual obligations to stakeholders such as suppliers, partners, and employees? Purchase contracts with suppliers, delivery and other performance contracts with partners, and union contracts and pension liabilities with employees?

Are there contracts with other companies that are triggered by the acquisition?

Has the possibility of the seller or seller employees setting up a competing business been considered?

Figure 6.2. Creating Shareholder Value from Acquisitions:
A General Manager's Checklist, Cont'd

recognize that integration is a challenging process, especially if the target company is big, but even when it is as small as 20 percent of the size of the acquirer. There are two broad integration issues: integration of human resources and integration of physical resources. It is the former that often gets short shrift in acquisitions. See the checklist in Figure 6.2 for human resource issues that need to be raised and addressed in the integration process. The issues related to physical resources (manufacturing, marketing, accounting, and IT systems) are obvious, but companies often underestimate the cost of integrating human resources.

Do the Legal Due Diligence

The importance of legal due diligence cannot be overstated. MCI WorldCom paid $2.3 billion for the Brazilian company Embratel during Brazil's privatization of Telebras, its state telecommunications concern. That price was a 46 percent premium to the government's minimum asking price. Brazilian tax authorities claimed the U.S. long-distance giant owed as much as $650 million in back taxes, interest, and fines.[13] MCI WorldCom maintained that it was not responsible for those debts since they were incurred by Embratel before its privatization. This dispute could have been avoided if the contract between MCI WorldCom and the Brazilian government had been clear on this liability. As the checklist in Figure 6.2 indicates, several legal and regulatory issues need to be considered if value is not to be lost in the course of future disputes.

Know When to Walk Away

Takeover negotiations can often get emotional, especially if there are competing offers or if the target resists. Executives can get carried away in the heat of the deal and may be loath to lose the target. Successful acquirers recognize this and build disciplining mechanisms into the acquisition process. Such mechanisms can include a price ceiling that can be broken only with approval of a superior, or a solid rule holding the executive making the deal responsible for delivering a threshold rate of return on the deal.

■ GreatDrill's Acquisition of TimTools

As GreatDrill's CEO, you wish to avoid the pitfalls that limit the value potential in acquisitions. Therefore, you decide to carefully evaluate the TimTools acquisition proposal forwarded by your strategic planning group by taking the following steps:

1. Confirm the strategic fit between this acquisition and GreatDrill's growth strategy.
2. Identify the value drivers and evaluate the specific targets set to extract value from the acquisition.
3. Evaluate the cash flows of the target company under GreatDrill management and any changes to GreatDrill's operational cash flows due to the acquisition.
4. Make sure that the nonoperational assets of the target company and its liabilities have been included in the analysis.
5. Consider the costs of integrating the target company.
6. Avoid overpaying by carefully evaluating how much and in what form to pay for the acquisition.

GreatDrill's Growth Strategy

GreatDrill's growth strategy is based on two foundations: innovation and geographic growth. It expects innovation to increase sales in its existing markets by introducing new products such as cordless and multipurpose tools. It also expects its innovation to provide footholds in new markets in which to sell its existing products. Based on this strategy, its acquisition program concentrates only on targets that either help GreatDrill add to its portfolio of products or provide access to new markets.

TimTools' Strategic Fit and the Value Proposition

GreatDrill has sales primarily in North America with an emerging presence in Latin America, but it has been exploring the possibility of entering the Western European market. TimTools came to its attention primarily because it has a strong European presence with an established distribution network there. The acquisition of TimTools appears congruent with GreatDrill's growth strategy of expanding into new markets. Upon careful analysis of TimTools' business, GreatDrill has recognized several other sources of value:

- TimTools has more of a presence in the industrial market whereas GreatDrill has more of a presence in the consumer market, especially because of GreatDrill's superior hand tools group. This complementarity reduces the potential of losses due to cannibalization of each other's products.

- TimTools has not been well managed. Its annual revenue growth has been an anemic 3.5 percent compared to the industry average of 6 percent. GreatDrill's marketing department believes it can increase TimTools' revenue growth to at least the industry average.

- The cost structure of TimTools has been too high. A TimTools effort to sell to every market segment has resulted in an excessive number of products, reducing manufacturing efficiency and increasing inventory costs. Rationalization of the product portfolio will increase manufacturing efficiency and reduce COGS.

▫ The rationalization of product lines will also decrease working capital needs as overall inventory is reduced.

▫ There is substantial overlap between the sales forces of the TimTools and GreatDrill hand tools divisions. Reduction in sales and advertising duplications would reduce SG&A.

Setting Targets for Value Drivers

The next step in your process is to examine how the strategic planning group has quantified the value added to GreatDrill from the acquisition of TimTools. To quantify the value added by the acquisition, the group first set specific targets for the value drivers in the acquisition. This process has not only enabled the quantification of the value of the acquisition, it has also provided the company specific targets to meet after the acquisition. The value drivers in the TimTools acquisition can be broadly classified into two categories:

▫ Greater revenue growth and reduction in COGS, SG&A, and working capital resulting from the increased efficiency of TimTools under GreatDrill management.

▫ Increased sales for GreatDrill products in Western Europe resulting from TimTools' European distribution system.

The strategic planning group has estimated the value of each of these categories separately. It is useful to evaluate each value driver separately so that the accuracy of these estimates can be verified, along with the feasibility of attaining them.

Increased Efficiency of TimTools Under GreatDrill Management
The strategic planning group has estimated the targets for the increased operating efficiency of TimTools as shown in Table 6.1. The primary implications are discussed in the list following the table.

Table 6.1. Free Cash Flow Estimates of TimTools Under GreatDrill Management ($ and share count, millions)

1   TimTools shares outstanding = 5.84
2   Cost of capital: TimTools (percent) = 10.0
3   Tax rate (percent) = 40.0

Before acquisition
4   Working capital/Revenue (percent) = 28.0

After acquisition
5   Revenue growth up to 2008 (percent) = 6.0
6   Working capital/Revenue (percent) = 24.0

	2003	2004	2005	2006	2007	2008	2009
7 COGS/Revenue (percent) =	67.5	67.0	65.0	65.0	65.0	65.0	65.0
8 SG&A/Revenue (percent) =	21.5	21.0	20.0	19.0	19.0	19.0	19.0
9 Working capital =	$155	$132	$140	$148	$157	$167	$167

Year	2003	2004	2005	2006	2007	2008	2009
10 Revenue	$553.0	$550.0	$583.0	$618.0	$655.1	$694.4	
11 COGS	($373.3)	($368.5)	($379.0)	($401.7)	($425.8)	($451.3)	
12 SG&A	($118.9)	($115.5)	($116.6)	($117.4)	($124.5)	($131.9)	
13 Depreciation	($21.0)	($21.0)	($21.0)	($21.0)	($21.0)	($21.0)	
14 Other deductions	($2.0)	($2.0)	($2.0)	($2.0)	($2.0)	($2.0)	
15 Taxable income		$43.0	$64.5	$75.9	$81.8	$88.1	
16 Tax		($17.2)	($25.8)	($30.4)	($32.7)	($35.2)	
17 NOPAT		$25.8	$38.7	$45.5	$49.1	$52.9	
18 After-tax operating CF*		$46.8	$59.7	$66.5	$70.1	$73.9	$73.9
19 Change in working capital		$22.8	($7.9)	($8.4)	($8.9)	($9.4)	$0.0
20 Capital expenditure		($21.0)	($21.0)	($21.0)	($21.0)	($21.0)	($21.0)
21 Free cash flow		$48.6	$30.8	$37.1	$40.2	$43.4	$52.9

After acquisition
Terminal value in Year 2008 = $529

22
23 Present value of cash flows, 2004–2008 = $152
24 Present value of terminal value = $328
25 Enterprise value = $480

Assumptions
1. Depreciation and other deductions are assumed to hold at 2003 levels.
2. GreatDrill will invest capital in TimTools only as replacement. To reflect this, new capital expenditures are assumed to be equal to depreciation.
3. After 2008, growth rate is assumed be zero. To reflect this, after-tax operating cash flow and capital expenditure are assumed to be constant at 2008 level. Changes in working capital are assumed to be zero.

- Revenue in 2004 will stay at about 2003 levels because of the reduction in the number of products (line 10). After that it will grow at the industry average level of 6 percent annually till 2008 (line 5).
- Through increased manufacturing efficiency, COGS could be brought down from 67.5 percent to 67 percent of revenue in 2004, and to 65 percent thereafter (line 7).
- Reduction in sales and advertising duplications would cut SG&A from 21.5 percent to 21 percent of revenue in 2004, 20 percent in 2005, and 19 percent thereafter (line 8).
- Due to the reduced number of TimTools products, working capital will be reduced from 28 percent of revenue in 2003 to 24 percent of revenue in 2004 and thereafter (lines 4 and 6).

Leveraging TimTools' European Distribution
For the second value driver, the additional European sales generated for GreatDrill products, the strategic planning group estimates the values shown in Table 6.2. Line 4 provides estimates of GreatDrill cash flows without the acquisition while line 6 provides the same with the acquisition of TimTools.

- The acquisition will increase GreatDrill's 2004 cash flows by 5 percent as GreatDrill starts selling its own products in Europe using TimTools' distribution system.
- In subsequent years, the cash flow from GreatDrill's European market will grow as indicated in Table 6.2, line 5, and by 2006 the European market will provide 25 percent of GreatDrill's cash flows from other products.

Value Added to GreatDrill by the Acquisition

Based on the target estimates, the strategic planning group has provided a free cash flow analysis of TimTools under GreatDrill management. Table 6.1 provides the details. Notice that the

Table 6.2. Valuation of European Distribution System to GreatDrill
($ and share count, millions)

1	Growth in pre-merger free cash flow up to 2008 (percent) = 6
2	Cost of capital of GreatDrill (percent) = 10
3	Shares outstanding = 10

Year	2003	2004	2005	2006	2007	2008
4 GreatDrill free cash flow without acquisition		$32.0	$33.9	$36.0	$38.1	$40.4
5 Increase due to merger (percent)		5	15	25	25	25
6 GreatDrill free cash flow with acquisition		$33.6	$39.0	$44.9	$47.6	$50.5
7 Increase in FCF due to acquisition		$1.6	$5.1	$9.0	$9.5	$10.1
8					Terminal value in Year 2008 = $101

Valuation of synergy gains

9	PV of 2004–2008 cash flows = $25
10	Terminal value = $63
11	Total value = $88

template used to calculate free cash flows closely resembles that used for resource allocation decisions (the cash flow template portion of Table 2.1). The assumptions are listed at the bottom of Table 6.1. The planning group made estimates for the first five years after acquisition on a yearly basis, phasing in the efficiency improvements, which it knew from previous experience take time to achieve. Typically, it takes a few years to fully digest a sizable acquisition.

After estimating the free cash flows for the first five years after the acquisition (or for the time period you believe it takes to fully assimilate the operations of the target), it is customary to put a "terminal value" to represent the value beyond the first five years (see Table 6.1, line 22). The terminal value represents the present value of all future free cash flows beyond the terminal year of estimation. It is calculated under the assumption that the cash flows will be perpetual, which is a reasonable assumption for the very long cash flow streams of companies. The following formula gives the present value of the perpetuity in the terminal year:

$$PV_T = \frac{CF_{T+1}}{r - g},$$

where

PV_T = Present value in the terminal year T.
CF_{T+1} = Cash flow in the year following the terminal year.
r = Cost of capital representing the risk of the cash flows.
g = Expected annual long-term growth rate of the cash flows.

The terminal value will be a significant component of the total value and therefore must be estimated carefully. Since it represents the value of the cash flows for a very long period into the future, we should be conservative about the growth assumptions that are made about these cash flows. Typically, we should use the long-run growth rate of the industry, which is likely to be close to the long-run growth rate of the economy. This will be only a few percentage points (0–4 percent). The planning group decided to evaluate the terminal value on the basis of no growth at all after 2008 (see assumption 3 in Table 6.1). This is quite a conservative assumption, and it has several implications. The after-tax cash flow will be constant after 2008, and so will be the capital expenditures, which will be made just to offset the depreciation of existing fixed assets. Since there is no growth, there is no need for additional working capital, and hence changes in working capital will also be zero. The present value of the first five years' cash flows (2004–2008) is $152 million (Table 6.1, line 23). The terminal value is calculated using the perpetuity formula (with $g = 0$). Since the projected cash flow in 2009 is $52.9 million (line 21), terminal value in 2008 will be $52.9 \div 0.1 = \$529$ million (line 22).

The 2003 present value of the 2008 terminal value is $328 million (Table 6.1, line 24). Therefore, the total value of all the cash flows (Table 6.1, line 25) is 152 + 328 = $480 million. This value is often called the **enterprise value**; it is the value of Tim-Tools' operations under GreatDrill management.

The next task is to value TimTools' European distribution system. For this, we move to Table 6.2. It is expected that next year (2004) GreatDrill's cash flows from its existing products and markets (without the acquisition) will be $32 million and this cash flow will increase at 6 percent till 2008 (Table 6.2, line 4). Based on the strategic planning group's estimates stated earlier, the increase in free cash flow resulting from sales of GreatDrill products in Europe is given on line 7. After 2008, it is estimated conservatively that the cash flows will stay at 2008 levels.

Using the same techniques as in Table 6.1, the present value of the first five years of cash flows at GreatDrill's cost of capital of 10 percent is $25 million (Table 6.2, line 9). Using the perpetuity formula shown earlier (with $g = 0$) we find that terminal value in 2008 = 10.10 ÷ 0.1 = $101 million (line 8).

The 2003 present value of this terminal value is $63 million (line 10). Therefore, the value added by the TimTools distribution system is 25 + 63 = $88 million (line 11).

We move on now to Table 6.3 to estimate the per-share value of TimTools to GreatDrill. Adding the value of a revitalized TimTools under GreatDrill management to the value added to existing GreatDrill products by the access provided by TimTools' distribution system to European markets, we get a total operational value of TimTools to GreatDrill as 480 + 88 = $568 million (line 3).

At this point, you note that the strategic planning group has not investigated whether GreatDrill could expand in Europe without acquiring TimTools. If indeed GreatDrill could achieve the expansion by itself, then the value added by TimTools' European distribution system would be only the difference be-

Table 6.3. Net Value of TimTools to GreatDrill
($ millions, except per-share value)

1 Value of TimTools under GreatDrill management	$480		
2 Value of European distribution system	$88		
3 Total operational value of TimTools to GreatDrill		$568	
4 Excess cash and marketable securities		$30	
5 Total value of TimTools to GreatDrill			$598
6 Total debt of TimTools	($100)		
7 Pension plan underfunding	($20)		
8 Total liabilities		($120)	
9 Investment banking and legal fees	($6)		
10 Severance payments to employees after merger	($23)		
11 Integration budget	($2)		
12 Total acquisition costs		($31)	
13 Total liabilities and acquisition costs			($151)
14 Net value of TimTools equity to GreatDrill			$447

15 Value of TimTools to GreatDrill per TimTools share = $76.55

tween the $88 million (the benefit of TimTools' distribution system) and any positive NPV that an organic growth in Europe would generate. The analysis as presented implicitly assumes that the NPV of an organic growth in Europe is zero or negative.

Other Assets of the Target Company

Continuing per Table 6.3, the figure $568 million represents the present value of the additional cash flows from the tools business expected to be generated for GreatDrill from its acquisition of TimTools. This does not include the value of assets owned by TimTools unrelated to the tools business. In particular, it does not include the value of financial investments that TimTools might have made. For example, TimTools might have excess cash and marketable securities (liquid securities such as government bonds) in excess of what it needs for working capital. TimTools might have also invested in the equity of other companies, both private and public. In an acquisition where the entire target company is being purchased, the acquirer obtains ownership of these assets and has to pay for them. In the case of TimTools, the only nonoperational assets are $30 million in cash and marketable securities in excess of its working capital needs (line 4). Adding this amount to the enterprise value of $568 million, we get 568 + 30 = $598 million (Table 6.3, line 5).

Liabilities of the Target Company

Now that we have estimated that TimTools brings a total value of $598 million to GreatDrill, we have to consider the liabilities that its acquisition would bring as well. Table 6.3 continues the tale.

The most common liability that a target brings is the debt on its balance sheet. Typically, the acquiring company takes over this liability. TimTools has drawn $25 million from its bank on a revolving line of credit of $30 million. It has also a public issue of debt of $75 million with 5 years' maturity. Therefore, the total debt for which GreatDrill will be liable after the acquisition is $100 million (Table 6.3, line 6).

It is important to investigate whether the company has any other liabilities (see "Legal Issues" in Figure 6.2). Typical liabilities to consider are legal liabilities (actual and potential) stemming from product liability and environmental litigation, underfunded employee pension plans, tax liabilities, and contractual obligations to partners and suppliers. In many of these cases, the future liability (both existence and amount) is uncertain and the firm will have to make an estimate of the potential liability and its present value. In the case of TimTools, the only such liability is a pension plan that is underfunded by $20 million (Table 6.3, line 7). GreatDrill will be liable for this amount after the acquisition. Therefore, the total liabilities of TimTools is $120 million (Table 6.3, line 8).

Acquisition Costs

In addition to the liabilities, the acquirer must consider the costs of acquisition. Some of these are transaction costs such as investment banking and legal fees. Other costs are also triggered by the acquisition event, such as golden parachutes and severance agreements of top executives. Finally, there may be integration costs that the company chooses to incur to make the acquisition work smoothly, such as voluntary retirement schemes or employee buyouts, buyouts of contracts with other stakeholders such as partners or suppliers, budget for the integration team, and the like. In the case of the TimTools acquisition, the investment banking and legal fees are estimated to be $6 million (Table 6.3, line 9). As for integration costs, there is substantial overlap between the sales forces of the two companies' hand tools divisions, and the reduction of the sales force is expected to result in a $23 million charge (line 10) due to severance payments. In addition, the strategic planning group has budgeted integration costs of $2 million (line 11). The acquisition costs, therefore, total $31 million (line 12).

In summary, the liabilities and the acquisition costs add up to $151 million (line 13). Subtracting this amount from the gross value created by the acquisition ($598 million), we obtain the net value created by the acquisition as $447 million (line 14). This works out to $447 \div 5.84 = \$76.55$ per TimTools share (line 15). Therefore, this is the absolute maximum that GreatDrill can afford to pay. If it pays any more, the acquisition will have a negative NPV and will be value destroying.

Having gone through this analysis prepared by your strategic planning group, you feel confident that at the right price this acquisition can create value for GreatDrill. Your confidence stems from the following:

- The acquisition is congruent with your growth strategy. TimTools allows you to grow your markets. In addition, you can add value by improving TimTools management.

- The value drivers were clearly identified based on the specific combination of GreatDrill and TimTools and are unique to this combination.
- The DCF analysis was based on input from your manufacturing and marketing personnel who identified areas of improvement and provided specific targets that they felt confident they can achieve. For example, marketing estimated that it can achieve a growth rate of 6 percent (GreatDrill's own growth rate) in TimTools' revenue. Similarly, manufacturing offered specific plans for trimming COGS and SG&A and provided targets for each. Setting such specific targets before the acquisition enables the company to follow up with the concerned groups later.
- The analysis is realistic in the sense that it recognizes that the synergy benefits will take time to achieve. This is partly because of estimated delays in integrating the two companies' systems, cultures, and people, but also because it takes time to make improvements.
- The analysis recognizes that it is difficult to sustain competitive advantage for long periods in the presence of competition and changes in technology. It is realistic in assuming that growth will taper off after some time unless major investments are made to sustain it. Since such investments are not foreseeable today, the analysis conservatively assumes that growth will stop after a few years.
- The analysis takes into account the costs of acquisition, such as severance packages to employees.
- The due diligence has identified unfunded pension liabilities that are not sufficient to destroy the value of the acquisition.

Paying for the Acquisition

Now that you know how much value TimTools brings to Great-Drill, you turn to the questions of how much to pay for the company and in what form to pay.

How Much to Pay

TimTools shares are currently trading at $37, so that is the lower bound of your offer. Theoretically, you can extract value from this acquisition if your offer is less than or equal to $76.55 per share. But you wish to retain some value for GreatDrill, and therefore the practical range is smaller. The first decision is to set an upper limit, or "walk away price," for your offer. Such a limit imposes a discipline on the negotiating team and reduces the probability of overpayment. After setting an upper limit, you will then need to decide on an opening offer.

One way to set an upper limit is to set a minimum rate of return you seek from acquisitions. Clearly this threshold rate of return must be greater than your company's cost of capital (assuming the acquisition's risk is in the same risk class as your company's operations). How much higher the threshold should be depends on your company management's goals regarding the rate of return it wishes to, and realistically can, deliver to shareholders. Given the pitfalls in acquisitions, it might be better to set a hurdle rate at least as high as that used to approve internal expansion projects. In the case of the TimTools acquisition, both companies are in the same business and are likely to have similar risk profiles as reflected by their identical costs of capital of 10 percent. Therefore, you believe that a threshold rate of return of about 12 percent would be reasonable and feasible.

Using this threshold, your team can find the upper limit of the range of offers to be made to TimTools. Table 6.4 illustrates the calculation. First, you need to find the present value at the threshold return of 12 percent for the cash flows estimated in Table 6.1 and Table 6.2—the cash flows resulting from TimTools under GreatDrill management plus the European distribution system. These cash flows are entered on Table 6.4, lines 2 and 3, and line 4 shows their total. Line 5 of Table 6.4 calculates the terminal value in Year 2008 of all cash flows beyond that year to be $524.7 million. The present value of the 2004–2008 cash flows is $168.2 (line 6). The

Table 6.4. Upper Offer Limit for TimTools ($ millions, except per-share value)

1 Threshold return = 12 percent   Terminal Growth = 0 percent

Year	2003	2004	2005	2006	2007	2008	2009
2 TimTools cash flow after acquisition		$48.1	$30.8	$37.1	$40.2	$43.4	$52.9
3 Cash flow from European distribution		$1.6	$5.1	$9.0	$9.5	$10.1	$10.1
4 Operational cash flows from acquisition		$50.2	$35.8	$46.1	$49.7	$53.5	$63.0

5   Terminal value in Year 2008 = $524.7

6 PV of cash flows 2004–2008 @ 12 percent =	$168.2
7 Present value of terminal value =	$297.7
8 Excess cash =	$30.0
9 Total TimTools debt =	($100.0)
10 Pension plan underfunding =	($20.0)
11 Investment banking and legal fees =	($6.0)
12 Severance payments =	($23.0)
13 Integration costs =	($2.0)
14 Upper limit of TimTools' equity =	$344.9
15 Upper per share offer limit =	$59.06

2003 present value of the terminal value is $297.7 (line 7). By adding TimTools' excess cash (line 8) and then subtracting its total debt (line 9) and unfunded pension (line 10), and the banking and legal fees (line 11), severance payments (line 12), and integration costs (line 13), we obtain the upper limit of the equity value for TimTools that you are willing to pay (line 14). Dividing this value by the number of TimTools shares yields the upper per-share offer limit of $59.06 (line 15). This upper limit results in a premium of about 52 percent over the current price.

As noted in the earlier section about setting targets for extracting value, it is useful to identify each value driver and to value each one separately. In the TimTools case, the two major value drivers are the operational efficiency improvement under GreatDrill management and the European distribution system. The benefits from efficiency improvement are more likely to be realized than the benefits from the European distribution system—the efficiency improvements are more under the control of GreatDrill, whereas the success of the expansion into Europe depends on market conditions and competition. Table 6.3 shows that the European distribution system brings $88 million to the deal. Without it, the value of TimTools to GreatDrill is only $447 − $88 = $359 million, which translates to 359 ÷ 5.84 = $61.47 per share. This provides the comforting news that even if GreatDrill paid the upper limit of $59.06 per share of TimTools and the European expansion did not succeed, the acquisition is unlikely to lose money.

After determining the upper limit of the offer, your company needs to arrive at an opening offer. Two relevant issues to consider are market conditions (comparable transactions) and competition for the target. The target shareholders and management are likely to base their expectations of the offer on comparable transactions. To compare offers made in recent acquisitions in the industry, the concept of *multiples* is often used. Four common multiples are used to evaluate the offer price:

- Price-to-EPS multiple (generally referred to as P/E)
- Price-to-Book value of equity per share multiple
- Price-to-Revenue per share multiple
- Enterprise value-to-EBITDA (Earnings Before Interest, Taxes, Depreciation, and Amortization) multiple

From the target management's perspective, it is easier to justify selling the company at the offered price if these offer multiples are in the range of recent transactions in the industry. To determine what types of offers are being made in comparable transactions, GreatDrill should investigate recent takeovers in the tools industry to determine the prices paid as multiples, as shown in Table 6.5.

Your strategic planning group has provided you the averages of the multiples based on three recent acquisitions in the tools industry. For the three, the average P/E, Price-to-Book, Price-to-Revenue, and Enterprise value-to-EBITDA multiples were 14.0, 2.0, 0.8, and 6.5, respectively, as given in line 1 of Table 6.5. From the recent financial statement of TimTools, you note that the net income, book value of equity, and revenue of TimTools are $20.58 million, $153 million, and $553 million, respectively (line 2 of

Table 6.5. Offer Price Based on Multiples

Comparable transactions multiples

	P/E	Price-to-Book	Price-to-Revenue	Enterprise Value-to-EBITDA
1	14.00	2.00	0.80	6.50

TimTools financials

	Net Income	Book Value of Equity	Revenue	EBITDA	Shares Outstanding
2 Total (millions)	$20.58	$153.00	$553.00	$60.83	5.84
3 Per share	$3.52	$26.20	$94.69	$10.42	

TimTools offer price based on multiples

4 Per share	$49.33	$52.40	$75.75	$46.99

Table 6.5). You know that TimTools has 5.84 million shares outstanding, so you can determine per-share figures for these three dollar values (line 3). For the first three multiples (P/E, Price-to-Book, and Price-to-Revenue) you can arrive at an estimate of the offer price based on each multiple by multiplying the per-share figures on line 3 by the corresponding transaction multiple. As shown on Table 6.5, line 4, the offer prices based on P/E multiple, Price-to-Book multiple, and Price-to-Revenue multiple are, respectively, $49.33, $52.40, and $75.75. The calculation of the offer price based on Enterprise value-to-EBITDA multiple for Table 6.5 is shown in Table 6.6.

When you multiply the Enterprise value-to-EBITDA multiple of comparable transactions by the EBITDA of TimTools, you get an estimate of TimTools' enterprise value based on this multiple (Table 6.6, line 3). To this value the excess cash and marketable securities is added and all the liabilities and acquisition costs are subtracted to find the equity value of TimTools (Table 6.6, line 10). Dividing this equity value by the number of Tim-Tools shares outstanding yields the estimate of the per-share offer price based on the Enterprise value-to-EBITDA multiple (Table 6.6, line 11).

Table 6.6. Value based on Enterprise Value-to-EBITDA Multiple
($ millions, except per-share value)

1	EBITDA: TimTools	$60.83
2	EBITDA multiple of comparable transactions	6.50
3	Estimate of enterprise value—TimTools	$395
4	Excess cash and marketable securities	$30
5	Total debt	($100)
6	Underfunded pension liability	($20)
7	Investment banking and legal fees	($6)
8	Severance payments	($23)
9	Integration costs	($2)
10	Value of equity	$274
11	Per-share value of equity	$46.99

Clearly the estimate based on the Price-to-Revenue multiple is out of line with estimates based on the other three multiples. Two different reasons might account for this discrepancy. One is that while the value of TimTools should depend on *future* expectations, the estimates are all based on financial statements of the last twelve months. In particular, the estimate based on the Price-to-Revenue multiple uses TimTools' recent revenue, which could have been high. But TimTools' future revenue *growth* is expected to be lower than the industry average and, therefore, the estimate based on its most recent revenue is likely to overstate TimTools' value. A second possible explanation is that the cost structure of TimTools is too high, a fact not taken into account by a value based purely on the revenue multiple.

The estimates based on the other three multiples are lower than the upper limit. Based on these three estimates, an opening offer of about $50 seems appropriate if GreatDrill foresees no competing offer for TimTools. This provides TimTools shareholders a premium of about 35 percent over the recent stock price of $37. This premium is in line with the usual premium of 30–35 percent offered in similar transactions. If another acquirer might be interested in TimTools (sometimes because of Great-Drill's interest in TimTools), it may be smart strategy to preempt the competing bidder by a substantially high opening offer. Such an offer signals to the competing bidder that GreatDrill is very serious about acquiring TimTools and that its upper limit is likely to be quite high. Such a high opening bid might discourage competing bidders from investing in an attempt to acquire TimTools (hiring investment bankers, doing due diligence and valuation of TimTools, and so on).

The Form of Payment

After determining the offer price, the next task is determining the form of payment. Most acquisitions use cash or common stock, or sometimes a combination of both. It is not uncommon to augment these two forms of payment with debt instruments, equity instruments such as preferred stock, and equity-linked instruments such as warrants and convertible debt. Even if the acquirer has enough cash to buy the target, cash may not always be the best form of payment. The trade-off between cash and stock is driven by several factors such as tax issues, mispricing of stock, risk-sharing issues, and control issues (see Figure 6.3).

Tax issues play a major role in determining the form of payment. Target shareholders must pay capital gains tax immediately if they receive cash payment for selling their shares. However, if they are paid in acquirer stock or other securities, taxes are due only if and when they sell the securities they receive. This allows them some flexibility in planning their tax strategies to minimize the tax payment. The tax issue is likely to be more important if the target shareholders are the firm's founders: their tax basis will be very low resulting in potentially high capital gains taxes. In the case of TimTools, the founders hold 20 percent of the stock and their basis is likely to be low, creating a preference for a stock offer based on tax considerations.

Whether the acquiring and target companies' stocks are correctly priced by the market is another factor that influences the form of payment. Lack of complete information and other market inefficiencies may cause the stock prices to diverge from their true value from time to time. It is imperative that the acquirer do an internal analysis of its stock, and that of the target, to detect mispricing. If the acquirer believes its stock is overpriced, it is clearly in its interest to use its stock as the form of payment. If the acquirer believes that both stocks are overpriced, it can mitigate the effect of the overpriced target stock by offering its own stock as the form of payment.

If the acquirer is uncertain about the value of the target because of inability to conduct an exhaustive due diligence (this could be because competitive pressures require a speedy acquisition), it can share this risk with target shareholders by offering

Factors	Issues
Internal cash is available	
Tax issues	If target shareholders are paid cash, the payment triggers an immediate capital gains tax. If the basis of the target shareholders is low, they will prefer a stock offer, which triggers a tax only when sold. This allows them better tax planning. This issue is likely to be very important in the case of founders selling their company, as their basis will be very low.
Misvaluation of stock	If acquirer stock is undervalued, use cash; conversely, if it is overvalued, use stock. If stocks are overvalued in general, use of stock offsets the overvaluation of target stock.
Risk sharing	Stock mergers that constrain target shareholders' ability to sell the shares they obtained in the combined firm for a period of time enable risk-sharing between the acquirer and the target. This issue is important if target management holds a substantial block of the target company's stock.
	Stock offers are often combined with ex-post performance-based payouts to offset risk to acquirers. Such post-acquisition payouts can be based on post-acquisition operating performance (for example, profit) in which case they are called *Earn-outs;* or based on stock price, in which case they are called *Contingent Value Rights (CVR).*
Market reaction	Market reaction typically has been more adverse to stock offers than to cash offers. This might be partly due to the market's belief that stock offers imply overvaluation of acquirer stock. If the acquirer is concerned about the adverse reaction (because it has to raise additional capital in the near term) it might be worth considering a cash offer.
Corporate control	Stock mergers dilute the ownership and control of acquirer shareholders. This could be an issue if a single or small group of target shareholders owns a significant fraction of the target and hence could effectively control the combined company. The problem can be mitigated by offering common stock with limited voting power, preferred stock, or debt instruments.
Internal cash is not available	
Availability of external capital	If company is overleveraged, issuing additional debt may be difficult. In a market downturn, equity markets may be closed to acquirers. In such situations, stock mergers may be advisable.
Cost of external financing	Raising external capital is costly since it involves adviser fees, as well as administrative costs and time. It is easier to offer stock or securities to the target.

Figure 6.3. Factors That Affect the Form of Payment

acquiring-company stock as the form of payment and requiring key target shareholders such as management to hold the stock for a period of time. If the benefits of mergers are not realized, the combined company's stock price will reflect that, and so the associated losses will be borne by both acquirer and target shareholders. By contrast, if the acquirer pays cash, it will bear all the losses.

Another way to mitigate the risk due to uncertainty involved in an acquisition is to incorporate an *earnout*, that is, a payment to target shareholders based on meeting certain ex-post operating performance measures. Such an earnout can be combined with either cash or stock offers.

The target and acquiring management often disagree about the value of a stock offer. The acquirer argues that the stock will be worth more than its current value once the market fully recognizes the benefits of the acquisition, and hence will want to offer a smaller fraction of the combined company to target shareholders. The target, on the other hand, is likely to value the acquirer shares closer to their pre-acquisition value and therefore to demand a greater fraction of the combined company. To settle such disagreements, some deals incorporate what is known as a *contingent value right (CVR)*, which gives the target shareholders additional consideration if the share price of the combined firm falls below a specified threshold over a defined period after the acquisition.

Markets react differently to different forms of payment. Market reaction to cash offers is, on average, positive while the reaction to stock offers is negative.[14] Acquirers must be sensitive to this, especially if they need to raise capital in the equity markets in the near future. More elaborate disclosure about the benefits of the acquisition to analysts and investors in the case of stock offers might mitigate the negative reaction.

The final issue in the determination of the form of payment is corporate control. Corporate control becomes an issue if the target company is not small relative to the acquirer and has one or more controlling stockholders who own substantial blocks of shares. These shareholders might end up with some control of the acquirer board. If the acquiring management does not wish the target's stockholders to have such control in its affairs, it might consider a cash offer or offer securities other than voting stock, such as nonvoting common stock, debt, and preferred stock.

In the event that the acquirer is short of cash, some additional considerations come into play in determining the form of payment. If the acquirer is not carrying too much debt relative to industry norms, it can raise cash by issuing debt and use it to pay the target. If the acquirer has too much debt on its balance sheet and if the markets are in a downturn, it may use a stock exchange to facilitate the acquisition. Since raising external capital is usually costly (underwriter fees, administrative costs, and time involved), it is easier to offer stock or securities to the target.

You consider all these issues while deciding the form of payment for TimTools. The largest shareholder of TimTools, the founding family, is likely to prefer a stock offer for tax reasons. However, other considerations argue against a stock offer. An internal analysis done earlier has indicated that your stock is undervalued by the market. Moreover, given your capital needs to implement the growth strategy, you have to guard against any further drop in your stock price, which might occur with a stock offer. Furthermore, you do not wish to give the founding family a large enough stake in your firm to have significant power since founding families have an emotional attachment to their firm and might oppose some of the changes you wish to implement to increase the efficiency of TimTools.

In view of these concerns, you lean toward making a two-stage offer. In stage one, you will buy the founders' stake using preferred stock. This takes care of the family's tax concerns without yielding any voting rights. At the same time, it avoids any negative signal to the market. It may be possible to structure the offer so that the founders can sell the stock back to GreatDrill (and only to GreatDrill) at full value over the next few years, which gives them some of the tax planning flexibility they are likely to seek. In stage two, you could raise cash through a debt issue (as your debt ratio is quite low relative to the industry) to purchase the remaining shares. You have to ensure that you can service the additional debt and that it will not hamper your future growth plans. You have to take care that the payments in both stages are identical, to avoid shareholder litigation. You plan to discuss this payment package with your investment bankers.

Other Issues

You notice several issues that the analysis of the strategic planning group has not addressed. This has to be a friendly acquisition, given the founders' control of 20 percent of the company. It is better to negotiate with the founding family first because their approval is likely to help convince financial institutions to agree to the acquisition. The analysis does not provide any information about possible takeover defenses TimTools might have. If the company has a poison pill (defined in the "FAQ" section), you will have to request the TimTools management to remove it.

You make a mental note that it is critical to retain the key managers involved with the European distribution since your company has no experience in Europe. It will be important to lock them in as soon as the TimTools founders give their approval.

FAQs About Acquisitions

I often hear that an acquisition should be accretive in current earnings per share (EPS), that is, it should increase current EPS. Do you agree?

Managers are often reluctant to undertake an acquisition that will dilute their immediate (current or next year's) EPS even though it might create value that will increase the firm's future EPS. Such dilution will occur if you buy companies that have relatively low current earnings (typically a growth company with a greater P/E multiple than yours). Of course, if the acquisition is expected to dilute even future EPS, it is value-destroying and should be avoided. The reason for the reluctance about short-term dilution is the concern that analysts might view the dilution as permanent and undervalue the stock. The evidence does not support this concern. Research has shown that in 47 percent of *dilutive* acquisitions the acquiring company's stock price has outperformed its industry average stock price return by more than 10 percent one year after the acquisition announcement; such outperformance was observed only in 34 percent of the *accretive* acquisitions.[15]

Furthermore, as shown earlier in Figure 6.1, current EPS can be increased without creating value. EPS can also be managed by using different financing techniques such as debt financing.

Often companies determine the value of the acquisition based on financial multiples such as P/E multiple or Price-to-Book multiple. Why do you advocate DCF analysis to determine value and multiples only as a guide for setting the initial offer price?

It is true that multiples of comparable acquisitions are often used to determine the value of an acquisition. The major drawback with this approach of valuation is that it does not take into consideration the synergy of the combination under consideration. In other words, the multiples technique implies that the value of the target is the same for every acquirer and that the relevant multiple for this transaction is the same for comparable transactions involving different acquirers and targets. Note that the multiples technique will yield the same values regardless of the acquirer. Moreover, use of multiples does not clearly identify the value drivers of the acquisition being considered and therefore does not enforce discipline on the management to identify the drivers, set target values for them, and follow up after the acquisition to ensure that the acquisition benefits are realized. The DCF technique, on the other hand, clearly identifies the value drivers and values them. The detailed analysis that the DCF technique entails also creates discipline in the acquisition process.

The multiples technique *is* useful as a frame of reference for negotiating with the target. By making offers with similar multiples as comparable transactions, it is easier to convince the target management that the offer is fair. It also facilitates the target management's job of making the case to its board and investors.

In the case, the DCF analysis to find the value of the company was forward looking, that is, based on future cash flows. To the value so computed, we added only the excess cash flow. Should we not add also the value of existing assets on the balance sheet, just as we subtracted the value of existing liabilities?

It is true that the DCF analysis finds the value of future cash flows. However, it assumes that the existing operating assets (fixed assets such as property, plant, and equipment, and working capital) are needed to create these future cash flows. This is the reason none of the existing operating assets are explicitly considered in the analysis. Considering them again would be double counting. Only nonoperational assets such as excess cash, marketable securities, financial investments in other companies, and the like must be added. Similarly, none of the operating liabilities such as accounts payable are to be subtracted as these are part of working capital needed to generate the future cash flows.

I often hear about "goodwill" in the context of acquisitions. What is it and how does it affect the value of an acquisition?

Goodwill is an accounting adjustment that is made to balance the books when an acquirer pays more than the fair value of the assets of the target. It must be noted first that there is nothing unusual about paying more than the fair value, and it can be value-creating if the future cash flows from the acquisition justify the purchase price. For example, if the fair value of the assets on the target's balance sheet is $100 and the acquirer paid $160 for those assets, then the excess of $60 must be split between the fair value of any intangible assets (patents, formulas for food products, rights to airport gates, licenses, customer lists, and so on) and goodwill. Suppose the intangible assets are valued at $20; then goodwill will be $40. According to current FASB rules, intangible assets need to be amortized over their useful life, but goodwill cannot be amortized. Firms, however, must check each year to see if there has been any impairment in the value of the assets purchased and, correspondingly, the goodwill, and write down any impairment of goodwill. Note that all these requirements apply for financial reporting. For tax purposes, goodwill and intangible assets must be amortized over fifteen years.

To summarize, the economic impact of goodwill is the tax break the acquiring company receives from amortization of the goodwill.

If we use our stock as the form of compensation, do we need to account for the expected rise in our stock price when the market realizes the benefits of the acquisition?

Absolutely. If we assume that market does not yet know that merger negotiations are on, the acquirer share price will not reflect the market's assessment of the benefits of the acquisition. Since the acquirer is paying the target with the shares of the combined firm, it must use the expected stock price after the market is informed of the acquisition to decide how many shares to pay the target shareholders. However, the two parties are likely to disagree about this expected price.

How does an earnout work? When is it appropriate to use one?

In an earnout, the acquirer makes part of the payment to the seller contingent on the performance of the target unit subsequent to the merger. The earnout is usually included to provide some insurance to the buyer about the future performance of the target. For example, in January 2001, Sunoco purchased all of the outstanding capital stock of Aristech Chemical Company from Mitsubishi Corporation. The purchase price was $695 million. Sunoco agreed to make contingent earnout payments with a net present value of up to $167 million to Mitsubishi if realized margins for polypropylene and phenol were to exceed certain agreed-upon thresholds over the next six years.

Earnouts are useful when it is difficult for the acquirer to obtain accurate and reliable information about the target. Such situations arise in the following circumstances:

- The target is a private company. Private companies have limited disclosure requirements.
- The target is a subsidiary or operating unit of a company. The financial statements of subsidiaries or operating units may inflate their financial health because of favorable cost allocations and transfer pricing.
- The target is located in a different country. Not only are the disclosure requirements more lax in many countries, the accounting standards are also different, making it difficult to discern the financial health of foreign companies.
- The target is a company in a high-growth industry (technology, biotech) with very little tangible assets. It is difficult to evaluate intangible assets such as intellectual capital.

The other requirement for a useful and successful earnout contract is feasibility of implementation. Earnouts work better in cases with few sellers, or when the seller is a well-defined entity such as a company. This makes it easier to resolve disputes and to renegotiate the contract if needed. Therefore, it is no surprise that more than 95 percent of earnouts written so far involve private targets and subsidiaries of companies.[16]

One of the drawbacks of earnouts is that the acquiring company can manipulate the performance measures of the target entity after the acquisition by cost allocations and transfer pricing techniques to avoid the contingent payments. Earnouts are likely to be successful when the purchased entity has operated fairly independently of the selling company and will operate independently after the acquisition.

How does a contingent value right (CVR) work?

The main difference between a CVR and an earnout is that the CVR, unlike the earnout, is based on a parameter not entirely within the control of the company. The CVR can insure the seller from losses resulting from a drop in share price of the acquirer after closing the deal, in acquisitions where the form of payment is stock. If the acquiring company's share price falls below a threshold level for a defined period of time after the closing, the seller will receive some additional payment. As stated earlier, when the form of payment is stock, disagreements are likely about the value of the acquirer's stock and about the prospect that the stock market will value the stock correctly. The CVR was a major factor in the outcome of Viacom's acquisition of Paramount and Blockbuster.[17]

It is not necessary that the contingency in the CVR be the acquirer's stock price. When Antigenics acquired Aronex Pharmaceuticals in 2001, it included a CVR that would be triggered if the U.S. Food and Drug Administration granted approval of Aronex Pharmaceuticals' drug application for Atragen on or before July 6, 2002. If the drug was approved before this date, Aronex Pharmaceuticals shareholders would receive additional payment. In this case, the CVR was included to reduce the risk of the acquirer, Antigenics, by allowing it to make part of the price it agreed to pay contingent upon the target's actually developing an element of value that was only potential at the time of the deal.

What are poison pills?

Poison pills are part of an arsenal of defensive measures that companies employ against takeovers. A poison pill can be adopted by the company's board without shareholder approval, and it generally works by giving target shareholders (except the acquirer) the right to purchase shares in the combined company at a huge discount (on the order of 90 percent or so) whenever a specific trigger event occurs, such as a potential acquirer's acquiring a specified fraction of the target company's equity. This clearly increases the cost of the acquisition to the acquirer. Because these pills can be waived only at the target management's discretion, they are a barrier to takeover attempts hostile to the target management. There is still no consensus regarding the benefits of poison pills to target shareholders. In many companies, target shareholders have voted to remove them. Target management usually claims that a poison pill provides management a bargaining chip and allows it to get a better price in an acquisition.

Besides poison pills, what other takeover defenses do companies employ?

There are a slew of them. They include charter amendments that require a super-majority shareholder vote to approve a takeover, a staggered board that makes it difficult for the acquirer to gain board majority through proxy contests, and dual-class shares with the control shares being closely held. Then there are state anti-takeover amendments that make it difficult for an acquirer hostile to the target management to effect a takeover.

SUMMARY

In this chapter, we provide a financial perspective on acquisitions and explain why such a large fraction of acquisitions do not create value to the acquiring company shareholders. The causes stem from a lack of strategic focus and confusion about the intermediate metrics that create shareholder value. In addition, there is a lack of discipline in evaluating the benefits and costs of the acquisition and in the process of determining the offer price.

Acquiring companies should be clear that a particular acquisition is congruent to their strategy and identify the value drivers and the problem areas. Based on this identification, a detailed financial analysis of the consequences of the acquisition should be conducted to determine the value generated by each of the drivers. Specific targets should be set for the value drivers which the acquiring company managers should strive to meet after the merger.

Using the illustrative case of GreatDrill's acquisition of TimTools, the chapter traces the steps to be followed to ensure that an acquisition will create value:

1. Ascertain that the acquisition makes strategic sense.
2. Identify the value drivers.
3. Set target benchmarks for each of the value drivers.
4. Based on the target benchmarks, use the DCF methodology to value the acquisition.
5. Set the walk away price based on a target expected rate of return from the acquisition.
6. Use multiples to benchmark the valuation and to aid in negotiation.
7. Choose a form of payment that creates the most value.

In this chapter, we discuss how acquisitions can be part of a value-creating growth strategy. In the next chapter, we discuss how divestitures can also be a value-creating growth strategy.

Divestitures

A s CEO of Imperial Spirits Corporation (ISC), you have just come from a contentious session with some of your firm's largest institutional investors. The message is blunt: institutional shareholders are unhappy with ISC's stock price performance and the fact that ISC remains a diversified firm. They argue that the value of ISC can only be unlocked by renewing the firm's commitment to its core business, producing and marketing premium alcoholic spirits. Under your predecessor, ISC had ventured into the faster-growing biotech industry. These assets are held by ISC through its fully owned subsidiary, Imperial Bio Products (IBP). The rationale offered at the time was that ISC's traditional market was growing slowly and that it would add value to reorient ISC's capital and managerial skills to other, unrelated industries.

You have been at the helm of ISC for only a few months. While you are not a fan of diversification, you are uncertain whether the benefits of divesting IBP would outweigh the costs of such a restructuring. The decision on divestiture needs to be made soon. At a board of directors meeting in a few days you are expected to make the case either to maintain the firm as currently constituted or to divest the subsidiary and refocus the firm on its core business. To make your decision, you want to get a better sense of the potential costs and benefits of such restructuring and why investors might attach a greater value to the firms if they were broken apart.

You wonder if there are less drastic ways than divesting the subsidiary to address investor concerns. You know, for instance, that some firms have issued separate targeted or tracking stock (so-called *alphabet stock*) on subsidiaries—without relinquishing control of the subsidiary. The purpose is apparently to improve the quality of information available with respect to subsidiary performance.

If ISC does decide to go ahead with divestiture of its subsidiary, the form of the divestiture will need to be resolved. Broadly, the subsidiary could be sold to another firm or spun off as an independent firm. Among the salient considerations are that a sale of the subsidiary will make ISC's investors subject to taxes on the gain in the value of the assets, though a spin-off would normally be tax-free. However, a spin-off can lead to other headaches. For instance, how viable is the IBP subsidiary as a stand-alone firm? And the divestiture could be structured to take place in stages, with a partial sale of subsidiary stock— an **equity carve-out**—followed by a spin-off of the rest of the firm. Would that be a good idea?

Another consideration that could weigh heavily in the divestiture decision is that ISC has investment plans that require an infusion of financing in the neighborhood of $100 million. If the financing could be raised as part of the divestiture process, it might prove a cost-effective way to raise funds as well as to refocus the firm.

In this chapter we explore the reasons—both good and not-so-good—to divest firm assets. With these in mind, the case proceeds through the initial divestiture decision and on to the question of how to structure the divestiture, paying attention to concerns like taxes and a possible infusion of cash. In the course of the chapter we draw upon several ideas from earlier chapters, particularly the notion from Chapter Four that capital markets are affected by information problems and other financial market imperfections.

■ Good and Bad Reasons to Divest

Firms divest assets or divisions by selling them or, alternatively, by spinning them off as independent firms. Divestitures often result from a decision to exit a particular industry and become more focused on core business. It is claimed, for instance, that a number of the divestitures and reorganizations that took place in the 1980s and 1990s were the result of firms' reversing the diversifying acquisitions done in the 1960s and 1970s. There are two main reasons to divest: to gain value by increasing the parent firm's focus, and to increase the productivity and profitability of the divested assets themselves—whether as an independent firm (after a spin-off) or as part of another firm (after a sell-off). A number of other reasons may be important in specific situations, as well. These include raising capital, meeting regulatory requirements, addressing liability concerns, and increasing opportunities for an upstream subsidiary. There are also some not-so-good reasons, discussed later in this chapter.

Increasing Focus on the Core Business

On the whole, there is little evidence that diversification has worked to the benefit of shareholders. Conglomerates that were allegedly put together to capture synergies and to enjoy greater access to capital on account of larger scale and diversified cash flows have, in general, delivered disappointing results. It is not surprising, therefore, that the stock market, seemingly enthusiastic about diversification in the 1960s and 1970s, is skeptical now about diversification strategies. This is indicated, for instance, by the typically negative impact on the stock price of acquiring firms when a diversifying acquisition is announced. Announcing the spin-off of unrelated units, on the other hand, is accompanied by a substantial increase in the stock market value of a diversified firm.

Several reasons have been advanced for why businesses may be more valuable as independent, focused firms rather than as divisions of a multidivision firm. The thrust of the arguments is that conglomerates are subject to problems that stem from their multidivisional structure: lower transparency, rent-seeking by divisional managers, investment distortions, and the like. Hence, unless the benefits from synergies or other factors are sufficiently large, the focused firm structure ought to be preferred.

The Transparency Problem

It is argued that there is greater transparency and accountability within focused firms relative to a more complex, multidivision firm. Within a multidivision firm it can be more difficult to disentangle the nature of the investments and the performance of individual divisions and their managers. If the firm were dismantled, it could be easier to evaluate the performance of the (former) divisional managers, as well as to provide them with stronger incentive contracts—based on the stock price performance and returns of their stand-alone firms, rather than incentive contracts that could have been offered when they were part of a conglomerate.

The Problem of Investment Distortions

The splitting up of a conglomerate can enhance shareholder value by reducing investment distortions. In principle, conglomeration should result in an **internal capital market** in which corporate headquarters allocates capital to divisions in response to their investment opportunities. It is well recognized, however, that capital budgeting between divisions can be subject to a political process by which divisional influences distort investment decisions. One can liken this, for instance, to budgetary battles between different agencies and departments of the federal government. Studies of investment patterns within conglomerates suggest that their investments may, at least in part, result from a type of corporate socialism. While divisions with relatively good prospects do tend to receive higher capital investment (and those with relatively poorer prospects tend to receive lower amounts), the effect of investment patterns in conglomerates is less responsive to investment opportunities than appears to be the case with investment decisions by more focused firms.

There is also some evidence that the greater the difference between investment opportunities among divisions, the greater the distortion and resulting loss in market value. When divestiture takes the form of spinning off a division, this will replace a distorted internal capital market allocation process with one in which each resulting firm (the parent and the spun-off unit) has to raise capital in external capital markets. The spin-off can enhance shareholder value if the benefits from greater scrutiny and discipline of external capital markets more than offsets the higher cost associated with both the parent and the spun-off unit having to separately raise capital in external markets.

The Value of a Positive Signal

The decision by a conglomerate to focus on its core industry can, on occasion, serve as a strong positive signal by the parent firm to its clients and to competitors of its commitment to its core business. By contrast, the choice of a diversified strategy may invite competition if it suggests to competitors that the firm is not going to be aggressive in terms of protecting market share in its core business. The reason why a diversified firm will be a weaker competitor—or, at least, perceived to be a weaker competitor—is that the firm no longer needs to be as committed to its core business, since it has additional avenues in which to expand its activities.

Employing Divested Assets More Productively

A significant source of the gain in divestitures is that the divested assets may be more productively employed elsewhere. In a sell-off the divested assets may be acquired by a firm that has the skills and commitment to employ them in a more productive manner than the divesting firm could do. A spun-off subsidiary may be more productive as well—its greater freedom of action as an independent firm and its reliance on external rather than internal capital markets can allow it to better exploit its investment opportunities. An independent firm can also provide its skilled employees with more opportunity to benefit from the performance of the firm by giving them equity and stock options. This can give the more talented and entrepreneurial employees the incentive to remain and contribute.

Spin-offs also represent a mechanism for commercial exploitation of a technology that was initially developed at the parent organization but has proven itself tangential to the parent's primary business. This type of divestiture was particularly evident in the late 1990s when many high-tech divisions and subsidiaries were divested and became independent firms—arguably because the firms were expected to have greater flexibility and discretion and hence market value as independent firms than as part of multidivision firms.

Other Motives to Divest

Other common motives to divest are the need to raise capital, to comply with regulatory requirements, and to address liability concerns. The spin-off of an upstream supplier can sometimes benefit a firm's equity-holders as well; as an independent firm, the spun-off unit can increase in value by expanding its client base and attracting its former parent's competitors.

Raising Capital

A firm may sell assets or a division when it finds it difficult or expensive to raise capital by other means. Consider the situation in which a risky firm is unable to sell debt or equity capital at prices that the management considers appropriate. This may be because investors have limited information and are concerned about the true state of affairs inside the firm (recall our discussion on external financing in Chapter Four). In such a situation the firm may find it attractive to raise capital by selling specific assets or divisions that it can sell at a favorable (or, at least, not unfavorable) price. These are likely to be assets with lower potential information problems and where the buyer and seller can more easily agree on terms of value, for example, tangible assets such as real estate. If there is a choice about which assets to sell, the firm will presumably want to sell those that have low synergies with the rest of its assets and relatively greater synergies with those of the acquirer.

Capital can also be raised when a firm spins off a subsidiary in a **two-step process**. In step one, the consolidated firm does an equity carve-out, which is the IPO (Initial Public Offering) of some of the shares of a wholly owned subsidiary (usually less than 20 percent). This step raises funds since subsidiary shares are being sold in the equity carve-out. In step two (usually after a wait of six or more months), a spin-off takes place in which the remaining shares of the subsidiary are apportioned in a tax-free distribution to the firm's shareholders. Such a two-step procedure is feasible only if there is sufficient demand for the subsidiary shares to do a successful IPO. The benefit of the two-step procedure of equity carve-out and spin-off is that it allows companies to raise capital and, at the same time, to divest unrelated businesses. Later in the chapter we discuss tax issues and their influence on the spin-off procedure.

Meeting Regulatory Requirements
A spin-off may sometimes be the result of antitrust laws when the Federal Trade Commission approves a merger, subject to the firms' divesting particular operations or establishments in order to maintain a healthy level of competition. For instance, the units to be divested may be in geographic areas where the commission is concerned that the merger may result in significantly lower product market competition. In the case of an airline merger, merging airlines may be required to alter routes and sell off terminals at airports where they provide the bulk of existing service.

Handling Liability Concerns
Another potential benefit from divestiture is that the separated businesses may be less exposed to legal liability arising from products sold by a legally vulnerable division. Under the U.S. legal system this may provide some limited degree of protection—especially if the spin-off is not regarded as a transparent effort to escape liability!

Divesting an Upstream Supplier
When a subsidiary supplies inputs to the parent firm, competing firms that might be potential customers of the subsidiary are

likely to be reluctant to purchase from it because it is controlled by a competitor. One way to ensure that the parent will not interfere with the operations of the subsidiary is to spin it off as an independent firm. A recent example of this is AT&T's divestiture of Lucent. This was apparently triggered by an effort on Lucent's part to attract competitors of AT&T, who were reluctant to purchase components from Lucent as long as it remained a subsidiary of AT&T.

Suspect Motives

On occasion, spin-offs have served as vehicles for improving the balance sheet of a parent by loading the divested unit with debt. This is possible because divestiture is subject to few guidelines and, depending on the nature of debt covenants, companies may have considerable discretion in the way debt is allocated to a spun-off division. However, a spun-off unit loaded with debt is a likely source of costly lawsuits and bitter conflicts between debt- and equity-holders—especially if the spun-off unit runs into financial trouble. This appears to have happened in the recent Lucent's IPO carve-out of Agere Systems. While setting up the new firm, the highly leveraged Lucent appears to have done two things: it used the carve-out to raise over $2 billion, and at the same time, it transferred over $2 billion of its debt to Agere's balance sheet. As it happens, Agere did run into financial trouble—caused, to an extent, by the high leverage it had to contend with.

Investors' suspicions about motives recently arose when Tyco International announced its spin-off of not just one but four of its major business units. The announcement triggered an unusually negative market reaction. Tyco stock plummeted, and the firm lost over a third of its market capitalization in a week. Investors were apparently concerned that Tyco was facing a severe cash problem and that the two-step spin-offs were intended to help it raise cash.

What happens when a spun-off unit performs well below expectations and starts to trade well below the IPO price at which the shares were brought to the market? Such outcomes can become an embarrassment to their corporate parents and, at least on some occasions, parent firms buy back the shares of their former division (a *spin-in*). For example, Walt Disney Co. sold about a quarter of the shares of its Internet division in an IPO in late 1999. After a dismal performance by its former division, Disney decided to buy back the issued shares in early 2001.

◼ Should ISC Consider Divesting IBP?

Now let's get back to our case. How do the several reasons outlined in the preceding sections bear on your decision of whether or not to divest your firm of its subsidiary, IBP? If you review the opening facts, you will see several reasons to expect shareholders to benefit from divesting IBP.

First, with regard to making your subsidiary more productive, you know that it has been difficult for IBP to attract and retain the talented employees it needs. In a research-intensive business such as biotechnology this is likely to be a severe handicap. If your biotech unit is spun off as an independent firm, it may find it easier to attract entrepreneurial and talented employees by providing incentives and compensation in the form of equity-related contracts. Even if IBP were divested in a sell-off, if the acquirer were another biotech firm, this could reassure potential employees who currently doubt commitment and ability of ISC to invest in and manage such an unrelated subsidiary.

Second, consider investment distortions. There appears to be significant potential for distortion in the way in which budgeting and investment allocation decisions are made at ISC. As discussed, investment distortions may be aggravated by substantial differences between the nature of investment opportunities among divisions of a diversified firm. The value creation and investment demands of ISC and IBP are rather different—one based on brand marketing and the other on capital-intensive product development. Table 7.1 indicates that the typical P/E and Market-to-Book ratios for firms in the biotech industry are more than twice as large as those for the beverages industry.

Third, as you've been aware, with regard to raising capital, ISC appears to be having trouble selling equity on the consolidated firm at a price that the managers consider appropriate. A diversified firm is generally viewed as being less transparent and harder for outside investors to disentangle. It is possible that both the parent and subsidiary will be more transparent after a spin-off and face fewer frictions in raising external financing. Also, while there is no specific mention in the case about threats from competitors, we have noted that spin-offs can be part of a strategy by a firm to signal commitment to its core business, and clearly your institutional investors are in need of some reassurance.

Finally, divesting the subsidiary can also provide a means of raising capital—while achieving focus. With your need for $100 million to invest, this is surely on your mind. Capital can be raised if the subsidiary is sold for cash or, in a spin-off, if the firm follows the two-step procedure and does an equity carve-out followed some months later by a spin-off.

Using Financial Data to Identify the Need for Divestiture

Divestiture is often part of a larger strategy—for example, to meet FTC requirements for merger approval, to avoid liability, or to enable greater sales for a subsidiary that is an upstream

Table 7.1. Industry Comparables (Medians) of Focused Firms

Industry	P/E Ratio	Market-to-Book	Debt-to-Equity
Beverages (wine and liquors)	19.2	1.5	.86
Biotechnology	54.2	3.9	.55

supplier to both the parent and its competitors. In these cases the need for divestiture is clear. In other situations, where the objective is to enhance shareholder value because of potential benefits from focus, it may be difficult to determine whether shareholders will actually benefit from a divestiture. In these cases, more quantitative measures can be useful.

Can financial criteria be used to identify situations in which focusing is likely to enhance shareholder value? Managers, despite their superior information about firm operations, may still benefit from the market's view of the firm's prospects. Capital markets are often very efficient at gathering and processing diverse information—information that the manager may not have such as prospects for the economy and the industry, potential impact of pending legislation, and so forth—that can affect firm value. Market-based information may also help the manager anticipate the reaction of the stock market if the firm were to announce its plans for a divestiture.

Let's look at two useful market indicators: **conglomerate discount** (the market value of a conglomerate relative to value imputed from focused firms) and diversity in opportunities among the firm's divisions.[1]

Measuring the Conglomerate Discount

A rough-and-ready way to examine whether investors would benefit from breaking up a conglomerate is to compare its market value to the value imputed from that of focused firms. Consider, for instance, a conglomerate that consists of two unrelated divisions. Let's represent the book value of assets of the two divisions as Book1 and Book2, respectively. Also, the term *Firm Market Value* denotes the market value of all of the firm's financial securities—the stock market value of the firm combined with the value of its outstanding debt claims (a similar definition of firm value was used in Chapter Four).

To obtain the imputed value of the firm (based on the market valuation of focused firms) we proceed by determining the typical (or median) **Market-to-Book** value (the ratio firm market value over book asset value) of focused firms in the industries of the two conglomerate divisions. Let's represent the median industry ratios by M1 ÷ B1 and M2 ÷ B2. The imputed value for the conglomerate is then given by the formula

$$\text{Imputed Value} = (M1 \div B1) \times Book1 + (M2 \div B2) \times Book2.$$

The imputed value, therefore, represents the anticipated market value of the multidivision firm. The calculation is based on the supposition that, once the conglomerate divisions are separated, each division's assets are going to be valued in the market according to the Market-to-Book value of the typical focused firm in the industry.

This imputed value can now be compared to the actual firm value of the conglomerate to determine how the conglomerate is being valued by the market, relative to the valuation of focused firms. When the market value of the conglomerate firm is substantially below its imputed value, this is an indication that shareholders might be better off if the firm became more focused on its core industry and divested its noncore operations.

Be careful, however—the constituent divisions of a conglomerated firm may be quite different from the median focused firm. For instance, the conglomerate may have acquired firms that, for a variety of reasons, are poor performers with relatively low Market-to-Book values. In this case, the market value of the firm may well be below its imputed value, but splitting up would not necessarily enhance shareholder wealth. Therefore, any information available about how a division differs from the typical focused firm in its industry can be useful in interpreting the difference between actual and imputed value of a conglomerate firm.

Here are examples to further illustrate the calculation and interpretation of imputed value.

A Numerical Example. A conglomerate with a stock market capitalization of $1.5 billion has two unrelated divisions. It also has $500 million of debt outstanding. The two divisions (call them divisions 1 and 2) have balance sheet assets of $.75 billion and $1.0 billion, respectively. Focused firms in the industries of divisions 1 and 2 have median Market-to-Book values of 1.5 and 1.2, respectively. It is believed that the divisions held in the conglomerate are fairly typical of firms in their industries. From this information we can obtain the imputed value and the conglomerate discount as follows:

Total market value of conglomerate firm =
Debt + Equity = $.5 billion + $1.5 billion = $2.0 billion.
Imputed value = (.75 × 1.5) + (1.0 × 1.2) = $2.325 billion.

Thus it appears that the actual market value of the conglomerate is discounted about 14 percent compared to imputed value.

On average, conglomerates tend to be valued at discounts of 10–15 percent, relative to focused firms—though about 40 percent of conglomerates tend to be valued above their imputed values. The average conglomerate discount suggests the possibility that many conglomerates enhance shareholder wealth by becoming more focused. As pointed out, however, a discount does not necessarily imply that focusing would create shareholder value.

The Imputed Value for ISC and IBP. For this second example we start with the information shown in Table 7.2.

Using the median industry Market-to-Book ratios for the parent firm's industry (1.5) and the subsidiary (3.9), we obtain:

Table 7.2. ISC and IBP ($ millions)

	ISC (Parent)	IBP (Subsidiary)	Consolidated
Market cap	—	—	$6,921
Total assets	$4,921	$841	
Long-term debt	$1,776	$200	$1,976
Capital Expenditure	$133	$170	
Revenue	$5,167	$60	
Operating Income	$799	$12	
After-tax Income	$607	$10	
Shares Outstanding	—	—	100 million
Return on assets (percent)	7.1	6.2	

ISC Imputed Value = (M/B of beverage industry) ×
(Book value parent assets) + (M/B of biotech industry) ×
(Book value subsidiary assets) = (1.5) × (4921 million) +
(3.9) × (841 million) = $10,661 million.

ISC Firm Market Value =
Debt + Equity = 1976 + 6921 = $8,897 million.

Thus, the firm is being valued by the market at a discount of roughly 16.5 percent compared to its imputed value, suggesting the possibility of substantial benefits (with the caveats mentioned earlier) from divesting the subsidiary. This is consistent with the earlier case observations about reasons to divest IBP.

We now turn to the second of our financial measures that can guide our decision to focus.

Diversity in Opportunities Among the Firm's Divisions
Evidence suggests that one of the reasons for the conglomerate discount is that investments made by conglomerates are often distorted—as divisional managers with fewer productive opportunities engage in influence-seeking activities to increase their

allocation of investment dollars.[2] The costs of such influence seeking and investment distortions are likely to be higher when there is a greater diversity in the investment opportunities across the divisions of a conglomerate. One reason why a conglomerate such as GE may be more successful than others is that it has tended to acquire and retain some of the more profitable entities in an industry—thereby lowering the potential for rent-seeking and costly lobbying by divisional managers.

The Market-to-Book ratio is often used as a measure of a firm's investment opportunities—the idea being that the market value in the numerator represents the present value of future cash flows, while the book value in the denominator measures the investment (or replacement) value of the assets employed to obtain these future cash flows. We would, for instance, expect a relatively high Market-to-Book ratio for firms in a new industry with the potential for rapid growth and future payoffs, relative to the investment indicated by the book value.

In your case, ISC appears to have significant potential for such distortions—as indicated by the difference in the Market-to-Book ratios of the focused firms in the relevant industries. Look again at Table 7.1. The relatively large difference in Market-to-Book ratios of firms in the two different industries suggests that ISC could be vulnerable to rent-seeking by managers from the beverage side of the firm. This suggests potential benefits from divesting IBP, as does the other financial measure.

On average, the announcement of a spin-off tends to increase the stock market value of a conglomerate by 7–10 percent. If this is the magnitude of the increase in the stock market value of ISP, it implies a shareholder wealth increase of $500–700 million—certainly a substantial increase in shareholder wealth.

We move on now from asking whether a divestiture should be done to how it ought to be structured.

Structuring a Divestiture

There are three customary ways to structure a divestiture: as a sell-off, a spin-off, or an equity carve-out. Each has its pros and cons. We raise three questions, the answers to which are relevant to the form of the divestiture. Beyond the questions, there is the issue of taxes.

Questions for Divestiture Deliberations

Is the business viable as an independent firm in terms of operations and management?

For a firm to be spun off it must be viable as a stand-alone company. Clearly, the spun-off unit must possess managers who can lead it as an independent firm. Such an executive and entrepreneurial management may not have been necessary when the firm was part of a larger diversified firm. If the assets and management are not viable as an independent firm, the divestiture will have to take the form of a sell-off.

Is it important to raise funds as part of the divestiture?

If it is important to be able to raise funds, then the divestiture can be done either through a sell-off or by the two-step spin-off described earlier in the chapter. In the two-step spin-off funds are raised in the first step, which involves selling some of the shares of the subsidiary in an equity carve-out. The choice between sell-off and carve-out/spin-off will be determined by three basic considerations.

- Is the firm viable as a stand-alone firm? A carve-out/spin-off can be done only if this is the case.
- Can shares of the divested subsidiary be sold in the equity carve-out for more than the price another firm is willing to pay for the divested assets? If the prices in both the sell-off and the spin-off IPO are unfavorable and a small IPO is

sufficient to raise the funds, the carve-out/spin-off route will be preferred since fewer shares are sold at an unfavorable price.

- What is the role of taxes? A sell-off will require the firm to recognize capital gains, while an equity carve-out/spin-off can usually be structured to be tax-free.

What if it is not necessary to raise external financing and the divested unit is viable as a stand-alone firm?

In this case, things to consider are the net costs, autonomy and incentives, and undervaluation.

Net Costs. The choice of method will be determined by the net costs and benefits to the parent firm, considering the relative costs of structuring a spin-off versus a sell-off. Both these costs can be relatively low, unless the spin-off entails an IPO round. The underwriting and other fees in an IPO can be large (about 7 percent of proceeds).

Autonomy and Incentives. If both spin-off and sell-off are feasible, the spin-off may be more desirable if an important reason for the divestiture is to attract downstream firms that may have been reluctant to purchase from a competitor. Since potential clients are concerned about the autonomy of the upstream firm, a spin-off is better than a sell-off to another firm with connections to the industry. The spin-off may be more desirable also when the reason is to obtain focus and to retain talented employees, especially if talented employees are seeking executive options and firm stock.

Undervaluation. If funds do not need to be raised and the firm is unable to obtain an attractive price in a sell-off or in an IPO (that is, it is undervalued), then the management will prefer to use a spin-off to divest. The usual spin-off (not the two-step spin-off) is desirable in these circumstances because it doesn't require the full or partial sale of the division at an unattractive price.

Taxes and Divestiture Method

Sell-offs and spin-offs with no equity carve-out are taxed quite differently from each other. For a sell-off, the parent firm is subject to a tax on the capital gains—that is, on the difference between the selling price and the tax basis of the assets. The tax basis of the assets is determined by the historical prices at which assets were purchased, adjusted for subsequent investments and depreciation. While the parent firm is liable for the taxes, there are no direct tax implications for investors unless the firm distributes some or all of the cash from the sale in a special dividend or share repurchase.

In the case of spin-off—one in which no funds are raised by an IPO in a first stage, the transaction is tax-free. The shares of the divested division are distributed to shareholders and are regarded as being equivalent to a stock dividend (not taxed) rather than a taxable cash dividend. The tax basis is determined by allocating the pre-spin-off basis between the parent and spun-off unit based on their relative fair market values. Figure 7.1 summarizes the main tax implications of these two methods.

Sell-off	Spin-off (with no equity carve-out)
▪ *Parent* recognizes gain or loss equal to difference between proceeds and tax basis. ▪ *Shareholders* recognize no gain or loss unless proceeds are distributed as a dividend.	▪ No gain or loss to *parent* or *shareholders*. ▪ Tax basis of subsidiary assets is unaffected. ▪ *Shareholders* allocate basis in pre-spin-off parent stock between subsidiary and post-spin-off parent based on relative fair market values.

Figure 7.1. Tax implications of Sell-Off and Spin-Off

☐

Preserving the Tax-Free Status of Two-Step Spin-Offs. The tax-free status of a spin-off can be preserved when the spin-off involves an IPO in the first stage. However, four conditions must be satisfied:

- The spun-off business must have been active for at least five years and not have been acquired in a taxable transaction in the past five years. Therefore, companies recently acquired in stock-for-stock exchanges may be spun off, but companies acquired in acquisitions involving cash payments may not.
- The parent must distribute all of the subsidiary's stock that it owns, and such stock must represent at least 80 percent of the subsidiary's voting stock. Hence, an IPO of subsidiary stock that is done prior to the spin-off must not exceed 20 percent of the subsidiary's voting shares.
- A spin-off is taxable if, after the spin-off, any person owns 50 percent or more of the stock of either the parent or the spun-off firm, and if that stock is disqualified stock. In general, stock is disqualified if it was purchased during the five years preceding the spin-off.
- The spin-off must have a substantial business purpose. A wide variety of business purposes are acceptable—including the reduction of taxes that are state, local, and foreign (in other words, anything but federal taxes!).

Tax-Free Spin-Offs and Voting Rights of Spin-Off Shares. In a two-step spin-off, as noted, the tax-free status can be preserved only if the voting rights of shares sold in the first-stage IPO do not exceed 20 percent of the voting rights of the subsequent spin-off. At first glance, this appears quite restrictive in terms of the proceeds that can be raised in the IPO prior to spin-off. However, the restriction is in terms of voting and not economic rights—suggesting that additional proceeds could be raised by issuing more than one class of stock, with shares sold in the IPO having low voting rights.

Precisely such a *High Vote/Low Vote* structure was adopted to allow a tax-free spin-off of ExpressJet by Continental. Under the plan, two classes of shares were created, Class A and Class B. While the two categories had the same economic rights, they had different voting rights. Class A shares were to be sold in the IPO—accounting for up to 50 percent of the economic rights, though only 20 percent of the voting rights. Six months after the IPO, at the time of the spin-off, the rest of the shares with a higher voting weight—with 80 percent of the voting control of the firm—were to be distributed.

Structuring Divestiture at ISC

Recall from the start of the chapter that you want ISC to raise $100 million as part of the process of divesting its subsidiary. As we have discussed, financing can be raised if the firm sells the subsidiary to another firm or if the firm does a spin-off in two stages: an equity carve-out followed by a spin-off of the rest of the subsidiary shares. The choice between the two methods will come down to a comparison between the net after-tax values received from the alternatives. The decision will also be affected by the manager's information and beliefs about the value of the subsidiary relative to the price at which the subsidiary shares can be sold in the IPO and by the offer received or expected from a firm interested in buying the subsidiary.

As it happens, no one in your company has a clear idea of what would be a fair valuation of the subsidiary. But if you assume that the Market-to-Book ratio of the subsidiary becomes similar to those of focused firms in the biotechnology industry (that is, 3.9 per Table 7.1), then the total (debt + equity) market value would be roughly:

Market Value = \$841 million × 3.9 = \$3279 million.

The subsidiary has debt of \$200 million. Therefore:

Equity value =
\$3279 million − \$200 million (debt) = \$3079 million.

This could serve as a guess of the value. A lower guess may be based on the notion that the market value increase post-spin-off tends to be in the range of 7–10 percent. Hence, because of reasons that are specific to the biotech subsidiary, even after the benefits of the spin-off kick in, its valuation may be 10 percent or so less than the valuation suggested by the median focused firm. Since the current conglomerate discount is about 16.5 percent, a conservative assumption is that even after the spin-off, the subsidiary will be valued at, say, a 10 percent discount relative to the valuation of \$3279 million that was based on a 3.9 Book-to-Market multiple. That discounted dollar value would be about \$2952 million. Subtracting \$200 million of debt leaves an equity value of \$2752 million.

For our discussion, let us assume that this \$2752 million is the lowest net (after taxes and other expenses) value that ISC would be willing to consider in choosing its method of divestiture. Since there are 100 million shares outstanding according to Table 7.2, the per share value would be \$27.52.

Choosing Between Carve-Out/Spin-Off and Sell-Off
What is the level of offer at which ISC might want to switch from doing a spin-off to selling off the unit? In other words, what price would yield a premium large enough to overcome the tax disadvantage associated with a sell-off because of the need to recognize capital gains? A buyer may be willing to pay such a premium (over an anticipated spin-off value) if it believes that owning the subsidiary would enhance its own existing activities or that it

would have the potential to enhance the revenue stream of the subsidiary given its own resources and technology.

For the minimum sale price that would be acceptable to the firm, let's use the letter P. Naturally, your firm will seek to negotiate a higher price, depending on just how valuable you believe the subsidiary is likely to be for the acquirer.

Assume that ISC's tax basis in the subsidiary is its asset value of $841 million (representing initial purchase price and net investments). With a minimum selling price of P and a tax rate of 40 percent, the seller will receive:

$$\text{Taxable Gain} = P - 841.$$
$$\text{Taxes} = .40 \times (P - 841).$$
$$\text{After-tax amount raised in sell-off} =$$
$$P - \text{Taxes} = P - .4 \times (P - 841).$$

We now compare this value (from sell-off) to what could be obtained by the alternative of a two-step spin-off.

According to the tax code, the subsidiary, with its 100 million shares, can sell at most 20 million shares in an IPO and still be able to retain the ability to do a tax-free distribution of the rest of the subsidiary shares. This limit is unlikely to be of concern here, given that the $100 million can be raised by issuing much less than 20 percent of the firm's valuation.

One way for the firm to determine the demand for the subsidiary shares in the IPO is to have its investment bank investigate market demand for the subsidiary shares. We assume that market demand is investigated in the usual way: the investment bank obtains indications of interest from its regular investors. A brief version of a possible demand analysis is given in Table 7.3. The exhibit provides summary information on the share prices that the investment bank's regular investors would be willing to pay, such that all offered shares are sold. Since ISC needs to raise $100 million, we can calculate from Table 7.3 that only 5 million

Table 7.3. Demand Indications from Investors for Three Possible
Offering Quantities in IPO (Equity Carve-Out) of IBP

Shares Sold in IPO	High Price	Median Price	Low Price
5 million	$29.0	$28.0	$27.75
10 million	$28.5	$27.75	$27.25
15 million	$28.0	$27.5	$27.0

shares will probably need to be sold in the IPO. Hence, there is
no difficulty with respect to satisfying the 20 percent limit on the
IPO shares sold to maintain the tax-free nature of the spin-off.

Assuming that the quantity of shares to be sold in the IPO
is set at 5 million, we could consider $28 per share (the median
price according to the demand indications in the table) as a possible offer price. To be more conservative, let us assume that the
investment bank insists on "leaving some money on the table"
for investors and the shares are sold for only $27/share. The
analysis can be carried out with different assumptions to obtain
a range of possible outcomes.

If 5 million shares are sold in the IPO at an offer price of
$27, the total proceeds raised would be

$$\text{Proceeds} = 5 \text{ million} \times \$27 = \$135 \text{ million.}$$

The amount actually raised by the firm will be less since
there are substantial underwriting and selling costs associated
with an IPO. Underwriting costs of IPOs tend to be in the range
of 7 percent. Using this figure, we find the amount of funds that
the firm will receive:

$$\text{Funds received by ISC} = \$135 \times (1 - .07) = \$125.5 \text{ million.}$$

The IPO represents only 5 percent of the subsidiary's equity. Hence, using the estimate obtained earlier of an anticipated

share value for the focused firm $27.52, we can surmise that the IPO route provides ISC with this total value:

Total value from IPO/Spin-off route: $125.5 + 27.52 × 95 million = $2739 million.

Note that the only transaction costs we consider are those associated with underwriting and with taxes. This is to simplify the discussion—the cost of doing a spin-off or arranging for asset sales is several times smaller than these two costs.

We now come back to the question of the amount that a buyer would need to offer in order to equal the amount anticipated from the spin-off route. As noted, if P is the sale price, then the after-tax amount received by ISC when it sells IBP is

After-tax payoff from sell-off = $P - (P - 841) \times (.4)$.

Equating the payoff from the two methods, we can obtain the minimum acceptable value of P:

$$\$2739 \text{ million} = P - (P - 841) \times (.4)$$
$$\text{or, } P = \$4014 \text{ million.}$$

Hence, to be indifferent between the sell-off and spin-off options, the (pretax) amount that you receive in the sell-off must be much larger than the anticipated offer price in a carve-out. In fact, the sell-off must occur at a price that is about $1.2 billion larger than the offer price in the IPO. This difference reflects the relatively large taxes associated with the sell-off. This suggests that the most likely route for you as CEO of ISC will be that of an IPO and that you may have little to gain from an extensive search for potential buyers of the subsidiary.

▪ Divestitures: A Checklist

Here is a sequence of questions that can guide your firm through the main decisions regarding divestitures.

1. Does the firm have one or more divisions (or significant assets) that are unrelated to the firm's core business? To evaluate whether the division should be divested, ask the following questions:

   a. Are the investment opportunities of the divisions very different from those in the firm's core business? The division is a stronger candidate for divestiture if the opportunities are quite different based on a comparison of the Market-to-Book ratios and other measures such as rates of return on investments or growth in overall industry investments. You would also want to take note of any information on whether attracting skilled individuals to divisions would be significantly affected by the possibility of offering them stock-based incentives in an independent firm.

   b. Is the firm being discounted by the stock market relative to value imputed from stand-alone firms? A substantial discount, above 10 percent to 15 percent, could indicate potential benefits from divesting unrelated divisions. Try to adjust, if possible, for divisional performance and valuation prior to its becoming part of the firm.

   c. Are there other potential benefits from divesting?
      - Might divesting unrelated, easy-to-value assets potentially be a cheap way to raise financing?
      - Is the ownership of particular assets likely to cause antitrust issues?
      - Are there potential liability risks from continued ownership of the assets?

- Is the division a potential supplier to competitors—who might be interested in purchasing from it if it were no longer a division of your firm?
2. If the decision is to divest the division, to determine the form the divestiture takes, you need to ask the following questions (see also Figure 7.2):
   a. Is the division viable as an independent entity that can be spun off? Is the divisional management prepared to lead an independent firm?
      - If it is not currently viable, can reasonable changes to the division's management or assets improve its viability?
   b. Is financing to be raised as well?
      - If yes, is the financing small enough to be raised in an IPO of less than 20 percent of shares the division? If not, how does the value from a sell-off (after-tax) compare to a spin-off (also potentially taxable here).
   c. Which of the potential methods—spin-off, two-step spin-off, or sell-off—is appropriate given the viability (or otherwise) of the division and your financing needs? If there are alternative ways to go, which one results in the lowest tax obligations?

FAQs About Divestiture

If refocusing tends to create value for shareholders, why do so many conglomerates continue to exist?

The evidence suggests that, on average, diversification has not tended to create value for firm shareholders. As mentioned, many of the conglomerates created in earlier years have refocused—and the refocusing has tended to be accompanied by shareholder gain. Also, the notion that the average conglomerate should be dismantled is bolstered by the fact that the average

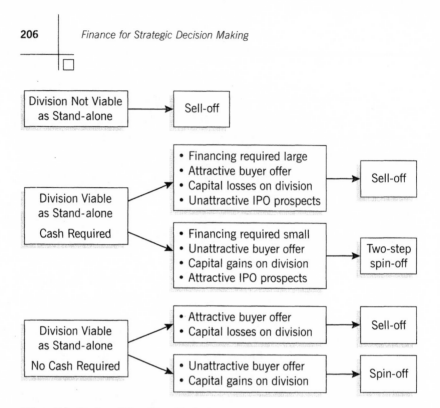

Figure 7.2. Choice of Divestiture Method

conglomerate is valued at a 10–15 percent discount relative to value imputed from single-segment firms.

At the same time, many conglomerates are apparently performing well—40 percent of conglomerates are valued in excess of their imputed values. Further, it's necessary to be careful about interpreting the conglomerate discount, since the discount is sometimes more reflective of the characteristics of firms that were conglomerated than of economic loss from the multidivisional structure itself. Bottom line, while there is value to be created from dismantling certain conglomerates, others have apparently been successful as conglomerates and it would be destructive of value to dismantle or refocus these firms.

The stock market tends to react negatively to the announcement of equity offerings. So why is there a positive stock price reaction when a conglomerate announces a two-step spin-off in which part of the unit to be spun off is sold in an equity carve-out?

There are some significant differences between the usual equity offering and an equity carve-out. An equity carve-out, in many cases, is a prelude to a spin-off that refocuses the parent firm. Hence, the positive reaction to an equity carve-out is partly a reflection of the anticipated benefits from the refocusing that might be expected to follow. A second reason is that the equity being sold is in the division that is about to be spun off and not equity in the parent firm (or consolidated firm). Hence, investors may not have concerns about the manager's taking advantage of the parent or the consolidated firm's being overvalued.

Is there a connection between the development and efficiency of capital markets and the benefits from divestiture and refocusing?

It is claimed that one potential benefit of the multidivision structure is that it gives rise to an internal capital market in which it is conglomerate headquarters that allocates capital among the divisions in response to their opportunities. This may be advantageous if allocation done inside the firm is much better than would be accomplished by external capital markets.

It follows, therefore, that as external capital markets become more efficient the benefit from having an internal capital market to allocate capital declines, given, for instance, the problems associated with divisional competition for investment resources. It is claimed that this is a factor that accounts for the prevalence of conglomerates in economies with less developed capital markets—and from the greater benefits from focus as capital markets in the United States have become more efficient.

What is a tracking stock or an alphabet stock? Does it provide an effective alternative to a spin-off?

A tracking or targeted stock (also called an alphabet stock since a letter of the alphabet is often appended to the stock name) has the flavor of attempting to—as the old saw goes—have one's cake and eat it too. A targeted stock is issued by a diversified firm and entitles the holder to the benefits of the earnings stream of a particular division or industry segment. The first example was GM's offering of tracking stock on EDS to accommodate the wishes of Ross Perot.

The catch, however, is that the division for which the targeted stock is issued still remains part of the consolidated company; the parent's board and management are fully in control of the subsidiary. The attempt, therefore, seems to be one in which managers of conglomerates seek some of the benefits of a spin-off—without yielding control. With criticism by the financial press and academics that there is no change in the decision-making structure—and hence no reason to expect any benefit—the enthusiasm for target stocks has declined and few new ones have been issued since the mid-1990s.

For ISC, could tracking stock be an effective alternative to divesting IBP?

Despite what you as ISC's CEO may have heard about targeted stocks, they do not offer an effective alternative to divesting the subsidiary—if the objective is to refocus the business and raise capital. A tracking stock is unlikely to satisfy the demands of institutional shareholders, in any case.

SUMMARY

In this chapter we outline the main reasons why divestitures can contribute to creating shareholder wealth. A firm seeking to refocus on its core business and regain its competitive edge will want to divest unrelated assets and divisions. Divestiture can also result in the division's assets being used more productively, as part of another firm (sell-off), or as an independent firm (spin-off). Converting a division into an independent firm through divestiture can be value creating—its managers have freedom of action and stronger incentives through stock-based compensation contracts.

In addition, a number of other reasons may be important in specific situations. These include needs to raise capital, meet regulatory requirements, address liability concerns, and increase opportunities for an upstream subsidiary. Divestitures have been used for dubious purposes as well: in some instances, parent firms have succeeded in reducing their liabilities by spinning off units loaded up with the conglomerate's debt.

Two useful market indicators help guide the divestiture process by evaluating the potential for value creation. One measure estimates the market value of the conglomerate relative to value imputed from focused firms. The second measure examines the difference in investment opportunities across divisions of the conglomerate—the notion being that greater diversity in investment opportunities is expected to be related to the loss in value from keeping the divisions in the same firm.

With regard to the manner in which a divestiture should be structured, the three customary choices in terms of how a divestiture is structured are sell-off, spin-off, or the two-step spin-off (an equity carve-out followed by a spin-off). The choices are affected by whether the divested unit is viable as a stand-alone firm, whether financing is to be raised, and whether the tax consequences of the gain or loss associated with selling the unit are significant. The various choices are laid out in Figure 7.2.

Risk Management

Y our firm has opportunities to undertake potentially valuable investments. However, new projects often carry considerable risk and may expose the firm to an undesirable
level of risk. Are there actions you can take to mitigate project
risk? If so, should you be taking them? In other words, does risk
management make sense given our objective of shareholder
value maximization? This chapter discusses risk management:
what risks you should seek to manage and how such risk management might be implemented. We begin by laying out a case
that embodies a risk management problem.

You are CEO of Prospecting Inc., a company that is mainly
involved in providing services for the oil industry. It is the first

quarter of 2003 and, of late, you have become increasingly concerned about the prevailing economic environment. While the firm has engaged in ad hoc efforts to manage risk, you believe that the firm may need to take stock of its risk exposures and decide if there are risks that should be reduced. In the meantime, you have received potentially interesting proposals from insurance companies suggesting that the firm should consider replacing various property and liability policies with an integrated insurance policy. They claim that such a policy would be better tailored to the firm's risk exposures and cost less than the existing insurance policies.

You and a few associates founded Prospecting in the early 1980s. At the time there was persistent demand for new and cheaper sources of energy. There was also a scarcity of skilled individuals familiar with advanced methods of analyzing and integrating information from soil and aerial surveys as part of the search for oil and gas. Over the years, the firm has carved out a niche as a reliable midsized provider of technical services and software to the oil industry. It has developed proprietary software that is recognized as an industry standard; it also provides customized software and other technical services to clients. Its customers include several major oil firms and some of their smaller rivals.

Table 8.1 is an income statement for the firm. Lines 1 and 2 of the table indicate that, in recent years, foreign revenues—primarily from European sources—have become more important. In 2002, they accounted for about 40 percent of total sales. As a consequence, the firm is now more exposed to foreign exchange risk. The table reflects the fact that demand for the firm's services is sensitive to conditions in the oil market, which presents another form of risk.

Figure 8.1 depicts the relation between average oil prices and the firm's sales for the four years from 1999 through 2002. The figure indicates that an increase in oil prices to above $30

Table 8.1. Income Statement ($ millions)

	1999	2000	2001	2002
1 Sales (U.S.)	157.20	191.20	153.60	154.40
2 Sales (Foreign)	56.15	78.47	64.79	62.19
3 Total Sales = (1) + (2)	213.35	269.67	218.39	216.59
4 Expenses − wages	64.57	83.11	67.55	66.59
5 Other expenses	98.38	120.83	100.78	84.95
6 Earnings (EBITDA) = (3) − (4) − (5)	50.41	65.72	50.05	65.05
7 Depreciation	10.50	12.00	14.50	12.50
8 Interest Expense	25.00	30.00	30.00	26.10
9 Taxes = .4 × ((6) − (7) − (8))	5.96	9.49	2.22	10.58
10 Income = (6) − (7) − (8) − (9)	8.94	14.23	3.33	15.87
11 Cash Flow = (7) + (10)	19.44	26.23	17.83	28.37
12 Average Oil Prices (per barrel)	$19.30	$30.30	$25.90	$26.10
13 $/Euro rate	0.94	1.08	1.11	1.06
14 (Total Expenses)/Sales = ((4)+(5))/(3)	0.76	0.76	0.77	0.70
15 Cash holding from last year = last year ((16) − (17))	10.00	1.44	0.68	0.00
16 Total cash available before investment = (15) + (11) + (18)	29.44	27.68	24.00	24.00
17 Investment	28.00	27.00	24.00	24.00
18 Short-term Borrowing	0.00	0.00	5.49	1.12

per barrel in 2000 was associated with a boost in total sales of about 25–30 percent relative to sales in other years.

Besides risk from volatility in oil price and foreign exchange, the firm has had to cope with considerable business and operational risks. A hazard to its prospects—and one inherently difficult to assess—is the constant possibility of technological innovation by a competitor or an entirely new firm that could deplete the value of your own proprietary software. To counter such possibilities the firm has been investing substantial resources in software development and in continually upgrading the skills of its

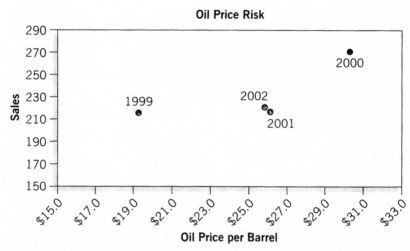

Figure 8.1. Plot of Sales Against Average Oil Prices for the Year

workforce. For the years 2000 through 2002, management had planned to invest about $27 million each year, but things did not go well in 2001 and actual investments fell somewhat short of the goal (line 17) in 2001 and 2002. Financial conditions were affected by the fact that the firm had to make relatively large interest payments in 2001 (line 8) and was hurt by a drop in oil prices (line 12). As a consequence, the firm had insufficient funds to achieve its investment objectives. It was forced to trim its investment plans and to arrange to borrow about $5.5 million in short-term funds (line 18) at fairly unattractive rates. To avoid such occurrences in the future, the firm has announced its intention to gradually reduce its debt burden.

At this time you would like to develop a risk management policy that explicitly recognizes the different types of risks that the firm must contend with, including business, financial, and liability risks. Managing these different kinds of risk will probably require a variety of actions. You also have questions about implementing a risk management policy. For example, should risks be managed internally or by a financial intermediary outside the firm? And are there downsides to risk management that you need to be aware of?

In the following sections we discuss what a firm can and should do about risk exposure. We begin by considering what kinds of risks are important to manage.

▥ Should All Risks Be Managed?

Prospecting Inc. faces several risks that can affect its value. Some are broad economic risks having to with oil prices and exchange rates; others involve risk of financial distress and the risk of losing its reputation for quality products and services. In addition, despite its efforts to stay at the cutting edge, the firm faces the risk of rival technological developments, loss of vital employees, and heightened competition.

Should you attempt to control all these (and other) risks as part of a risk management strategy? Simply because a risk can be managed is not a justification to do so. The standard for risk management is the same as that for any other corporate activity—it should be tied to a potential increase in shareholder value. At Prospecting Inc. some of the risks are intimately tied to the core activities of your firm—its reputation for quality, of being a technology leader, of dealing with competition, of developing its human capital. Clearly these risks affect shareholder value, though it may not be feasible, for the most part, to obtain insurance or to transfer such risks. This is because the entity that is best informed and best able to influence the outcomes is the firm itself and, in particular, the management team—including you. The discussion on information problems in Chapter Four suggests that an outside insurance provider with poorer information and little control is not going to be well positioned to bear such risks (or, what is effectively the same thing, will charge an arm and a leg for such insurance). These business and operating risks will therefore largely be retained by the firm. However, the firm can take steps to reduce its business and operational risk in various ways—for instance, through building flexibility into its business strategy—which we discuss a bit later.

On the other hand, risks such as those involving oil prices and exchange rates are of another kind entirely. These risks are not integral to the core value-creating activities of the firm. However, they can be, as in Prospecting's case, significant risks that a firm might want to manage in defense of shareholder value. Such risks can easily be transferred through financial securities or financial intermediaries to others more willing to bear them. The transfer of such risks is subject to few market imperfections since oil and exchange rate prices are easily verified and, in general, cannot be manipulated by an individual firm.

However—to repeat—simply because a risk can be managed is not a good reason to manage it! In general, risk management will always cost some money and should be employed when poor outcomes can have strong negative consequences—such as financial distress or constraints on the firm's ability to invest. Risks without such negative consequences are best retained by the firm. Hence a firm with substantial assets has little reason to buy, say, automobile insurance. The potential losses would not put the firm in jeopardy or disrupt its ability to invest. At the same time, the costs of third-party insurance would exceed the expected payback from such a policy (after all, for the insurance company to survive, it has to be taking in more than it expects to pay out).

■ Risk Can Be Reduced, Retained, or Transferred

A firm basically has three things that it can do with risk. It can try to reduce the amount of risk by altering operations or taking other specific actions to improve control and flexibility. Beyond reducing risk, a firm can either retain whatever risk remains or arrange to transfer some part of the risk to others in the economy as, for instance, through the use of insurance contracts or other financial instruments. We begin by considering ways to reduce risk.

Risk Reduction

Risk can be reduced by making changes in the firm's operations or else by changing its financial structure.

Changes in Operations
Firms can modify their operations in numerous ways to manage risk. Principally, they can increase flexibility, invest to maintain their competitive edge, make organizational changes, and standardize.

By introducing greater flexibility into the production process firms can put themselves in a position to respond quickly to changes in economic conditions. One way to do this may be through greater reliance on temporary workers. The downside, of course, is that the quality of work may suffer. An idea under consideration at Prospecting is for the firm to prepare for future growth opportunities by having a somewhat larger skilled team than strictly necessary. The idea is that skilled individuals can be assigned to somewhat routine jobs when demand is slow. When demand picks up, the firm can respond quickly, while relying on temporary hires for backup on more routine tasks.

Maintaining a competitive edge can also serve to reduce risk. A central aspect of Prospecting's competitive strategy is maintaining its reputation for quality products and services. The firm has been making investments explicitly intended to keep it at the cutting edge in terms of technology. Its training and recruitment programs are intended to retain and develop skilled workers. If some of the senior employees were to leave, this could have a drastic impact on the firm's ability to deliver its products and services, making it hard to recruit and train new skilled personnel and damaging its reputation. The firm has a no-compete policy to prohibit former employees from working with a competitor for a year after leaving.

Another way to lower business risk may be for the firm to become more diversified and reduce exposure to conditions in a specific industry. However, as discussed in connection with divestitures (Chapter Seven), evidence on the performance of diversified firms is not encouraging, and several multidivision firms have been disassembled in recent years to create more focused firms. Firms can also limit their risk—especially where large projects are involved—by using project financing. That is, they set up such projects as independent concerns that raise their own debt financing, which does not have recourse to the assets of the parent firm. Meanwhile, the parent firm typically retains some or all of the equity in the project-financed venture.

Prospecting's main competitor is another U.S.-based firm that is somewhat larger and more diversified. However, organizational changes—such as adding a new division—are not under active consideration at Prospecting. Still, given the sensitivity of the firm's earnings to oil prices, there may be advantages to Prospecting from extending its expertise in oil to other commodity or energy-related businesses, as appears to be the strategy of its more diversified competitor.

The competitor has an advantage in being able to serve some of its foreign clients through offices and personnel located in Europe. In response, Prospecting is considering the possibility of eventually establishing its own subsidiary in Europe. The logic is that its European sales are already important and such a move would protect the firm against unfavorable exchange rate movements and, presumably, allow it to serve the European market better. It would also improve its competitive position relative to its main rival. This is, however, a relatively expensive option, especially in the firm's current situation, though it may be good in the long run, given the importance of foreign markets for the firm.

Standardizing is yet another way to reduce operational risk. This is the model-T approach—Henry Ford's old maxim that consumers can choose any color of car, so long as it's black. Offering customers less choice reduces operational risk by reducing unknowns in demand, worker retraining costs, and production setup and technology. The problem, of course, is that such a strategy is workable only when competitors are unable to move ahead technologically. While some standardization can help, Prospecting is in a technological business where the benefits of standardization may be quite limited. After all, the moral of the model-T story is that after a period of domination, Ford was unable to compete with newer car models from other companies and lost much of its market share.

Reducing Leverage

As you know from our discussion of capital structure (Chapter Four), debt introduces financial risk for the firm's stockholders, on top of the firm's underlying business or operational risk. Capital structure choice can involve trade-offs such as between tax shields and other benefits of debt versus potential costs of financial distress.

Table 8.1 (lines 16 and 17) shows that Prospecting faced a cash crunch in 2001. The firm had to pay $30 million in interest payments that year (line 8), which, given a low cash position and average revenue, led to the firm's cutting back on its planned investment of $27 million despite some short-term borrowing. Hence the firm suffered from being unable to fully fund its investments and was forced to borrow at disadvantageous rates.

Under pressure from its debtholders, the firm has promised to reduce its leverage over time. This may be a desirable goal if the reduction in tax shield is more than offset by the lower probability of financial distress or financial crunch. Such a decision should, in general, be based on the firm's projected investment needs and uncertainty in its cash flows. The firm does not necessarily have to reduce leverage to avoid future liquidity crunches. It may be able, for instance, to enter into contacts with banks for lines of credit (LOCs) that it can draw upon in the event of a liquidity crunch. While the firm will have to pay a small fee to maintain an LOC, the advantage is that at crunch time the firm is quickly able to obtain financing at a predetermined rate. This will enable the firm to maintain higher leverage (and tax shields) than would have been appropriate otherwise. Alternatively, if the firm can effectively manage the risk of oil prices and foreign exchange rates by stabilizing the cash flows, this may allow the firm to maintain greater levels of leverage.

The nature of Prospecting's business suggests that financial distress could be very costly in terms of shareholder value, because intangible assets such as reputation appear to be critical to its business strategy. As you know from Chapter Four, whereas tangible assets such as plant and equipment tend to lose some value in bankruptcy, nontangible assets such as reputation can simply disappear. Financial distress might also induce several of the firm's most skilled employees to leave, making it quite difficult to retain the rest and to attract new skilled employees.

Risk Retention

After reducing risks where it can, a firm can simply decide to self-insure, that is, to retain the rest of its risk. This is especially likely when the risk is small relative to the firm's equity capital and unlikely to cause financial disruption or liquidity problems. The main benefit from retaining risks—compared to transferring them—is that it is usually cost-effective to self-insure. This is because information asymmetry and other frictions (recall the market imperfection framework in Chapter Four) drive up the costs of insurance provision by a third party. Insurance providers are cautious for two good reasons. First, the provider is concerned that those seeking insurance are likely to be of greater-than-average risk (the lemons problem), and, second, that the presence of insurance may affect the behavior of the insured (moral hazard). Think about how having very good car insurance may induce a car owner to be careless about choosing a parking place.

Of course, the concern at Prospecting is that the firm may be retaining too much of its risk exposure—especially risks such as exchange rates and oil prices over which the firm has no control. Such economy-wide risks are often the ones for which hedging (or another form of risk management) is most appropriate.

Risk Transfer

Financial contracts allow for an efficient sharing and transfer of risk to those in the economy who are most willing to bear the risk (in other words, to those that require the lowest rate of return as compensation for bearing the risk). Risk transfers are generally classified as hedging or insuring.

Hedging refers to a situation in which the firm transfers both the upside and downside of a risk. For a portfolio that moves with the stock market, a hedging of the market risk would imply that the value of the portfolio was no longer sensitive to stock market movements. If the stock market risk is only reduced, the portfolio may be regarded as being partially hedged.

In contrast to hedging, *insuring* is a contract by which only the downside risk—bad outcomes and losses—is transferred. The insured entity retains the possibility of an upside. Hence, insurance against a fall in the stock market would provide protection in the event of a negative outcome, while allowing for gains to be retained. Of course, such an insurance policy would be correspondingly more expensive than a contract that fully hedged stock market risk and took away the upside while protecting against the downside.

For Prospecting, hedging and insuring can be used to reduce exposure to oil and exchange rate risks. Let's take a brief respite from the case to introduce financial instruments that the firm may want to use.

Derivatives as Financial Instruments

Derivative securities are financial instruments widely used for risk management. As the name suggests, *derivatives* are financial claims with payoffs linked to—derived from—the prices of other securities or assets. There are a large variety of derivatives. For example, payoffs of derivative securities can be linked to exchange rates, to interest rates, commodity prices, stock prices, and many other types of price risk. Some derivatives are traded on an exchange and are very liquid, while others tend to be placed privately (that is, not traded publicly) or are customized claims provided by investment banks to their clients.

Why do derivatives exist? Since these securities are claims on other assets, why not directly invest in the underlying assets? The reason is that derivative claims allow investors and firms to implement investment strategies—whether for speculation or risk management—that would be much more difficult or expensive to achieve by directly taking positions in the underlying assets. Two broad classes of derivatives are often employed to manage risk. One class is that of futures and forward contracts; the other is options.

Futures and Forward Contracts. The essential feature of futures and forward contracts is that they are firm commitments to deliver an underlying asset at an agreed-upon price on a particular delivery date—or else pay a settlement price in lieu of actual delivery. There could, for instance, be a futures (forward) contract for the delivery of 1,000 ounces of gold on January 7,

2005, at a **futures price**—also called a **forward price**—of $300/ ounce. In general, little money changes hands when the contract is entered into; the parties simply agree on the terms and the buyer makes a token payment. The contract will usually specify various details regarding the delivery location, quality of the asset, and so on.

Futures and forward contacts have some of the flavor of being side bets or a **zero-sum game** between investors on opposite sides of the contract. This is because for every investor who holds a futures position that requires delivering the goods on the stated date, there is someone else on the other side of the contract who is obliged to take delivery of the goods (the **long** position) under the terms of the contract.

Forward contracts tend to be customized, private contracts. In our discussion we therefore focus on futures contracts, which are traded on exchanges and are standardized with respect to delivery dates, contract size, delivery location, and other contractual terms. Depending on demand by market participants, there may be several exchange-listed futures contracts on the same underlying commodity, though with different delivery dates: hence (in, say, November 2004), there may be five or more different futures contracts for wheat, the first one for delivery in January 2005, the second one for delivery in March 2005, and so forth. The market-determined futures price for the January 2005 futures contract represents the futures price at which buyers and sellers of wheat are willing to enter into contracts for the delivery of wheat in January 2005. Similarly, today's futures price on the March 2005 contract represents the price at which buyers and sellers are willing to buy or sell wheat as of March 2005.

Hence, someone who wants to be sure of obtaining wheat in March 2005 at a predetermined price (today's futures price) can enter into a sufficient number of futures contracts for delivery of the desired quantity of wheat. By entering into the futures contracts for delivery, the purchaser agrees to take delivery of the wheat in March 2005 at the price stated in the futures contracts. The use of such a contract for hedging is explained below.

Establishing a position in a futures contract requires only the pledging of an initial margin amount (which may be just 5–10 percent of the delivery amount). No other investment is required. However, all profits and losses on the futures position are settled on a daily basis, in a procedure called **marking to market**. For instance, suppose you take a long position (that is, you are committed to take delivery of the underlying good) in a single futures contract in which the good to be delivered is a specific quantity and type of oil. Let's denote the futures oil price at which you establish your position, say for the February 2005 contract, by F_0. Let us denote the futures price on the same (February 2005) contract the next trading day by F_1. Then, as of that second day, you have made a profit or loss of $F_1 - F_0$. This is the change in value of your contract, since the futures price (F_1) at which investors are willing to buy oil in February 2005 has changed from the price (F_0) at which you had been promised delivery. If the futures price is now higher (or lower), you have made a profit (loss) since you will be paying a lower (higher) price (F_0) than what investors are willing to pay today (F_1):

Profit (or loss) to long (side taking delivery)
futures position = $F_1 - F_0$.

Since futures contracts are like side bets, for the investor on the other side (obligated to supply the goods) the profit or loss is precisely the reverse of what you have made. Figure 8.2 illustrates the relationship between the change in price of a futures contract and the profit or loss on a contract.

For a numerical example, take 100 troy oz. to be the standardized size for a futures contract on gold that is traded on the futures exchange. On December 19, 2004, you take a long position in three gold contracts maturing in April 2005. Hence, you

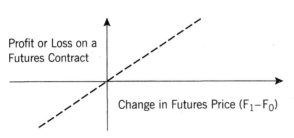

Figure 8.2. Pricing and Profits on a Futures Contract

have entered into contracts that require you to accept delivery of 300 oz. of gold in April 2005. The futures price for the April 2005 contracts on December 19 is $275.50/oz. It costs nothing (other than the margin) to establish the position. Now, suppose that the very next trading day, the futures price rises to $276/oz. The profit you make is

$$(\text{position} \times \text{contract size}) \times (F_1 - F_0) =$$
$$(3 \times 100) \times (276 - 275.5) = \$150.$$

The $150 profit will be deposited into your margin account. This will happen each trading day (marking-to-market) as long as you maintain your position (you can close out your position at any time) or the contracts mature. The effect of marking to the market is to ensure that investors on the exchange are solvent—since the exchange is the final guarantor that the futures contracts will be honored. If you make a loss, the loss amount is withdrawn from your margin account. If funds are insufficient, you receive a call to deposit additional funds—otherwise your position is closed automatically.

Hedging with Futures. Let us now consider a situation in which the objective is to manage the risk of a firm's cash flow. Continuing with the gold example, let us say that your firm is a supplier to the gold mining industry and your cash flows are *positively correlated* (move in the same direction) with changes in the price of gold.

To implement a hedge, you will need to determine the sensitivity of the firm's cash flow to changes in gold futures prices. The sensitivity can be estimated, for instance, by using statistical analysis. The usual technique would involve finding the linear relation (by fitting a linear regression or the "best" straight line) between cash flows and the gold futures prices. The sensitivity of your cash flow to gold prices is indicated by the slope of the straight (regression) line that represents the relation between the two. We discuss the estimation of cash flow sensitivity further in the FAQs at the end of the chapter. Now, suppose that on the basis of your analysis you determine that, on average, this is how futures prices tend to affect the cash flow:

$$\text{Change in firm cash flow} =$$
$$30 \times (\text{Change in value of gold futures contract}).$$

This relation suggests that in order to manage the risk of the cash flow, you need to take a position in the futures contract that offsets the changes in the firm's cash flow. The cash flow (on average) tends to increase by about thirty times the change in the value of a long position in the futures contract, so—to offset the risk—you will need to take a position that has precisely the opposite effect in terms of profits and losses. In other words, you need to enter into thirty futures contacts for the delivery of gold—such a position will result profits (losses) thirty times as large as the fall (increase) in the futures price of gold.

Options: Puts and Calls

As a financial contract, an option is the right to buy or sell a specified asset on or by a specified maturity date at a price agreed on today. A right to buy an asset is called a **call** option. The right to sell an asset is called a **put** option. The underlying assets can be

financial assets like stocks and stock indices or tangible commodities like oil and coffee. The price at which the holder of the
option has the right to buy or sell the underlying asset is called
the **strike** or **exercise price**. The price at which a call or put option can be purchased in the market is called the call or put
option premium.

The next two figures represent the payoffs that come from
exercising calls and puts. Figure 8.3 relates to the call option on
an asset with exercise price X and maturity date T. Let the market
value of the underlying asset at maturity be denoted by S_T. If
the value S_T is greater than X, the owner of the option obtains
$S_T - X$ upon exercising the call option (this is the payoff from exercising—and not the overall profit or loss of the investor from
buying the option since we are not taking into account what the
investor originally paid). On the other hand, if the value of the asset is less than X, the option is worthless and will be allowed to
expire without exercise. The figure shows the payoff at maturity.

Now consider Figure 8.4: a put option with exercise price
X that matures at date T. Since a put option is the right to sell,
the option will be exercised at maturity only if the value of the

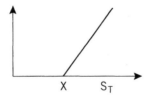

Figure 8.3. Call Option Payoff at Maturity

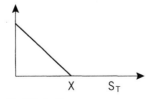

Figure 8.4. Put Option Payoff at Maturity

underlying asset S_T is less than (or equal to) the exercise price X. When the value of the asset is larger than X, the option is worthless and will be allowed to expire without being exercised. Again, the figure shows the payoff at maturity.

Managing Risk with Put Options

Let us consider the use of a put option to manage the risk of the underlying asset, say a stock. The exercise price is X, which gives the owner of a put option the right to sell the stock at maturity for a price of X to the person on the other side of the option contract. As with futures contracts, options are a zero-sum game between those buying and those selling the option contract.

Consider the use of a put option as insurance against the drop in the price of an asset. Suppose you own a hundred shares of stock and purchase put options on the shares to protect your position. The put options mature in six months and have an exercise price of $100. The payoff in six months from owning the shares and the put options is as follows:

- If the share price exceeds $100/share at the end of six months (say, it rises to $120/share), you won't exercise the option to sell the shares at $100/share because your 100 shares will be worth $12,000 rather than the $10,000 the option would bring in.
- On the other hand, if the share price is $90/share at the end of six months, you will want to exercise your put options and sell the shares at $100/share. Your position will be worth $10,000, which is better than the $9,000 otherwise available.

Hence, by using put options, you have been able to ensure that at the end of six months (the maturity date of the options) you receive at least $10,000 or $100/share. Similar to an insurance policy, the put options limit the amount of losses you suffer.

Note the basic difference between futures and options in terms of how they help you manage risk. Futures contracts are low cost. However, when used to hedge risk they have the effect of eliminating not only the downside but also the upside. On the other hand, put options are like insurance contracts. They are more expensive to use than futures contracts. However, in a fashion similar to insurance, they can be used to eliminate downside risk while maintaining the possibility of an upside gain. Later in the chapter we discuss ways you can use futures and options to help manage Prospecting's risks. We turn for now to a discussion of when risk management with financial contracts contributes to value creation.

When Should You Manage Risk Using Financial Contracts?

As noted, only certain types of risk—those that do not derive from the core business and operating risks of the firm—may be worth hedging, using financial contracts to transfer the risk to other investors. When a risk can be transferred by the use of derivative contracts, there are two primary situations in which risk management enhances value: when the effort reduces bankruptcy risk and financial distress costs and, second, when it improves the matching between the firm's cash flow and its investment needs, thereby reducing costly external financing or making it unnecessary to forgo profitable investments. Risk management can also be beneficial by lowering expected taxes and improving corporate governance in some circumstance.

In the presence of significant bankruptcy costs, it is obvious that stabilizing the firm's cash flows can beneficially reduce the probability of financial distress. The greater stability may allow the firm to take on more leverage and thereby benefit from the additional tax shields. While Prospecting is not on the verge of bankruptcy, it has had its share of problems in recent years and is planning to move to a less leveraged capital structure. Hence, Prospecting could benefit from managing its exposure to oil prices and exchange rates. Drawing upon our discussion of capital structure choice (Chapter Four), financial distress is likely to be of particular concern for a firm such as Prospecting—given the importance of intangibles such as its reputation and the human capital of its skilled workers.

As we noted in the discussion on external financing (Chapter Four), rather than raising cash externally by issuing debt or equity, companies prefer internally generated cash to finance their investments. In this respect, shocks that reduce a company's cash flow can compromise its ability to undertake value-creating investments. This was precisely the situation Prospecting faced in 2001. Hence, risk management can create value by better matching internally generated cash flow with the firm's investment and overall cash flow needs. This reduces the need for access to costly external financing and can improve the firm's investment decisions.[1]

An implication of the foregoing is that the importance of risk management depends on the strength of a firm's balance sheet. A company with lots of cash or spare debt capacity (relative to its investment needs) does not need to worry much about risk management—it will have enough resources to bear risk and maintain its investment policy.

It should be noted that the risk of any particular investment or cash flow should always be thought of in terms of its incremental contribution to a firm's net or overall exposure. For example, it is common for certain risky cash flows to be inversely correlated with each other and therefore to provide, in effect, a natural hedge. Prospecting, for instance, has what appears to be a natural hedge for its overall earnings in the relation between total sales and expenses (lines 3 through 5 of Table 8.1). Hence, although wages and other expenses appear risky, you might end up making the firm's earnings (line 6) riskier if you were to somehow reduce the fluctuation in annual expenses. Though wages are risky, they move in line with revenues and in a sense are reducing the net risk rather than increasing it.

▣ Using Derivatives to Manage Risk at Prospecting, Inc.

Now we discuss the use of futures contracts and put options to manage risk at Prospecting Inc., using information from the income statement in Table 8.1. In terms of assessing risk management we are especially interested in knowing whether risk management would have helped the firm avoid the liquidity crunch in 2001. Let us first examine the impact of hedging the $/euro exchange rate risk (line 13).

Foreign Exchange Risk Hedging

Changes in the $/euro exchange rate can affect Prospecting's cash flows in different ways. If the euro weakens against the dollar, for instance, this makes Prospecting's products relatively more expensive in the foreign currency and may reduce the demand for its products. A weaker euro will also weaken the firm's competitive position relative to its competitor, which has a subsidiary in Europe and is therefore less affected by changes in the exchange rate. However, we would not expect a stronger euro to necessarily give Prospecting an advantage either, since the competitor has operations in the United States as well.

In the absence of more detailed information, let us analyze the effect of hedging some of the firm's foreign exchange risk, say half, in a fairly simple way. This will give us some sense of the potential benefits to Prospecting, if any, from hedging foreign exchange risk.

Information on average exchange rates and foreign sales is given in line 13 and line 2, respectively, in Table 8.1. The four-year average $/euro rate is $1.04/euro. To determine if there are benefits from hedging, we examine the difference it makes to the firm's earnings if half of its euro earnings, in each year, are converted into dollars at this average rate, compared to the exchange rate for that year. In lines 1 through 3 in Table 8.2 we provide the sales in euros and the conversion into dollars at a fixed (hedged) rate (line 2) and at the prevailing rates for the year (line 3). Finally, line 4 provides the cash flow effect of a 50 percent hedge of the foreign exchange earnings.

The results of the hedging exercise may strike you as being somewhat unexpected. If you examine line 4, you realize that hedging the exchange rate would not have helped at all in 2001—if anything, hedging could have made the liquidity position worse (by about $2 million). It is easy to see why hedging exchange rates would have made matters worse in 2001: the $/euro exchange rate that year averaged $1.11/euro, which is high relative to other years, indicating that the dollar figures for the foreign sales were already being helped by the dollar's relative weakness (more dollars per euro) in 2001.

The bottom line here is that the exchange rate risk, though present, may be offsetting the other major risk here, the oil price risk. We have only four years of data to go on, but the optimal action may be to leave the foreign exchange risk unhedged. If

Table 8.2. Effect of Hedging $/Euro Risk ($ millions)

	1999	2000	2001	2002
1 Sales in euros = (line 2, Table 8.1/ line 13, Table 8.1)	53.90	38.73	58.84	70.93
2 Foreign sales in dollars at fixed rate $1.04/euro = 1.04 × Line 1	62.12	75.56	60.70	61.02
3 Foreign sales in dollars (line 2, Table 8.1)	56.15	78.47	64.79	62.19
4 Adjustment for 50 percent hedging ($ million) = .5 × (line 2 − line 3)	2.99	−1.45	−2.04	−0.59

the nature of the relationship between oil prices and the exchange rate continues to hold through time, we may want to consider increasing the firm's foreign exchange risk exposure (by, for example, entering into futures or forward contracts for the delivery of euros or in options contracts that paid off when the $/euro rate was higher).

Earlier in the chapter we mentioned that Prospecting was toying with the idea of opening up offices in Europe, partly in order to hedge exchange rate risk. However, since the $/euro exchange rate risk should probably not be hedged, Prospecting should open offices in Europe only if its decision is based on business considerations such as market access or efficient delivery of services, and not for reasons having to do with foreign exchange hedging.

Managing Oil Price Risk

As mentioned earlier in the chapter, the revenues of Prospecting are sensitive to oil prices. While we have sales and oil prices for only four years, Figure 8.1 indicates that the one year (2000) when sales experienced a substantial increase was when the oil price crossed above $30/barrel. In Table 8.3, we examine the consequences of buying put options on oil with an exercise price of $28/barrel (recall that the exercise price is the price at which the holder of an option has the right to buy or sell an asset). The amount of options contracts are assumed to be such as to allow the firm to sell 2 million barrels of oil (remember it's a put option) at $28/barrel. Hence, in 2000, with average oil prices at $25.90 (line 8, Table 8.3), at which price the firm is assumed to exercise its option contracts, the firm obtains hedging revenues of $(28 − 25.9) × 2 million = $4.2 million. Such option contracts are usually settled for cash rather than a delivery of the physical commodity underlying the option contract. (For simplicity, these figures ignore the costs of purchasing options.)

Table 8.3. Income Statement Adjusted for Hedging ($ millions)

	1999	2000	2001	2002
1 Earnings (EBITDA) = line 6, Table 8.2	50.41	65.72	50.05	65.05
2 Earnings + Hedging Flows = (line 1 + line 9)	50.41	65.72	54.25	67.90
3 Depreciation	10.50	12.00	14.50	12.50
4 Interest expense	25.00	30.00	30.00	25.59
5 Taxes = .4 × (line 2 − line 3 − line 4)	5.96	9.49	3.90	11.92
6 Income = (line 2 − line 3 − line 4 − line 5)	8.95	14.23	5.85	17.89
7 Cash flows = (line 6 + line 3)	19.44	26.23	20.35	30.38
8 Average oil prices per barrel	$19.30	$30.30	$25.90	$26.10
9 Hedging (options on oil futures)			4.20	2.85
10 Cash from last year	10.00	1.44	.68	0.00
11 Cash available	29.44	27.68	21.03	30.38
12 Investment	28.00	27.00	24.00	27.00
13 Short-term borrowing	0.00	0.00	2.97	0.00

Hence, the use of such option contracts would have given the firm significant additional revenues in 2001 and 2002 at a time when oil price and the firm's revenues were lower. It is a matter of speculation, since we have only four years of income information, as to whether the firm's revenues will continue to follow the type of pattern exhibited in 1999–2002 and whether such put option contracts will prove to be a good oil price hedge. However, the exercise does highlight the potential benefits from oil-price risk management. As indicated in Table 8.3, the hedging profits (line 9) have the effect of raising available cash flows (line 7 and line 11) for 2001 and 2002. With the higher available cash flows, the firm would have been able to decrease its short-term borrowing (line 13) to $2.97 million in 2001 and zero in 2002 if investment levels were maintained (line 12). Alternatively, the firm could have decided to increase its investment levels closer to its original plan of $27 million in 2001 and 2002.

The bottom line is that Prospecting faces a significant risk from oil price movements. Using put options on oil is one way to limit this risk and enhance cash flows when oil prices fall below a certain range.

■ Other Potential Benefits from Risk Management

So far, we have focused on two significant benefits from the use of financial instruments to manage risk: lowering the likelihood of financial distress and achieving a better matching of the firm's cash flows with its investment needs. There are other potential benefits, as well, including reducing taxes and improving incentive schemes and corporate governance.[2]

Taxes and Risk Management

As noted, risk management, whether by risk reduction or transfer, is warranted when, for a particular risk, the potential benefits on the upside are significantly less valuable than the potential losses on the downside. This is the situation, for instance, when a firm is concerned about the possibility of financial distress with the associated large downside costs. Corporate taxes can have an asymmetric effect on corporate income in a somewhat similar fashion, the asymmetry coming from the different way in which a firm's profits and losses are effectively taxed. To see this, suppose that when a certain firm is profitable it is taxed at a corporate tax rate of 40 percent, resulting in the firm's receiving only $.60 for each additional dollar of taxable income. On the other hand, if the firm loses money, it suffers a loss of $1.00 for every dollar of loss unless it can carry forward its losses and offset future taxes. Let us consider a simple example to illustrate why the asymmetric tax treatment matters.

Consider a firm that has an expected pretax cash flow of $100 million. The firm is, however, exposed to a large cash flow risk—say, the outcome of a critical legal trial. There is a 50 percent chance that things will go well and the firm will experience an additional gain of $200 million, resulting in a profit of $300 million. If things go badly, which can happen with a 50 percent chance as well, the firm will lose $200 million, resulting in a net loss of $100 million. Assume also that the firm faces a tax rate of 40 percent when it has taxable earnings and that it is unable to carry its losses forward.

For this firm let's compare the after-tax cash flow with and without risk management by looking at these four equations:

1. Expected after-tax value without risk management if firm *cannot* use losses to reduce taxes elsewhere:

$$.5 \times (1 - .4) \times 300 \text{ million} - .5 \times (100 \text{ million}) = \\ \$40 \text{ million}$$

2. Expected after-tax value without risk management if firm *can* fully take advantage of losses for tax purposes:

$$.5 \times (1 - .4) \times 300 \text{ million} - .5 \times (1 - .4) \times \\ (100 \text{ million}) = \$60 \text{ million}$$

3. Expected pretax cash flows with risk management:

$$.5 \times 300 \text{ million} - .5 \times 100 \text{ million} = 100 \text{ million}$$

4. Expected after-tax value with risk management:

$$(1 - .4) \times (100 \text{ million}) = \$60 \text{ million}$$

Assume that with risk management the firm is able to remove the uncertainty of its pretax cash flows and obtains its average or expected cash flow of $100 million for certain. Equations 1 and 2 indicate the expected after-tax values without risk management. Equation 1 represents a situation in which the firm is unable to use its losses for reducing taxes elsewhere, while 2 indicates a situation in which the firm can fully take advantage of the losses for tax purposes by lowering its taxable income elsewhere.

With risk management, our assumption is that the firm is able to obtain its expected pretax cash flows of $100 million for certain (equation 3). With the pretax cash flows being risk managed, equation 4 indicates that the after-tax value of the firm is $60 million. Hence, relative to a situation (as in equation 1) in which the firm is unable to use losses to offset taxes, the firm is now able to lower its expected tax payments by stabilizing its pretax cash flow. In fact, as indicated, its expected after-tax value with risk management here is identical to what it would have been if the firm did not manage risk but was able to fully employ its losses to reduce taxes (equation 2).

Incentive Schemes and Corporate Governance

Incentive schemes should expose managers to risk they can control and minimize exposure to risks they cannot control. If the earnings of a firm are stabilized with respect to economy-wide or industry-wide risks, its earnings are likely to more truly reflect the skills of the current management. By this argument, if managers are compensated based on firm earnings or stock performance, reducing the exposure of the firm to economy-wide risks can make incentive programs more effective.

Another argument made in favor of risk management starts from the premise that large shareholders are desirable and that their presence increases the value of the firm. By their shareholding they signal their confidence in the firm to other investors as well as keep an eye on (that is, monitor) the functioning of the firm and its management. By reducing the volatility of its cash flows by an appropriate risk management policy, a firm can more easily attract large shareholders—who may otherwise be reluctant to bear the risk associated with assuming a large position in the firm. In the case of Prospecting, we know that the firm is held to a large extent by its founding managers and reducing stock price risk may induce managers to continue holding a substantial stake.

■ Some Concerns with Implementing Risk Management

While risk management is meant to control risk, unless the process is implemented with care and monitored properly, it has been known to degenerate into speculation. This can happen if, for instance, the objectives of the risk management group are not well specified and the unit pursues profits rather than risk reduction. In this connection it should be noted that one of the potential problems with the use of certain derivative contracts for risk management is that they are *off-balance-sheet* items. This raises a legitimate concern about the extent to which a firm's income and balance sheet information may be distorted by the presence of off-balance-sheet items ostensibly being used to manage risk.

In other firms, managers will sometimes choose risk management strategies in an effort to stabilize accounting earnings or stock prices rather than to maximize shareholder value. There is no reliable evidence that such strategies create value for the shareholders in the long run—even if the manager believes that such actions may assist the firm's stock price or analyst ratings in the short run.

Finally, and this was an issue that arose in connection with Prospecting's foreign exchange risk: what matters is a risk's contribution to the firm's overall risk. Efforts to minimize a particular risk may inadvertently increase the overall risk of the firm.

◼ Bundling Insurance—Integrated Risk Management

One way to transfer risk is through the use of insurance policies. Prospecting has received proposals to consider bundling various property and liability insurance policies (and possibly other types of risk) into an integrated policy. Such integrated insurance products have become increasingly available and are regarded as a cost-effective alternative to traditional forms of coverage. Why would such integrated insurance potentially represent a better form of insurance?

The main benefit of bundling insurance is that it can reduce unnecessary coverage that the purchase of separate policies entails. Purchase of a number of separate policies results in the firm's being insured against a series of smaller losses, irrespective of its overall financial health. The advantage of an integrated policy is that the firm can choose to be insured against large aggregate losses, which, as noted earlier, is what a firm should be most concerned about in terms of its risk management. Let us consider a simple example.

Suppose that a mining firm faces two significant risks that it would like to insure against. The first risk is flooding at its main mines. Such a flood can occur with a probability of 5 percent (about once in twenty years) and can cause a loss of $20 million. Another risk is a large rock slide that could disrupt the movement of materials and people from the mines. Let us assume that such an event also can occur with a probability of 5 percent each year (independent of whether or not there is flooding) and also cause losses of $20 million.

Should the firm buy two separate insurance policies or a bundled insurance policy? The answer depends on the level of losses that the firm can absorb (that is, the amount it is willing to self-insure) without, for instance, facing a situation of financial distress or a liquidity crisis. Suppose the firm decides that it can suffer a loss of up to $20 million, but any greater loss could create significant liquidity problems. If the firm goes with two separate insurance policies, the deductible could be set at $10 million for each policy, to avoid exceeding an aggregate loss of $20 million in the case that both losses occurred. As indicated in Table 8.4, if separate insurance policies are purchased, the combination of the policies can result in the firm's receiving insurance payments even when the aggregate losses do not exceed $20 million (lines 2 and 3). The cost of the separate insurance policies will reflect the fact that payments of $10 million are expected to be made on each policy, with a probability of 5 percent. However, the premium will be greater than simply the expected payouts since, at a minimum, the insurance company will need to recover its costs of processing and verifying claims.

Table 8.4 also shows that the results of a bundled policy are better (last column). That policy will require payout from the insurance provider only when the firm's aggregate losses are $40 million—the low-probability event in which the firm is in truly dire straits. For the mining firm, the bundled policy is more appropriate here since it allows the firm to self-insure to the extent it can, thereby minimizing the frictions and costs of third-party insurance.

How widely has the practice of bundling risk been adopted? While some firms have moved in that direction, most observers believe that the movement toward such risk integration has been

Table 8.4. Payouts on Bundled Insurance Versus Separate Policies ($ millions)

	Probability	Risk-1 Outcome	Risk-2 Outcome	Insurance Payout: Separate Policies ($10 million deductible each)	Insurance Payout: Bundled Policy ($20 million deductible)
1	(19/20) × (19/20)	$0	$0	$0	$0
2	(1/20) × (19/20)	–$20	$0	$10	$0
3	(19/20) × (1/20)	$0	–$20	$10	$0
4	(1/20) × (1/20)	–$20	–$20	$20	$20

slower than it should be. One reason for slow integration may be that different parts of a firm tend to deal with their own risks, quite independent of the rest of the firm. Hence, while a firm's treasury department may be dealing with exchange and interest rate risk, it may be the purchasing department that is actively concerned about the price of commodities and other inputs to the firm's production process. This suggests that risk integration is likely to happen only when senior managers make the strategic decision to implement such policies.

As CEO of Prospecting, you should be open to adopting bundled insurance. If an insurance provider is willing to offer such policies, the bundling of oil price risk insurance with traditional property and liability insurance may be the best way for the firm to manage its risks. The firm may also want to consider the interaction between its capital structure decision and an integrated risk policy. We would typically expect the firm to be able to carry more debt than otherwise, to take advantage of tax-shield benefits, given the lower financial distress risk on account of its insurance on the downside. While we have mentioned such proposals as coming from insurance providers in this case, similar bundled products are likely to be available from other types of financial intermediaries as well.

■ Key Questions for Your Firm

What's the right risk management strategy for your firm? Answers to the following questions can help you to decide:

- Has the firm made a detailed analysis of its risk exposures?
- What are the most significant business and operational risks in terms of firm value:

  Industry competition?

  Technological changes?

  Loss of key personnel?

Lawsuits?

Security issues: domestic and foreign?

Labor disputes?

- Of the major risks, identify and prioritize them in terms of probability of occurrence. Also ask:

How would the firm respond in various scenarios?

Who does contingency planning?

Are the contingency plans well integrated into the firm's overall strategy?

- What is the firm's level of debt financing? Is it consistent with the firm's business strategy and the risk it faces?

Does the firm have access to some funds in the event of a liquidity crunch?

Does the firm have access to multiple sources of financing—public markets, private placements, international sources?

Does the firm have a well-developed relationship with one or more significant banks?

- What are the broader economic and market risks that the firm faces?

How large is the firm's exposure to market risks?

What action is the firm taking to lower the exposure?

- Does the firm have a number of liability and property insurance policies?

Are the risks too large for the firm to self-insure against them?

Has the firm investigated using an integrated insurance policy?

FAQs About Corporate Risk Management

For hedging with futures contracts we need to know how a firm's cash flows, for instance, are affected by changes in futures prices. How should the sensitivity be estimated?

In most cases, we have a so-called statistical relation between futures contracts and the cash flow that we are interested in hedging. This statistical relation is usually estimated using historical data on the cash flows we are seeking to hedge, as well as the movements in futures prices at that time. The objective is to use the historical data to estimate the best linear (regression) relation we can between the futures prices and the cash flow that we are attempting to hedge.

If the data is not particularly complicated, we can use the statistical functions in spreadsheet programs such as MS Excel to estimate the regression equation.

Let us assume that, on the basis of several years of historical data, you have been able to estimate a regression model of the following kind:

$$C = 8.0 \times 10^6 - 3.3 \times 10^3 \times F.$$

Here, C represents the cash flow (say in $ millions) that we are interested in hedging, while F represents the futures price. The regression equation, in effect, is saying that a change in the futures price by $20 decreases the cash flow by $66,000. The regression coefficient of F is the sensitivity of the cash flow to changes in the futures price.

Now, if we want to hedge the impact of changes in the futures price on the cash flow, we need a position in futures contracts that offsets the effect indicated in the regression equation. Hence, our position in futures contracts should be long (that is, on the side obliged to take delivery) so that an increase in the futures prices increases the value of our position—and offsets the losses in the cash flow.

Let us assume that we have entered into futures contracts so that, for $1 increase in the futures price, we gain $3,300. When we combine our position in futures contracts with the cash flows we will have:

Total cash flow = Cash flow to be hedged +
Futures position = C + 3.3 × 10³ × F.

Now, let us say that the futures price increases by $1. By the regression equation, we expect that the cash flow C will decrease in value by about $3,300. At the same time, our position in the futures contracts gives us a gain of $3,300, thereby providing a hedge against the fluctuations in the cash flow that are linked to changes in the futures price.

How effective is the hedge that we can get by using a futures contract? In other words, can we entirely eliminate the risk of a cash flow that we are hedging?

The hedge can only be as good as the relation between the cash flow that we are trying to hedge and the futures prices. Continuing the example in the first question, for instance, let us suppose that we estimate the regression equation and find that the fit, or the R-square, is 30 percent. (*R-square* is a measure of the fraction of the variation in cash flow C that can be explained by the changes in futures price F; any statistical package, including spreadsheet programs like MS Excel, will provide the R-square of a regression equation.) This R-square then tells you just how good your hedging will be—in this case, if you hedge in the way described in the preceding question, you will be able to reduce the risk (its variance) by 30 percent.

Hence, the only way that your hedging can be 100 percent—so that all risk is removed by the hedge—is if you have a perfect correlation (that is, an R-square of 100 percent) between the cash flow and the futures price.

Should my firm hedge when my competitors do not appear to be hedging industry- or economy-wide risks?

Think about Prospecting and its main U.S. competitor, which is somewhat more diversified and provides technical services in areas other than just oil. The competitor has an advantage in being able to service some of its foreign clients by having offices and personnel located abroad. We don't know whether the competitor is hedging oil price and other risks, but if it isn't, that only strengthens the case for hedging for Prospecting. The reason is that if there is an economic shock that pushes the competitor in the direction of financial distress, then Prospecting—if it is hedged—is well positioned to grab market share or to acquire the competitor's human and other assets.

What is VAR and why is it used as a measure of risk?

While VAR (Value-at-Risk) arose in the context of risk management in the banking industry, it is now used more broadly for both managing and measuring risk. The VAR is a dollar figure that conveys the largest loss that a firm or investment portfolio might be expected to suffer, with a specified probability (or confidence level) over a certain period. Hence, if a particular activity has a monthly VAR of $1 million at the 99 percent confidence level, this indicates that we expect monthly losses to exceed $1 million only in one out of a hundred months (that is, on average once every eight or nine years).

There are some good reasons for firms to use this figure. VAR provides an aggregate measure of risk—a single dollar number related to the maximum loss that might be incurred—and it is aggregate loss that firms need to be concerned about, since aggregate loss is what determines whether a firm is in financial distress or facing a liquidity problem. The simplicity of having the single dollar figure given by VAR is that it can be easily translated into a capital requirement. For instance, the VAR can be interpreted as the lowest level of equity capital that might be required to keep the probability of financial distress low.

A second reason for using VAR is that it provides a common, consistent, and integrated measure of risk across various financial and nonfinancial risks that a firm or operation might face. This leads to greater risk transparency and a consistent treatment of risks across the firm.

What is RAROC? Why is it used?

Risk Adjusted Return on Capital (RAROC) is a commonly used measure of the return on a firm's or project's VAR (the return on its so-called risk capital). For the firm to maximize shareholder value, it should seek to maximize this return. By definition, RAROC = (Profit and loss)/VAR.

SUMMARY

This chapter explains when and how risk management contributes to shareholder value creation. One class of risks consists of those that are related to a firm's core business and operational strategy; these risks cannot be insured against. A number of actions, however, can moderate a firm's exposure to such risks; for instance, the firm can modify its operations to enhance its ability to respond to developments such as heightened competition or technological developments.

Another class consists of risks of a broader nature, such as economy-wide risks, that are not integral to the firm's core business but can expose it to considerable potential for loss or damage. These are the risks that should be managed, especially if they may be large enough to cause financial distress or to constrain a firm's ability to undertake profitable investments. Some basic derivative contracts, in particular futures and option contracts, can be useful for risk management. The chapter also describes other possible benefits from risk management, reducing taxes in certain situations as well as improving managerial incentive contracts and attracting large shareholders—all of which can enhance firm value.

The chapter also discusses the use of integrated insurance policies, which can be more effective than the usual policies since they are designed to protect the firm when its losses are truly large—rather than providing insurance in situations where it may be more efficient for the firm to self-insure.

Performance
Evaluation

A s the newly promoted Chief Operating Officer of Flurox
Corporation, a cleaning products company, you have at-
tended a workshop at the University of Michigan Business
School on leading change. One of the issues stressed at the workshop was the importance of the link between performance evaluation and shareholder value. The speaker argued that even
company managements that focus on shareholder value and allocate resources accordingly, using rules such as NPV, do not always evaluate performance on metrics congruent to shareholder
value. Indeed, although some of the performance metrics used by
companies, such as EPS, profit, and **Return on Capital Employed
(ROCE)**, to name a few, appear to be consistent with shareholder

value, their link to shareholder value is suspect. The speaker warned that even value-based resource allocation methods will be ineffective in allocating capital efficiently if the performance metrics are not based on shareholder value. Managers will corrupt or manipulate the resource allocation to maximize the performance metric used to evaluate their work at the possible expense of shareholder value.

Flurox uses EPS as the primary metric for evaluating senior management, and ROCE for divisional managers. You were under the impression that these performance measures were consistent with shareholder value, though the precise link was not clear to you. You also heard from some of the other workshop attendees about a measure called **Economic Profit (EP)**, which their companies have started using. Some of them claimed that the introduction of EP has cleaned up many of the past inefficiencies in capital allocation, though there has not been enough data to evaluate the long-term effects on stock price.

You want to learn about EP and compare it to the current metrics that Flurox uses. Since it already uses NPV and IRR for resource allocation decisions, you also want to understand how EP is related to these measures to ensure consistency between resource allocation and performance evaluation. You also want to get a better understanding of the link between the performance evaluation metrics Flurox uses (EPS and ROCE) and shareholder value.

Starting with a simplified concept, this chapter builds a useful definition of economic profit, shows how it is superior to earnings or return-based measures for evaluating performance, and demonstrates how it is in line with our theme of shareholder value creation.

■ An Introduction to Economic Profit

As the workshop speaker warned, resource allocation methodologies and performance evaluation metrics must be consistent with each other and with shareholder value. Therefore, to start it is important to understand how EP works as a resource allocation tool, and its relation to other resource allocation tools such as NPV and IRR, discussed in Chapter Two. We begin with a basic concept of EP, and gradually make it more sophisticated throughout the chapter.

The Basic Concept

The concept of economic profit is simple. Fundamentally, it is value added. As Chapter Three points out, a company needs to maintain a minimum rate of return on capital—referred to as the Weighted Average Cost of Capital, or WACC—that would satisfy the capital providers (both lenders and stockholders) just to stay even. To make an economic profit (as opposed to accounting profit), the company must earn a return greater than this cost of capital.[1] The number of percentage points the company earns above the cost of capital, scaled by the capital employed, yields a dollar value for the EP. We illustrate the concept of EP with a simple example.

An Example with Perpetual Cash Flows

Consider a project proposal that requires $100 of capital, is expected to provide a cash flow of $15 forever, and has a WACC of 12 percent. Is this project worth doing?

One way to answer the question is to use the resource allocation rules we already know (NPV and IRR). The NPV is calculated as the present value of all the expected future cash flows ($15 a year, forever) discounted at 12 percent, minus the capital of $100:

$$NPV = 15 \div 0.12 - 100 = \$25.$$

Since the $15 per year is forever, we use the perpetuity formula (introduced in Chapter Six) to find the present value of the expected future cash flow stream. It is useful to recall that the NPV of $25 represents the total wealth created by the project, expressed in present dollars. Since this is positive, the project is worth taking.

Similarly, we can evaluate the project by calculating the IRR. We can calculate the IRR of this project easily. Recall that the IRR is the average expected annual rate of return. Since the project yields the same cash flow every year, its annual expected rate of return and average expected annual rate of return are both $15 \div 100 = 15$ percent. Since this is greater than the WACC of 12 percent, the project is worth taking.

Now, instead, let us use the concept of EP to decide if the project is worth undertaking. The capital providers have supplied $100 of capital and expect a minimum average annual rate of return of 12 percent. One way to provide an average annual rate of return of 12 percent is to provide a rate of return of 12 percent every year. A 12 percent rate of return on a $100 capital base translates to $100 \times 0.12 = \$12$ every year. Since the project is forever, the $100 capital is always required and hence never recovered. The $12 return that would minimally satisfy the capital providers is called the **capital charge**. It is also called the **dollar cost of capital**. Therefore:

Capital charge = WACC × Capital employed.

To add value to investors, the project will need to generate more than the capital charge. In this simple example, the project is expected to generate $15 annually. This value added is the EP and is calculated as follows.

Annual cash from project = $15
− Annual capital charge = $\underline{\$12}$
Annual value added (EP) = $3

It is important to recognize that EP measures the value added during a period of time such as a year. In this example, all years are identical. (A later example illustrates what happens when the expected EP differs each year, as typically occurs in practice.)

Note that both expected EP and NPV are measures of value added (or wealth created). While NPV measures the entire value added from the project, expected EP measures the value added in a time period such as a year. This means that if we aggregate the annual expected EP over the life of the project we should obtain the NPV. This is indeed the case in this example, as can be seen if we calculate the present value of the annual expected EPs of the project by using the perpetuity formula:

$$PV \text{ of expected EP} = 3 \div 0.12 = \$25.$$

As in the NPV calculation we have divided the annual expected EP by the WACC since the project is a no-growth perpetuity.

What we see by this example is that if NPV is the whole loaf of bread, expected annual economic profits are the expected annual slices. This relation between NPV and EP tells us that using either method for resource allocation decisions will result in consistent decisions that maximize shareholder value. It also means that EP has no particular advantage over NPV as a methodology when it comes to allocating resources. This is because you need only know the size of the loaf to make the resource allocation decision. Knowing the annual slices does not provide any additional information from the resource allocation perspective.

Then why should you know about EP at all? The utility of EP comes not in resource allocation but in performance evaluation, which must be done periodically for several reasons. For instance, managers need to monitor the performance of a project periodically so that they can intervene if expectations are not realized. This is not only true for projects that underperform, in which case managers might wish to abandon or shrink the project. Projects that outperform should be expanded to extract more value. In addition to its use in guiding intervention, periodic evaluation is required to provide incentive compensation for the employees involved in the project. Since such compensation is usually paid annually, there is value to knowing the annual slices.

Refining the Definition of EP as a Performance Evaluation Tool

The first example dealt with a resource allocation problem; its cash flows were estimations and the annual economic profits were expectations. The example can easily be extended to a performance evaluation context if we view the cash flows as realizations, in which case the annual economic profits are actuals. However, the first example had one important limitation. It considered a perpetual cash flow stream, whereas in practice all cash flow streams, however long, are finite. The finiteness of the project cash flow stream makes it necessary to consider repaying the capital, which was not an issue in the example. Therefore let us consider some examples with finite cash flow streams to understand how this affects the estimation of EP.

An Example with One Cash-Flow Period

Consider the following one-period example. A project requires a capital of $100 in Year 0 and produces an operating cash flow of $115 in Year 1. The WACC is 10 percent. Suppose the entire capital of $100 was borrowed at 10 percent. In this case, it is easy to see that the value retained by the owner of the project (that is, the EP) will be the operating cash flow of $115 less the principal ($100) and interest ($10 = $100 × 10 percent). In general, capital is supplied in the form of both debt and equity. However, the concept is the same. Since *principal* and *interest* are terms applied only to debt financing, we can use *capital recovery* and *capital charge*, respectively, for similar functions in the context of EP. Using this concept, we obtain the following working definition of EP:

EP = Operating cash flow − Capital recovery − Capital charge
 = 115 − 100 − (0.1 × 100) = $5.

Note that in the earlier example with perpetual cash flows, there was no capital recovery since the initial capital was required to generate the cash flows in perpetuity. The working definition given here is more useful for dealing with the finite cash flow streams observed in practice. To further refine the working definition of EP for practical applications, we start with the following example.

An Example with Two Cash-Flow Periods

Consider a project with a WACC of 10 percent that requires a capital investment of $100 in Year 0 and produces operating cash flows of $60 and $70 at the end of the first and second years, respectively. In this example, in order to calculate EP using the working definition, we need to decide the rate at which the capital will be recovered. Being a multiyear project, the possibilities are infinite. Consider the two options shown in Table 9.1.

Option 1 involves recovering all capital at the end of Year 2. Since the entire capital of $100 is being used by the project till the termination of the project, the capital charge of $10 ($100 × 10 percent) has to be paid in each year. In addition, the entire capital of $100 has to be returned at the end of the project. This results in EP of $50 in Year 1 and −$40 in Year 2, their present value given by

Table 9.1. **Practical definition of EP: An Example with Two Cash-Flow Periods**

Option 1

	Year 1	Year 2
Operating cash flow	$60	$70
Capital recovery	$0	$100
Capital charge	$10	$10
EP	$50	($40)
PV of EP = $12.40		

Option 2

	Year 1	Year 2
Operating cash flow	$60	$70
Capital recovery	$40	$60
Capital charge	$10	$6
EP	$10	$4
PV of EP = $12.40		

$$\text{PV of EP} = 50 \div 1.1 + -40 \div 1.1^2 = \$12.40.$$

Option 2 involves returning capital in two installments. In this case, $40 of the capital is recovered at the end of the first year and the remainder is recovered at the end of the second year. In the first year, the capital charge is $10 ($100 × 10 percent). However, since $40 of capital is returned at the end of the first year, only $60 of capital is being used in the second year, for which a capital charge of $6 ($60 × 10 percent) has to be paid. This results in EP of $10 in Year 1 and $4 in Year 2, their present value given by

$$\text{PV of EP} = 10 \div 1.1 + 4 \div 1.1^2 = \$12.40.$$

Comparing the two options we can see that while the time pattern of EP depends on the rate of capital recovery, the PV of EP is unaffected. This is because the PV of EP (aggregating the slices) equals the NPV (the loaf). While the size of the slices may be different, they must add up to the same loaf, which is the value created by the project. In other words, the value created by this project is unaffected by how quickly the capital is recovered.[2] Therefore, we can choose any pattern of capital recovery that suits our purpose without affecting the measurement of the value created. Thus the assumed pattern of capital recovery need not have any relation to how capital is actually recovered, since the value created is unaffected by the assumption. However, to maintain a common definition of EP that everyone can use, there must be a standard assumption about how capital is recovered. Otherwise, one could get different *year-by-year* patterns of EP based on different assumptions about how capital is recovered.

The common assumption about capital recovery is quite simple: it is assumed that capital is recovered at the rate of depreciation. Let us apply this assumption to the working definition of EP. We had

$$EP = \text{Operating cash flow} -$$
$$\text{Capital recovery} - \text{Capital charge.}$$

Now we have

$$EP = \text{Operating cash flow}$$
$$- \text{Depreciation} - \text{Capital charge.}$$

Or

$$EP = \text{NOPAT} - \text{Capital charge.}$$

This is true because NOPAT (Net Operating Profit After Taxes) = Operating cash flow − Depreciation, as shown in Chapter Two. This last version is the definition of EP that is used in practice. Using the fact that capital charge is the product of WACC and capital employed, we can write EP as:

$$EP = \text{NOPAT} - \text{WACC} \times \text{Capital employed.}$$

Another variant of the definition is as follows:

$$EP = NOPAT - \text{Capital charge}$$

$$= \text{Capital employed} \times \left[\frac{NOPAT}{\text{Capital employed}} - \frac{\text{Capital charge}}{\text{Capital employed}} \right]$$

Since NOPAT/Capital employed equals the ROCE (Return On Capital Invested), and Capital charge/Capital employed equals WACC, we can also rewrite this formula as

$$EP = \text{Capital employed} \times (ROCE - WACC).$$

Why do experts agree on the assumption that capital is recovered at the rate of depreciation? It satisfies the essential criteria for performance evaluation to be used for incentive compensation: simplicity, transparency, and smoothness.

Simplicity implies that the performance evaluation measure must not be complicated to compute and must be easily communicable to all concerned employees. With this assumption, capital employed each year will be just the net fixed capital (that is, fixed capital less accumulated depreciation) plus working capital.

Transparency is probably the most important criterion. A measure should be easily verifiable to avoid any perception of manipulation by senior management. Depreciation is set primarily by accounting and tax rules, leaving little room for legal manipulation by management. Since depreciation is listed in the balance sheet, it is transparent to everyone.

With regard to smoothness, business conditions are likely to introduce variations in performance from year to year and any valid performance measure will reflect this variation. It is counterproductive to introduce further variation to the performance measure by design. When we compare the two options in Table 9.1, we can see that the EP swings dramatically in option 1: $50 in the first year and –$40 in the second year. In the second option, the EP declines steadily. If we used the first pattern for incentive compensation, it is easy to see that it would create perverse incentives. Managers who earned huge bonuses in the first year would have an incentive to leave that job (either quit the company or seek other assignments within it) to avoid the consequences of the poor performance expected in the following year. The first pattern also limits the company's ability to reassign managers, as no other manager would want to step in at the end of the first year of such a sequence.

Assuming that capital recovery equals depreciation computed using the straight line method provides a smooth decline in the capital employed and therefore avoids introducing volatility into the EP pattern over time.

▣ Measuring EP at Flurox from Its Financial Statements

Let's return now to your situation at Flurox and your desire to measure the company's performance in terms of economic profit. The NOPAT definition of EP is the best way to measure EP from Flurox's financial statements:

$$EP = NOPAT - \text{Capital charge}$$
$$= NOPAT - WACC \times \text{Capital employed}.$$

It is relatively easy to measure the economic profit of an entity (company, division, or business unit) if we have a balance sheet and income statement for that unit. We can obtain the NOPAT from the income statement and the capital employed from the balance sheet. The only input that is not available from the financial statements is the WACC, which can be obtained using the techniques described in Chapter Three.

Figure 9.1 provides an overview of the drivers of EP. The overview helps identify the balance sheet and income statement items needed to measure EP. Chapter Two discusses how to measure NOPAT from the income statement. To reiterate, include only operational items and ignore any financial items such as interest paid and interest or dividend earned from holdings in other companies. By ignoring such items, we measure the pure operating profit, which is an appropriate measure of the operating performance of the unit.

Also recall from Chapter Two that businesses employ two types of capital: fixed capital and working capital. Since our EP definition assumes that capital is being recovered at the rate of depreciation, for fixed capital we need the amount net of accumulated depreciation in the year the performance is being measured. As for working capital, the important thing to keep in mind is that we need the *operating* working capital, which equals current operating assets less current operating liabilities.

Figure 9.1 lists the most common current operating assets and liabilities. These are not necessarily the same as the current assets and liabilities listed on the balance sheet. For instance, the current assets listed on the balance sheet represent the cash on hand, not the cash that is part of the working capital needs. For companies not short on cash, one would expect the cash on hand to be far greater than what they would need for working capital. Furthermore, current assets in the balance sheet include marketable securities that are not part of working capital. Similarly, current liabilities in the balance sheet typically include short-term debt and the current portion of the long-term debt (principal amount due within the next twelve months). These are actually *sources* of capital (possibly working capital), while we

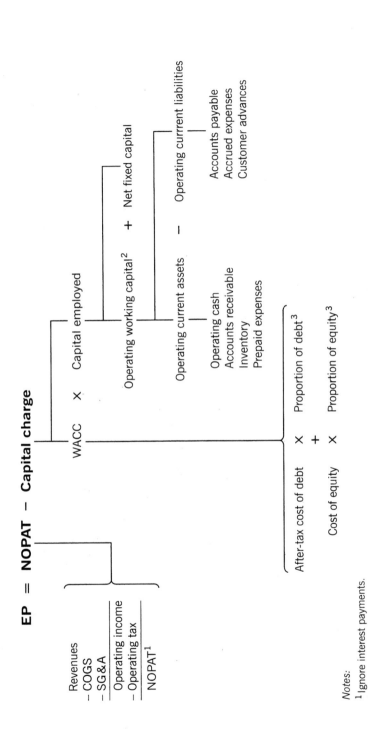

EP = NOPAT − Capital charge

Revenues
− COGS
− SG&A
—————
Operating income
− Operating tax
—————
NOPAT[1]

NOPAT[1]   Capital employed   × WACC

Operating working capital[2] + Net fixed capital

Operating current assets − Operating currrent liabilities

Operating cash
Accounts receivable
Inventory
Prepaid expenses

Accounts payable
Accrued expenses
Customer advances

WACC   After-tax cost of debt × Proportion of debt[3]
       +
       Cost of equity × Proportion of equity[3]

Notes:
[1] Ignore interest payments.
[2] Ignore interest-paying assets and interest-bearing liabilities.
[3] Proportions based on market values.

Figure 9.1. Overview of the Drivers of Economic Profit

are trying to estimate the working capital needs based on how it is *used*. In principle, we could have estimated the working capital needs based on the sources as well (though it is more cumbersome). However, mixing the sources and uses of working capital would be inappropriate. Adding the net fixed capital to the operating working capital gives us the capital employed as of the date of the balance sheet.

Equipped with this general understanding, you ask your CFO to evaluate the EP earned by Flurox last year based on last year's financial statements. You want to see how well Flurox performed in the year 2003. Its balance sheet and income statement are given in Table 9.2 and Table 9.3, respectively.

The determination of the EP from your operations (ignoring any EP from financial investments such as marketable securities, stock holdings in other companies, and so on) is explained in Table 9.4. From Figure 9.1, we know that the three drivers of EP are NOPAT, capital employed, and WACC. The upper portion of Table 9.4 (lines 1–13) relates to capital employed during 2003, calculating the average of the working and fixed capital at the ends of years 2002 and 2003. Both types of capital can be computed from the data in the balance sheet provided in Table 9.2. Working capital is computed as the difference between current operating assets—accounts receivable (line 3), inventory (line 4), and prepaid expenses (line 5)—and current operating liabilities. The latter consist of accounts payable (line 12), accrued expenses and taxes (lines 13 and 14), and advance customer payments (line 15). Operating cash is part of current operating assets, but it is usually difficult to estimate and likely to be small, so it is often ignored. The working capital figures for years 2002 and 2003 are $1017 million and $1134 million, respectively (line 10, Table 9.4). The fixed capital is the sum of several items: property, plant, and equipment net of depreciation (line 9 in Table 9.2—$2074 million in 2002 and $2167 million in 2003) and the

Table 9.2. **Flurox Corporation: Balance Sheet**
(year ending December 31; $ millions)

	2003	2002
ASSETS		
CURRENT		
1 Cash and cash equivalents	$467	$455
2 Marketable securities	$17	$18
3 Accounts receivable	$971	$939
4 Inventory	$764	$767
5 Prepaid expenses	$575	$476
6 TOTAL CURRENT ASSETS	$2,794	$2,655
7 PROPERTY, PLANT, AND EQUIPMENT	$2,830	$2,686
8 Less allowances for depreciation	$663	$612
9 NET PROPERTY, PLANT, AND EQUIPMENT	$2,167	$2,074
10 TRADEMARKS AND OTHER INTANGIBLE ASSETS	$645	$479
11 TOTAL ASSETS	$5,606	$5,208
LIABILITIES AND SHARE-OWNERS' EQUITY		
CURRENT		
12 Accounts payable	$864	$908
13 Accrued expenses	$56	$68
14 Accrued income taxes	$213	$150
15 Advance customer payments	$43	$39
16 Loans and notes payable	$936	$1,198
17 Current maturities of long-term debt	$39	$5
18 TOTAL CURRENT LIABILITIES	$2,151	$2,368
19 LONG-TERM DEBT	$1,305	$1,209
20 OTHER LIABILITIES	$240	$251
21 DEFERRED INCOME TAXES	$111	$90
22 SHARE-OWNERS' EQUITY	$1,799	$1,290
23 TOTAL LIABILITIES AND SHARE-OWNERS' EQUITY	$5,606	$5,208

□

Table 9.3. Flurox Corporation: Statement of Income
(year ending December 31; millions)

		2003	2002
1	NET OPERATING REVENUES	$5,094	$4,972
2	Cost of goods sold	$1,511	$1,551
3	GROSS PROFIT	$3,583	$3,421
4	Selling, administrative, and general expenses	$2,174	$2,138
5	Other operating charges	$0	$361
6	OPERATING INCOME	$1,409	$922
7	Interest income	$81	$86
8	Interest expense	$164	$159
9	INCOME BEFORE TAXES	$1,326	$849
10	Income taxes	$423	$306
11	NET INCOME	$903	$543
12	Average shares outstanding	622	619

trademarks and other intangible assets (line 10 in Table 9.2—$479 million in 2002 and $645 million in 2003). The intangible assets figures represent amounts paid by Flurox for acquiring trademarks and patents, and the goodwill (the premium in excess of fair value of assets—see Chapter Six) paid in past acquisitions. As Table 9.4 shows, the fixed capital was $2553 million in 2002 and $2812 million in 2003 (line 11). The total capital employed was $3570 million in 2002 and $3946 million in 2003 (line 12).

The financial statements only tell us how much capital has been employed *as of the end* of each year, 2002 and 2003. To evaluate the performance for 2003, one needs to know the capital employed *during* 2003. For simplicity, it is assumed that the *additional* capital employed during 2003 (over and above the capital employed at the beginning of 2003) is employed at midyear. Therefore, the capital employed during 2003 is simply the average of the capital employed at the end of 2002 and that employed at the end of 2003. Table 9.4 shows this amount as $3758 million (line 13).

Table 9.4. Phrox Corporation, Economic Profit Calculation ($ and ... in millions)

CAPITAL EMPLOYED

Current Operating Assets	2003	2002	Notes
1 Accounts receivable	$971	$939	From Balance Sheet-line 3, Table 9.2
2 Inventory	$764	$767	From Balance Sheet-line 4, Table 9.2
3 Prepaid expenses	$575	$476	From Balance Sheet-line 5, Table 9.2
4 TOTAL	$2,310	$2,182	Sum of lines 1–3
Current Operating Liabilities			
5 Accounts payable	$864	$908	From Balance Sheet-line 12, Table 9.2
6 Accrued expenses	$56	$68	From Balance Sheet-line 13, Table 9.2
7 Accrued taxes	$213	$150	From Balance Sheet-line 14, Table 9.2
8 Advance customer payments	$43	$39	From Balance Sheet-line 15, Table 9.2
9 TOTAL	$1,176	$1,165	Sum of lines 5–8
Capital Employed			
10 Working capital	$1,134	$1,017	Current operating assets – current operating liabilities
11 Fixed capital	$2,812	$2,553	Net PP&E + Trademarks and intangibles-lines 9 and 10, Table 9.2
12 Total capital	$3,946	$3,570	Line 10 + Line 11
13 Average capital employed	$3,758		Average of 2003 and 2002 total capital

NOPAT AND ECONOMIC PROFIT

	2003	Notes
14 Revenues	$5,094	From Income statement-line 1, Table 9.3
15 Cost of goods sold	($1,511)	From Income statement-line 2, Table 9.3
16 Selling, administrative, and general expenses	($2,174)	From Income statement-line 4, Table 9.3
17 Other operating charges	$0	From Income statement-line 5, Table 9.3
18 Taxable Operating Income	$1,409	Sum of lines 14–17
19 Tax	($493)	At 35 percent
20 NOPAT	$916	Line 18 + Line 19
21 Capital Charge	($353)	Average capital employed × WACC – line 13 × line 16, Table 9.5
22 Economic Profit	$563	NOPAT – Capital charge (Line 20 + Line 21)
23 Return On Capital Employed (ROCE, percent)	24.37	NOPAT ÷ Average capital employed (Line 20 ÷ Line 13)

The NOPAT calculations are shown in the lower portion of Table 9.4. When computing the NOPAT from operations only, you ignore any income from financial investments (in your company's case, the interest income). Also as shown, the taxable operating income is computed by deducting COGS, SG&A, and any other operating expenses from revenues. All these figures are available from the income statement in Table 9.3. Deducting the taxes on this operating income provides a NOPAT of $916 million for 2003 (line 20).

The WACC calculation for 2003, shown in Table 9.5, is similar to that discussed in Chapter Three. Your company's cost of debt during 2003 is 6.98 percent (line 3) and its beta during this year is estimated to be 0.85 (line 4). Using the commonly accepted market risk premium of 6 percent (see Chapter Three) and the 2003 risk-free rate of 5.12 percent, Flurox's cost of equity is computed as 10.22 percent.

Note that we are trying to compute the cost of the capital employed during 2003. Since the financial statements do not reveal the precise pattern of capital employment during 2003 (they only provide data at the end of each year), an average WACC is computed based on the average values of debt and equity during the year. To compute the average equity, the average of the beginning and ending year share prices is multiplied by the shares outstanding (line 10). To compute the average debt outstanding, the average of the year-end debt for 2003 and 2002 is used (line 13). As Table 9.5 concludes, the WACC for Flurox in 2003 is 9.40 percent (line 16).

The capital charge (line 21 of Table 9.4) is calculated as the product of the WACC and the average capital employed. It equals $353 million (9.40 percent × $3758 million). As noted, EP is then calculated as the difference between NOPAT and capital charge. For Flurox it equals $563 million ($916 million − $353 million).

Table 9.5. Flurox Corporation: WACC Calculations for 2003 ($ except share price and number of shares in millions)

1	Risk-free rate (percent) = 5.12	Average of year-beginning and year-end 10-year T-bond rate
2	Market risk premium (percent) = 6	Based on long-term estimates
3	Cost of debt (percent) = 6.98	Company's borrowing rate
4	Stock beta = 0.85	Estimated
5	Cost of equity (percent) = 10.22	Risk free rate + β × Market risk premium
6	Shares outstanding = 622	From Income statement
7	Share price on 1/2/2003 = $26.81	From Market data
8	Share price on 12/31/2003 = $18.15	From Market data
9	Average share price = $22.48	Average of year beginning and ending share prices
10	Average value of equity = $13,983	Average share price × Shares outstanding
11	Value of debt in 2002 = $2,412	Loans, notes, current maturity of long-term debt and long-term debt
12	Value of debt in 2003 = $2,280	Loans, notes, current maturity of long-term debt and long-term debt
13	Average value of debt = $2,346	Average of debt values in 2002 and 2003
14	Tax rate (percent) = 35	
15	Debt ratio (percent) = 14.4	Average value of debt/(Average value of debt + Average value of equity)
16	WACC (percent) = 9.40	

The CFO informs you that the EP measure shown in Table 9.4 is a simplified calculation to illustrate the concept. Additional adjustments are usually made to both NOPAT and capital employed for several reasons. Often items that are treated as expenses for accounting purposes are viewed as investments from an economic perspective. Examples are R&D expenditure and advertising costs, which are then amortized over several years (similar to depreciation of investments in fixed assets) to reflect the fact that the benefits from these expenditures take time to accrue. Treating them as expenses might cause spikes in the EP pattern. Another kind of adjustment arises from items that are booked as current expenses from an accounting perspective, but are actually incurred in the future. Examples are pension benefits and warranty liabilities. Finally, adjustments are made to reconcile the differences in the treatment of depreciation between financial reporting and tax reporting (straight line depreciation is used for the former while accelerated depreciation is used for the latter). However, the basic EP computation without these adjustments does provide a fairly useful representation of the performance of the company.

■ EP Versus Other Performance Measures

Having obtained a good understanding of EP, you now wonder how it differs from other performance measures you are familiar with. And is it better, as we are proposing? For example, your company uses EPS to evaluate senior management and ROCE to evaluate divisional managers. You have also seen companies use accounting profit (that is, net income or earnings) and return measures such as **Return on Net Assets (RONA)** and **Return on Equity (ROE)** for performance evaluation. Let us see how these measures compare to EP in measuring shareholder value.

Table 9.6 lists performance measures used by firms, categorized as *flow* (based on income or cash flow), *return* (based on rates of return), and *value* (based on shareholder value) measures.[3] Flow measures are computed on the basis of information contained in the income statement; examples are sales, net income, and EPS. Return measures, on the other hand, use information contained in both the income statement and the balance sheet; examples include ROCE and ROE. It can be seen from Table 9.6 that flow measures are the most popular while the only value measure (EP) is used by a minuscule fraction of the firms in the sample. Let's explore the limitations of the flow-based and return-based categories, in contrast with EP. Note that **ROIC (Return on Invested Capital)** reported in Table 9.6 is identical to ROCE, defined earlier.

Flow-Based Measures

All flow-based measures suffer from a common drawback: they do not consider the risk involved in generating the flow. Recall that the risk of future cash flows is incorporated in the cost of capital, which is an element in value-based measures such as EP. If performance is measured only according to flow measures, managers have the incentive to choose investments that are expected to increase the flow measure, regardless of whether the investment creates shareholder wealth. Typically the expected value of these flow measures is positively related to the risk involved. Therefore, managers can use a high-risk strategy to boost the value of a flow measure such as expected cash flow or expected earnings. Managers reap the benefits from increased expected flow measure, without paying the price for increasing shareholders' risk.

Two questionable tactics allow managers to boost measured performance if performance is measured using a flow measure.

Table 9.6. Performance Measures Used in Annual Bonus Contracts

Firms using the measure as one of the performance measures (percent)

Flow measures

Earnings per share (EPS)	28.5
Net income (or Earnings)	27.2
Operating income/income before tax	25.3
Sales	13.7
Cash flow	12.8
Cost reduction	7.6

Return measures

Return on equity (ROE)	19.5
Return on assets (ROA)	9.6
Return on invested capital (ROIC)	5.4
Stock price return	4.4
Return on sales (ROS)	3.8

Value measures

Economic Profit (EP)	0.9

Source: Christopher D. Ittner, David F. Larcker, and Madhav V. Rajan, "The Choice of Performance Measures in Annual Bonus Contracts," *Accounting Review* 72, no. 2 (1997): 231–255.

Note: Sample consists of 317 firms in forty-eight different two-digit SIC code industry classifications.

Classification of measures into flow, return, and value measures is not by the authors of the article.

The first tactic works for all flow measures and involves increasing the operating risk to shareholders by choosing higher-risk investments that increase the expected flow measure, regardless of whether such investments create shareholder wealth. In addition, if the flow measure is an equity measure such as net income or EPS, managers may increase the financial risk to shareholders by increasing leverage (debt-equity ratio): they can fund new investments with more than the optimal amount of debt, or can suboptimally restructure the capital by issuing debt and repurchasing equity. Such a change in capital structure increases the financial risk to shareholders even if the operating risk is unchanged, and might be value-decreasing even if the equity flow measure in question is actually increased.

All flow-based measures except EPS also suffer from another drawback. They do not factor in all the capital required (and its associated costs) to generate the flow. For example, measures such as sales or operating income do not consider any of the capital costs. Measures such as net income or cash flow to stockholders do consider the cost of debt since interest payments are deducted before computing them. However, they do not consider the cost of equity capital. Therefore, managers can boost these measures by investing large amounts of the requisite type of capital (equity capital if the flow measure used is net income or cash flow; or debt or equity capital if it is sales or operating income) without adding any value to shareholders or, worse still, even destroying value.

EPS, though listed as a flow-based measure, is not strictly tied to flow. It does factor in the equity capital employed since it is a per-share measure. In fact, it can be shown that EPS is an adequate measure of performance if the company has no excess cash and is financed entirely by equity. In such a setting, long-term increase in EPS will occur only if the company invests in value-added projects. However, as stated earlier, EPS does ignore the risk factor. Therefore, it provides an incentive either to undertake risky investments or to increase the risk to equity by increasing leverage. When a project with IRR greater than what can be earned on internal cash (typically the rate on Treasury bills) is financed by cash, the EPS increases. Similarly, when a project with IRR greater than the cost of debt is financed by debt, the EPS increases. However, this does not mean that the project necessarily adds value. If the IRR is less than the cost of capital but greater than the yield on marketable securities or the cost of debt, undertaking the project increases EPS but destroys value.

How does a project destroy value when it increases the expected EPS? This happens because both these financing choices (financing by cash or debt) effectively increase the debt-equity ratio of the company, thus increasing the risk to equity. The increase in expected future EPS is being offset by the increase in the risk to equity. If the increased risk more than offsets the increase in EPS (as it would in a negative-NPV project), value is destroyed.

Rate of Return Measures

At first glance, rate of return measures appear to be superior to flow-based measures since they take into account both the capital invested and the return obtained. However, unless used correctly, they can also result in value-destroying decisions.

Since there is no consensus regarding the definitions of many of these rates of return, it is useful to clarify what we mean by each of these terms. Return on Capital Employed (ROCE) is defined as before:

$$\text{ROCE} = \frac{\text{NOPAT}}{\text{Capital employed}},$$

where *NOPAT* is as defined earlier and in Chapter Two and *Capital employed* is the sum of fixed capital and working capital. As noted, some companies call the same ratio Return on Invested Capital (ROIC) or Return on Net Assets (RONA).[4]

For Flurox, the ROCE in 2003 was 24.37 percent (NOPAT ÷ Average capital employed = 916 ÷ 3758, line 23, Table 9.4), which is greater than the WACC (9.40 percent). In fact, the difference between ROCE and WACC, scaled by the capital employed, is the EP:

$$(0.2437 - 0.0940) \times 3758 = \$563 \text{ million.}$$

As long as the ROCE is greater than the WACC, the EP for that year will be positive. You can see the similarity between ROCE and EP on one hand and IRR and NPV on the other. The difference between these two pairs is that while the IRR and NPV measures provide estimates of value of a stream of expected cash flows, the ROCE and EP figures provide estimates of value based on a single year's (or, in general, a single period's) performance.

If the performance measure is the difference between ROCE and WACC scaled by the capital employed, then the performance measure is effectively EP. However, companies sometimes use ROCE itself as a performance measure and encourage maximizing it. If ROCE is used in this manner, then the company is ignoring risk. As in the case of EPS and profit, this usage creates the incentive to undertake riskier investments. If managers are encouraged to maximize ROCE, they might be reluctant to invest in low-ROCE projects even if the ROCE of these projects exceeds their WACC. Such projects create value but lower the average ROCE of the firm. Similarly, managers will be tempted to invest in high-ROCE projects even if the ROCE falls below their WACC. Such projects destroy value but increase the average ROCE of the firm.

It must be pointed out that because ROCE is an operating measure based on all capital employed it is less susceptible to changes in financing methods than EPS, which is an equity performance measure. For example, the choice between debt and equity does not affect ROCE because neither NOPAT nor capital employed is affected by this choice. It must be noted that for ROCE to be unaffected by the choice between internal and external financing, NOPAT needs to be measured excluding any income from marketable securities and working capital needs to be measured ignoring excess cash.

The most popular return measure in Table 9.6, Return on Equity (ROE), is defined as

$$ROE = \frac{\text{Net income}}{\text{Shareholders' equity}}.$$

Whether ROE is a good performance measure (that is, consistent with shareholder value) or not depends on how it is used. If the performance measure goal is to maximize the difference between ROE and the cost of equity, scaled by the equity employed, it is consistent with shareholder value. Such a measure essentially attempts to compute EP but is more cumbersome to implement than the methodology described earlier. However, if the goal is maximizing ROE by itself, then the measure suffers from all the problems of ROCE.

Another return measure used for performance evaluation is Return on Assets (ROA), which is defined as

$$ROA = \frac{\text{Net income}}{\text{Total assets}}.$$

ROA suffers from all the same problems as ROCE and more. For instance, by using total assets to scale the net income, ROA does not correctly account for the capital employed. Total assets do not always measure the capital employed, since total assets overstate working capital by ignoring the operating liabilities. In addition, ROA relates an equity measure (net income) to a nonequity measure (total assets). This leaves it open to manipulation by changes in the capital structure. For example, if a manager decreases debt below what is optimal, that action destroys shareholder value but increases net income and therefore ROA. Return on Sales (Net income/Sales) is an even worse measure as it excludes operating costs.

We hope that this discussion has convinced you that EP is superior to conventional earnings and return measures.

■ EP and Share Price

In keeping with the theme of this book, it is important that you understand the relation between EP and the stock price. You already know from Chapter Two that projects whose expected cash flows have a positive NPV create shareholder value. Since NPV is identical to the present value of expected EP over the project's lifetime, you also understand the link between *expected* EP and shareholder value. To the extent the particulars of the project have been communicated to the shareholders, the stock price will reflect the NPV of the project or, equivalently, the present value of the annual expected EP over the project's life (both on a per-share basis).

When using EP as a performance measure, what is being measured is the *realized* EP. What is the link between realized EP and stock price? Will a company that realizes positive EP year after year see its stock price go up? Since it is your management's objective to maximize shareholder value, any internal performance measure you adopt should be directly correlated to stock price, as stock price and cash dividends are the two measures of value creation from the shareholders' perspective.

To understand the link between realized EP and stock price, it is important to recognize that the stock price is based on market expectations of the future. These expectations may differ from reality on occasion, but in an effort to simplify the discussion here, we have assumed that investors are rational and fully informed and have ignored the impact of larger market fluctuations. When a project is announced, investors form expectations about the future cash flows from the project, and based on their estimate of the NPV, they revise the stock price. This means that the market's estimate of the NPV or, equivalently, the present value of the expected EP over the project's lifetime, is already incorporated in the stock price. If the realized EP each year is exactly as expected (an unlikely event!), there is no new information and hence, the stock price will not change. Only if the realized EP deviates from the market's expectation will the stock price change. This means that the realized EP has to exceed the expected EP for the stock price to rise. It follows that a company that creates positive EP year after year need not necessarily see its stock price rise. In fact, there could be situations where a company creates positive EP for several years but its stock price steadily declines because the realized EP is lower than the EP expected by the market.

To summarize, EP measures value created over and above the capital employed. However, since the stock market capitalizes its expectations about future value in the stock price at the time the capital is employed, only if EP exceeds expectations will the stock price increase. In other words, management is on a value treadmill. You have to work hard to produce the expected EP just to keep the stock price at the current level. To increase it, you have to run harder—beating the market's expectations. A corollary is that stock prices can increase even if past EP levels have been low or negative, if the market believes that the company has discovered value-creating opportunities that will add value in the future. It is important to recognize that stock price changes reflect unexpected news about the present or the future, while EP simply reflects past performance. A well-designed EP-based compensation system should recognize this and be structured such that managers receive a target bonus if the expected EP is achieved—plus an extra bonus if the realized EP exceeds the expected value and minus some penalty if the realized EP falls short.

■ Drivers of EP and the Measurement of Employee Performance

While company or unit performance can be measured by EP, it might not be appropriate to use EP to measure every employee's performance. Most employees contribute only to some facets of value, so it may be more appropriate to measure their performance on the basis of what they can affect. For example, it might be more appropriate to measure the performance of salespeople on the basis of the revenue per unit they bring in. It is important, however, that everyone's performance be measured using drivers of EP. Figure 9.1 showed the EP drivers. Among the three major elements of EP (NOPAT, capital employed, and WACC), few general managers have direct control over WACC. Minimizing WACC is in the domain of the CFO. From a general manager's perspective, that leaves NOPAT and capital employed as the critical value drivers. The value drivers for NOPAT are given in Figure 9.2.

While the general manager's goal is to increase the operating profit margin, defined as NOPAT ÷ Revenue, the employees' performance must be measured (at least partially, if not wholly) by the component of the operating margin over which they have the most control. Several taxonomies of the operating margins are possible, but Figure 9.2 provides one based on drivers that increase revenues and decrease costs. The list is representative rather than exhaustive. Individual employee performance can be measured by one or more of the component drivers of NOPAT, based on how much control they have over these drivers.

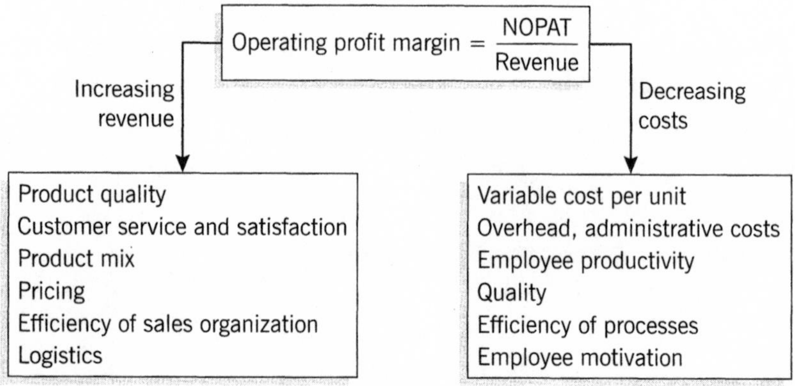

Figure 9.2. EP Drivers: NOPAT and Its Components

The value drivers for capital employed are given in Figure 9.3. As before, while the general manager's goal is to increase asset turnover, defined as Revenue ÷ Capital employed, the components of asset turnover are the ones that are appropriate for individual employees. Asset turnover can be improved by decreasing both fixed and working capital. Two general tactics for reducing fixed capital are better utilization of existing assets (better maintenance, more flexible manufacturing systems, multiple shifts, and the like) and outsourcing. With regard to decreasing working capital, the major drivers are inventory turns, collection period, and payable period. In some cases, working capital reductions can be achieved by increasing accrued expenses and reducing prepaid expenses.

Be aware that there are often trade-offs between drivers of NOPAT and capital employed. Attempts to improve one measure might worsen the other. Employees rewarded on the drivers of only one of the measures might attempt to boost their performance at the expense of the drivers of the other measure. For example, consider outsourcing. While it will reduce your capital employed, the profit margin of the vendor might also de-

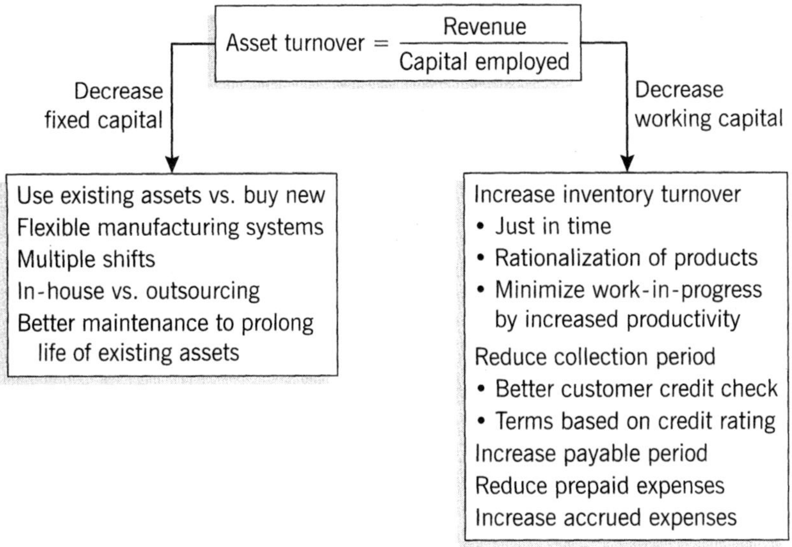

Figure 9.3. EP Drivers: Capital Employed and Its Components

crease your NOPAT. Care must be taken to ensure that any decline in NOPAT is less than the saving in capital charge due to reduced fixed capital. This can happen only if the EP to the vendor of producing the product or service is greater than the EP to you of producing it in-house.

Similarly, while some of the strategies listed in Figure 9.3 might reduce working capital, they might also decrease NOPAT. For instance, employing just-in-time inventory practices reduces your company's inventory and thus working capital merely by shifting the costs to a supplier. If there is no net benefit to the supplier in holding the inventory instead of your company, and if you do not have any special bargaining power over the supplier, the supplier will react by raising prices, reducing your company's NOPAT. For your company's EP to increase, this decrease in NOPAT should not eliminate the benefit of lowered capital charges.

◼ Other Issues in Using EP as a Performance Measure

As with any performance measure, EP has its own practical problems. They come in two basic types: measurement problems and incentive problems. The former involve the difficulty of measuring the components of EP accurately, and the latter involve adverse incentives caused when EP is used as a performance measure.

Measurement Issues

The three measurement problems discussed in this section (as well as some discussed later) are not unique to EP. All performance measures are likely to be susceptible to these problems, but they're worth considering here to avoid the implication that EP might escape them.

Accounting Issues

The only serious measurement issue if one wishes to measure the EP of a company arises from the deviation of accounting systems from economic reality. For instance, accrual accounting requires that a company treat as current any cost it expects to incur in the future due to a current action. Warranties provide an example of such a treatment. The company estimates future warranty costs when it provides a warranty and deducts this expected value from operating income, which results in lowering NOPAT in the current year. The after-tax warranty cost is then booked as a liability. While the company has incurred a future liability because of the warranty, it has incurred no current costs and some adjustment of NOPAT is in order to reflect this. When computing NOPAT and capital employed using financial statements, it is necessary to make several such adjustments to deal with accounting issues (deferred taxes, restructuring charges, goodwill, and pension liabilities are other examples).[5] By contrast, other items—such as R&D and advertising—are cash outflows (and treated as expenses in the financial statements) but are better viewed economically as investments instead of expenses.

Cost Allocation

When evaluating the performance of a division of a company, cost allocation issues typically arise. Unless the company is a true conglomerate, with no common resources such as fixed assets, R&D, marketing, information systems, and human resources shared by its units (Berkshire Hathaway comes close), it is difficult to estimate how much of the common resources to allocate to the various divisions. However, almost all multidivisional companies have resources common to the divisions, because synergy across divisions is often created by such sharing. Yet the rules of thumb used to allocate the common resources (revenue-based or profit-based allocation of shared costs) are often inefficient. For example, if shared costs are allocated according to profits, the result may be that profitable divisions are viewed as unprofitable while unprofitable divisions are viewed as profitable.

The cost allocation problem is not easy to resolve. Any attempt to eliminate or mitigate it is likely to have side effects. One potential way to eliminate the problem is to avoid measuring EP of individual divisions and measure the EP of groups of divisions that share resources. In doing so, however, information about individual divisional performance is lost and profitable divisions might end up subsidizing unprofitable ones. Activity-based costing (ABC) techniques attempt to allocate shared costs in proportion to the true economic costs incurred by the divisions, which might somewhat mitigate this problem.[6]

Transfer Pricing

In companies with divisions that are part of a vertically integrated value chain, transfer pricing policies between the divisions might also distort the measurement of divisional performance.

If the transfer is not at the market price, the result is distortions in the performance of the buying and the selling divisions. For instance, if the transfer price is lower than market, the selling division is penalized and the buying division is subsidized. Several attempts have been made to mitigate this problem; these attempts themselves are difficult and costly to administer, and the biggest challenge in implementing them is to obtain the acceptance of the managers involved.[7]

Incentive Issues

Most of the incentive issues that arise from the introduction of any performance measure (EP or another) are a result of the different decision horizons of shareholders and the manager. Shareholders collectively have a longer horizon than the managers.[8] Managers might get promoted, get transferred to a different position, or just leave the company in a few years. Therefore, they have a greater incentive to maximize short-term results at the expense of the long term.

Myopic Investment Decisions
If profit or EPS is used as a performance measure, the cost of equity capital is ignored. One of the first effects of instituting a performance measure such as EP (or any other measure based on shareholder value) is that managers become acutely aware of the capital charge and try to minimize the use of capital because that will tend to increase EP. A side effect is that they are likely to resort to postponing required capital improvements and R&D expenditure to boost short-term EP, even if postponement hurts the long-term performance of their division or unit.

Indiscriminate Cost Cutting
Since another way to improve EP is to increase NOPAT, managers are likely to focus on cutting costs upon the introduction of EP as a performance measure. The problem is that managers

with shorter horizons might be overzealous about cost cutting, postponing much-needed maintenance to keep current EP high at the expense of future EP.

In response to this problem, compensation plans are often designed to minimize problems arising from managers' shorter decision horizon. A popular compensation structure is to pay only part of the incentive compensation in any given year (say 25 percent) and bank the rest. If future performance is below expectations, the bank is debited—that is, the incentive compensation disappears from the books without being paid. This structure effectively lengthens the decision horizon of the manager. Often, stock-based compensation (stock options and restricted stock) is used, in addition to EP-based compensation, to mitigate managerial myopia and bridge the gap between the decision horizons of the manager and shareholders.

FAQs About Performance Evaluation

Why should my firm ignore interest and dividend receipts from a company's investments when computing NOPAT? Since some of the capital is locked up in financial investments, should we not consider the return from such investments?

When evaluating the performance of a nonfinancial company, we are interested in its operating performance. It is from operations that the company is expected to create value. Nonfinancial companies are unlikely to have any expertise in financial investments, without which such investment will yield only a zero net present value. Therefore, any value created ex-post is attributable more to luck than to expertise. Moreover, these companies have financial assets often for strategic reasons, not for investment purposes. They hold marketable securities to park excess cash temporarily. They hold stock in other companies because they have a strategic interest in the companies.

If nonfinancial companies believe that they can create value through financial investments, we suggest that they measure the

EP of their operating and financial activities separately. Such companies can be viewed as a portfolio of operating assets and financial assets. Effectively, each asset can be viewed as a division or operating unit. Then, the EP can be computed for each unit separately using its own capital employed, NOPAT, and WACC.

How do I estimate operating cash?

As we explained, it is nearly impossible to estimate operating cash from the financial statements, and so it is not uncommon to use the assumption that the required operating cash is zero. However, this assumption is not always correct. In an operating cycle, working capital takes many forms: inventory, receivables less payables, accrued items, and cash, for example. Therefore, if we estimate working capital needs on the basis of the company's operating experience, ignoring operating cash (a form that working capital takes some of the time) will underestimate the working capital requirements. Some estimate operating cash as a percentage of revenues, based on past experience.

How do I estimate WACC for a business unit?

This is achieved using the pure-play technique described in Chapter Three.

Why not estimate capital employed on the basis of the sources of capital (that is, where it came from), instead of uses (how it is used—fixed assets, working capital, and so on)?

It is true that the capital employed by the firm can be estimated by summing either the sources (short-term debt, long-term debt, equity) or the uses (fixed and working capital). However, two reasons favor the latter approach. First, operational managers have more control over the uses of capital than over the sources. Therefore, breaking down capital employed on the basis of how it is used makes it easier for them to assess the reasons for changes in performance and to figure out what they can do to improve performance if necessary. Second, if the capital is employed for more than one use (for example, some of the capital is in financial investments and the rest in operational investments, a case discussed earlier in the chapter), we need to apportion capital among the various uses to estimate the performance of each use. Such an apportioning can be done only on the basis of how the capital is used.

What are Economic Value Added (EVA) and Market Value Added (MVA), and how do they relate to EP?[9]

EVA is identical to EP. MVA can be measured in one of two ways depending on the information available. If we wish to measure the MVA of a decision before it is implemented but after it has been conceived, it can be measured as the PV of all expected future EP from the decision. In other words, MVA in this context is identical to NPV. In this case, the MVA is based on the information that the company has but is unavailable to the market. If we wish to measure the MVA of a company based on market information, it can be measured as the difference between the market value of all its securities (debt, equity, and other securities) and the capital employed (which can often be computed as the book value of its securities). The difference tells us the value the market has assigned to the wealth created by the company's investments based on the market's estimate of the future cash flows. If the market is efficient, the value calculated by the second method will be equal to the PV of the expected future EP of the company.

SUMMARY

In this chapter, we define and demonstrate a value-based performance measure called Economic Profit (EP) and show how it is linked to shareholder value. EP is intimately connected to the resource allocation criteria discussed earlier, such as NPV and IRR. The present value of expected EP is NPV. The PV of EP is positive if IRR exceeds WACC.

EP can be measured as the difference between NOPAT and capital charge if we make the assumption that capital is recovered at the rate of depreciation. The capital charge is measured as the product of capital employed and WACC. EP can be calculated from financial statements (balance sheet and income statement), and the chapter provides an illustrative example.

The chapter also discusses several other performance measures, both flow-based and return-based. A value-based measure such as EP has advantages over these measures, as they are more susceptible to manipulation by financing methods and ignore risk in general.

EP measures current (and past) performance while stock price is a measure of future expected performance (and hence, future expected EP). Therefore, it is no surprise that the link between current EP and current share price is not necessarily strong.

While EP might be an appropriate measure of performance for senior managers, it is less appropriate for subordinate managers who have control over few of the levers of value. Therefore, it is recommended that they be evaluated on the basis of the drivers of EP over which they have direct control.

EP does have some limitations. Like any performance measure, EP is imperfect. Its limitations include measurement issues and perverse incentives caused by measuring performance using EP.

Notes

Chapter 2

1. We put the *average* in quotation marks in the definition of IRR to signify that this is not a simple average.
2. Financial calculators and spreadsheet programs use this rule to calculate IRR. They use a trial-and-error method to find the discount rate that makes the NPV zero.
3. The term *internal rate of return* arises from the fact that IRR is the expected rate of return of an internal opportunity, in contrast to the cost of capital, which is expected rate of return of alternative investments, typically external to the company.
4. See any elementary textbook on financial management or corporate finance for examples where IRR and NPV rules give contradictory recommendations.

5. NOPAT is conceptually similar to net income, with one key difference. NOPAT excludes financing items such as interest payments and investment income.

Chapter 3

1. See, for example, R. Brealey and S. Myers, *Principles of Corporate Finance,* 7th ed. (New York: McGraw-Hill, 2003).

Chapter 4

1. F. Modigliani and M. H. Miller, "The Cost of Capital, Corporation Finance and the Theory of Investment." *American Economic Review* 48 (1958): 261–297.
2. E. I. Altman, "Financial Ratios, Discriminant Analysis and the Prediction of Corporate Bankruptcy," *Journal of Finance* 23, no. 4 (1968): 589–609.
3. The notion of agency costs of "free cash flow" was developed in an influential paper by Michael Jensen, "Agency Costs of Free Cash Flow, Corporate Finance and Takeovers," *American Economic Review* 76 (1986): 323–329.
4. The effect of information asymmetry on the sale of equity was first analyzed by S. Myers and N. Majluf in their paper, "Corporate Financing and Investment Decisions When Firms Have Information That Investors Do Not Have," *Journal of Financial Economics* 13 (1984): 187–221.
5. The post-offering performance of firms selling equity remains a controversial topic in academic finance. For a 2003 survey article on the finance literature in the area, see J. Ritter, "Investment Banking and Security Issuance," in *Handbook of the Economics of Finance,* edited by G. Constantinides, M. Harris, and R. Stulz (Amsterdam: North-Holland, 2003, pp. 253–304).

Chapter 5

1. The pattern of dividend payouts in recent years is discussed in E. Fama and K. French, "Disappearing Dividends: Changing Charac-

teristics or Lower Propensity to Pay," *Journal of Financial Economics* 60 (2001): 3–43.

2. For an early and influential survey paper on dividend payments by U.S. corporations, see J. Lintner, "Distribution of Incomes of Corporations Among Dividends, Retained Earnings and Taxes," *American Economic Review* 46, no. 2 (1956): 97–113.

3. The academic literature on the rationale for payouts is extensive. Here are two well-known papers: F. Easterbrook, "Two Agency-Cost Explanations of Dividends," *American Economic Review* 74 (1984): 650–659; and M. Miller and K. Rock, "Dividend Policy Under Asymmetric Information," *Journal of Finance* 40 (1985): 1031–1051.

4. For the choice between stock repurchases and dividends our discussion draws upon the arguments in M. Brennan and A. Thakor, "Shareholder Preferences and Dividend Policy," *Journal of Finance* 45, no. 4 (1990): 993–1019; and B. Chowdhry and V. Nanda, "Repurchase Premia as a Reason for Dividends: A Dynamic Model of Corporate Payout Policies," *Review of Financial Studies* no. 2 (1994): 321–350.

5. For our discussion on market reactions to dividend initiations and cessations we draw upon P. Healy and K. Palepu, "Earnings Information Conveyed by Dividend Initiations and Omissions," *Journal of Financial Economics* 14 (1988): 149–176.

Chapter 6

1. R. F. Bruner, "Does M&A Pay? Survey of Evidence for the Decision Maker," Working Paper 01-23, Darden Graduate School of Business Administration, 2002.

2. A. R. Lajoux and J. F. Weston, "Do Deals Deliver on Postmerger Performance?" *Mergers and Acquisitions* (September/October 1998): 34–37.

3. E. Berkovitch and M. P. Narayanan, "Motives for Takeovers: An Empirical Investigation," *Journal of Financial and Quantitative Analysis* 28, no. 3 (September 1993): 347–362.

4. "Merger Integration: Delivering on the Promise," *Booz-Allen Hamilton Report,* 2001.

□

5. N.W.C. Harper and S. P. Viguere, "Are You Too Focused?" *McKinsey Quarterly* (2002 Special Edition): 28–30.
6. M. M. Bekier, A. G. Bogardus, and T. Oldham, "Why Mergers Fail," *McKinsey Quarterly* no. 40 (2001): 6–9.
7. B. E. Eckbo, "Mergers and the Value of Anti-Trust Deterrence," *Journal of Finance* 47, no. 3 (July 1992): 1005–1029.
8. Bekier, Bogardus, and Oldham, "Why Mergers Fail."
9. "CEO Roundtable on Making Mergers Succeed," *Harvard Business Review* (May-June 2000): 145–154.
10. See, for example, Berkovitch and Narayanan, "Motives for Takeovers."
11. P. Berger and E. Ofek, "Diversification's Effect on Firm Value," *Journal of Financial Economics* 37, no. 1 (January 1995): 39–65.
12. "Flying Lessons: With TWA, American Plots Course to Avoid Airline-Merger Pitfalls," *Wall Street Journal* (April 20, 2001): A11.
13. "Brazil-MCI Tax Spat Deepens Doubt on Privatizations," *Wall Street Journal* (October 28, 1999): A18.
14. T. Loughran and A. M. Vijh, "Do Long-Term Shareholders Benefit from Corporate Acquisitions?" *Journal of Finance* 52, no. 5 (December 1997): 1765–1790.
15. D. Harding and P. Yale, "Discipline and the Dilutive Deal," *Harvard Business Review* (July 2002): 2–3.
16. N. Kohers and J. Ang, "Earnouts in Mergers: Agreeing to Disagree and Agreeing to Stay," *Journal of Business* 73, no. 3 (July 2000): 445–476.
17. B. Wasserstein, *Big Deal* (Warner Books, 1998).

Chapter 7

1. The diversification discount measure was proposed in a paper by P. Berger and E. Ofek, "Diversification's Effect on Firm Value," *Journal of Financial Economics* 37 (1995): 39–65. A recent survey that discusses the academic literature in the area is J. Stein's 2001 paper, "Agency, Investment and Corporate Investment," in *Handbook of the Economics of Finance,* edited by G. Constantinides, M. Harris, and R. Stulz (Amsterdam: North-Holland, 2003).

2. The argument that diversity can result in investment distortion is made in R. Rajan, H. Servaes, and L. Zingales, "The Cost of Diversity: The Diversification Discount and Inefficient Investment," *Journal of Finance* 55, no. 1 (2000): 35–80.

Chapter 8

1. This argument is made in K. A. Froot, D. S. Scharfstein, and J. C. Stein, "A Framework for Risk Management," *Harvard Business Review* (1994): 91–102.
2. Several authors have contributed to the literature on the value enhancement from risk management. An overview of the literature is available in chapter 3 of R. Stulz, *Risk Management and Derivatives* (Mason, Ohio: South-Western, 2003).

Chapter 9

1. Accounting profit (also known as net income or earnings) does take into account the cost of debt capital by deducting interest expenses from the operating income. However, it does not account for the cost of equity capital.
2. The value created is unaffected by how quickly the capital is recovered because of the implicit assumption that capital is raised at fair market rates. Therefore, there is no advantage or disadvantage in paying the capital back sooner or later.
3. The table is based on C. D. Ittner, D. F. Larcker, and M. V. Rajan, "The Choice of Performance Measures in Annual Bonus Contracts," *Accounting Review* 72, no. 2 (April 1997): 231–255. The classification of the measures is done by us.
4. RONA is sometimes defined as net income divided by fixed capital plus net working capital, which will yield a different number.
5. See S. David Young and Stephen F. O'Byrne, *EVA and Value-Based Management* (New York: McGraw-Hill, 2000).
6. See R. S. Kaplan and R. Cooper, *Cost and Effect* (Boston: Harvard Business School Press, 1998).

7. M. Hodak, "The End of Cost Allocations as We Know Them," *Journal of Applied Corporate Finance* 9, no. 3 (Fall 1997): 117–124.

8. This statement might come as a surprise for many managers, who tend to think that shareholders are only concerned about short-term earnings because they do not expect to hold any company's shares for long. However, this view is flawed. Even if individual shareholders have short holding periods, they do wish to maximize the selling price, which is based on future expectations. Therefore, shareholders collectively do have the incentive to maximize long-term expectations.

9. EVA is a registered trademark of Stern Stewart & Company.

The Authors

M. P. Narayanan is a professor of finance and chair of the finance area at the University of Michigan Business School. His primary research interests are in corporate finance, and he has published extensively in the top finance journals. Narayanan teaches extensively in executive education programs in the United States and abroad. He has served as a consultant to several organizations such as IBM and Johnson & Johnson on financial decision making and monitoring.

Vikram "Vik" Nanda is an associate professor of finance at the University of Michigan Business School. His primary research interests are in corporate finance and financial intermediation, and he has published extensively in the top finance and economics journals. Nanda has taught in executive education programs in the United States and has consulted in connection with litigation matters and risk management.

Index

CPSIA information can be obtained at www.ICGtesting.com
Printed in the USA
BVOW07*1035120714

358825BV00001B/1/P